Working Party on Library Holdings
of Commonwealth Literature

Commonwealth Literature Periodicals

A bibliography, including periodicals of
former Commonwealth countries, with
locations in the United Kingdom

Compiled and edited
by
Ronald Warwick

MANSELL · LONDON
1979

ISBN   0   7201   0800   4

Mansell Publishing, 3 Bloomsbury Place, London WC1A 2QA

First published 1979

British Library Cataloguing in Publication Data

Commonwealth Institute. *Working Party on Library
   Holdings of Commonwealth Literature*
   Commonwealth literature periodicals.
   1. English literature — Commonwealth of Nations
   authors — Periodicals — Bibliography — Union
   Lists
   I. Title   II. Warwick, Ronald
   016.82′08′09171241   Z2013.5.C/
   ISBN 0—7201—0800—4

Text set in 9/10 pt IBM Press Roman, printed and bound
in Great Britain at The Pitman Press, Bath

Commonwealth Literature
Periodicals

Contents

Contents

Foreword

NAMES AND REALITIES

'Commonwealth Literature' is an inaccurate though convenient piece of shorthand for a number of national literatures written wholly or in part in English, which themselves can be distinguished as consisting of three broadly different kinds of national literatures (about which I say more below). It could be argued that for centuries the term 'English Literature' has similarly involved a certain measure of ambiguity, for it has included four national literatures in English of the British Isles; an argument not without point, in view of internal political developments in Scotland, Ireland, and Wales in the 1970s. Neither should one forget the not always distinctly drawn boundaries that would divide 'English' and 'American' literatures. Since the Second World War, writers, critics and academics have become increasingly uneasy about the concept of 'English Literature' as a semantic holdall into which is stuffed also, for different journeys and different destinations, the literatures in English of Australia, Canada, New Zealand, South Africa — and what about the Caribbean, India, Kenya, Nigeria, Sri Lanka and Fiji, to mention only some? To include all these national literatures under the generic term 'English Literature' is surely to imply that all are written in the same kind of English and that its use imposes a more general cultural homogeneity upon those literatures than any investigation of the facts bears out. Apart from the obvious differences in vocabulary and idiom (for example, 'elevator' as used in Britain and Canada), there are rather more subtle deviations, of which one simple example must suffice here: however closely modelled on the Westminster House of Commons they may once have been, can it be claimed that the Canadian House of Commons or the South African House of Assembly function in the same way as each other or as the British prototype and to what extent, therefore, does the phrase 'parliamentary democracy' carry equal semantic or cultural weight in these three countries? The continued generic use of 'English Literature' would also have implied differences merely of the kind recognizable as 'regional', related only to locale, setting, background. Again the facts will not bear out such an implication. The mind of Raja Rao is steeped in Vedantic philosophy; to what extent is his Vedantism mere exotic 'background' in his novel *The Serpent and the Rope*, to what extent at the very heart of his fictional purpose? (One might pause here to wonder how important such a question would have seemed fifteen or even ten years ago.)

That the academic study of the literatures of Commonwealth (excluding the United Kingdom) and ex-Commonwealth countries has been initiated and fostered in university departments of English in many countries has tended to obscure further the *differences* among 'English Literature', 'American Literature' and 'Commonwealth Literatures'. Nevertheless, various expedients of nomenclature have been evolved to point the distinctions, however inadequately; thus, 'Commonwealth Literature' itself, 'Literature in

English', 'World Literature Written in English' and, somewhat fancifully, 'The Literature of Terranglia', which sweeps all, including the United States, into a gigantic holdall (though not without a certain attractive logic). But before this panoramic process began in the mid-1950s, it had already been under way for each of the national literatures separately. As early as 1905 the South African novelist Pauline Smith attended a lecture in a small South African country town on 'South African Literature'. Between the world wars phrases like 'Canadian Literature' and 'New Zealand Literature' were in use in those countries to distinguish literary creations composed in the British Isles and the United States from literature written by local writers.

It seems reasonable to argue that to the extent that English as spoken in each of the countries of the Commonwealth differs from British English and American English in pronunciation, vocabulary, idiom and cultural references, it is right and proper to think of a separate national literature. The New Zealand poet Kendrick Smithyman put this problem of terminology very clearly in the opening paragraph of an article published in the *Journal of Commonwealth Literature* in June 1971:

> The idea of Commonwealth literature is a handy fiction. If we go back to its elements, individual writers and individual literary works, we are unlikely to find a man who is a Commonwealth writer or find a piece of professedly Commonwealth writing. But, if we put aside the conscious products of late nineteenth-century Imperialism, or things written in the nascent if abortive spirit of Imperial Federation, we may readily find writing from one hand which may properly be claimed by more than one part of the Commonwealth. Then too there are the literary sports like Maugham or Lawrence, metropolitans in the main who arrive and pass but are not insignificant, and there are others who arrive, stay longer (even permanently) but whose commitment or affiliation or relevance a more ardent nativist may query. The idea of the Commonwealth and, by implication, of a correspondent literature, is monolithic and, in a determinable sense, unitary although not static. As for the literature, the condition is patently not unitary. It is diverse, and dynamic.

There seems little doubt now that, whatever its advantages, say, twenty years ago, the monolithic approach has ceased to be truly helpful or even practicable. It must, almost of necessity, skim over the diverse and therefore minimize the dynamic. In searching for commonalty it must generally over-simplify; it must underplay the relationship between a writer and the community he grew up in; in trying to precipitate the best simultaneously out of so many divergent backgrounds it must tend to make literary judgement belletristic, that is, concentrate unduly on writing for its own sake and merely scratch at the other considerations that are normally brought to bear in the discussion of literature. In such an enterprise, it is always more tempting to go for the universal rather than the particular, about which the Nigerian novelist Chinua Achebe has a very pertinent comment:

> But the dogma of universality . . . is so patently false and dangerous and yet so attractive that it ought not to go unchallenged. For supposing 'events all over the world' [he is quoting from a critic] have *not* shown 'in the new generation a similar dissatisfaction . . .' would it truly be invalid for a Nigerian writer seeing a dissatisfaction in *his* society to write about it? Am I being told for Christ's sake that before I write about any problem I must first verify whether they have it too in New York and London and Paris?
>
> (*Morning Yet on Creation Day: Essays*, London 1975 p. 52)

Of course, Achebe is not trying to justify parochialism or provincialism. He is taking issue with what he sees as timorous critical judgement of the kind which is over-anxious to show that the local product is as good as anything produced in the outside world. He is attacking literary criteria that depend upon international fads and fashions of taste which are no less provincial for being provincial across many national frontiers. He is reminding us that a literary work is to be reacted to for what it in fact is and for what it is trying to do.

Although other problems in turn rise immediately, perhaps it is more sensible nowadays to think of Commonwealth literatures, or of the national literatures of the Commonwealth and ex-Commonwealth countries. As I have argued elsewhere,[1] linguistic considerations alone can help to crack the Commonwealth Literature monolith into at least three *kinds* of national literatures:

1. The literatures of those countries where British settlement took place on a considerable scale and a local variant of English is therefore the mother tongue. One thinks of Australia, Canada, New Zealand and white English-speaking South Africa (though in each of these cases the matter is complicated by the presence of, respectively, the Aborigines; the French, the Indians, even the Eskimos; the Maoris; the Bantu-speaking peoples and the Afrikaners — each group with its culture affecting the native speakers of English in different degrees, and each group producing some non-native speakers of English who write in English).
2. The literature of the former British West Indies, where as a result of slavery and colonialism very distinct regional varieties of English have become the mother tongues of people of mainly African and Indian origin.
3. The literatures of the African and Asian countries of the former British Empire, where there was some British settlement (Kenya) or virtually none at all (for example, India, Nigeria and Malaysia). In this group, English is still widely used as a utilitarian language of communication, usually in a multilingual situation, and as a literary language has been acquired by writers whose mother tongues were pushed into the background by a British style of education, or whose deliberate choice it has been to write in English and not their mother tongues (though an Indian writer like Kamala Das uses both). Moreover, in these countries literature in English forms only part of the national literature and exists alongside writing in other languages also. In India, for example, writing in English is decidedly a minority activity, with writing also going on in languages like Hindi, Bengali, Kannada and Tamil. In such situations the mutual interaction among literatures in different languages is an important facet of the overall concept of a multilingual national literature. One sees why Kendrick Smithyman lays stress on the words 'diverse' and 'dynamic'.

And yet, even as one emphasizes the divergences, one is aware of certain common features in all these literatures in English. At the spoken level of usage, especially pronunciation and accentuation, the differences among the variants of English (English as spoken, for instance, by Australians and Trinidadians) are naturally more conspicuous than those that appear in the respective *written* literatures. However much Chinua Achebe may use Igbo proverbs translated literally into English, or Gabriel Okara may apply the grammatical structures of Ijaw to English sentences, or Raja Rao may use Indian—English words and forms of address, their written work still remains largely open and accessible to anyone with an educated knowledge of English, just as the literatures in English of the British Isles and the United States remain open to such writers as well as to their readers. Whether this large area of mutual accessibility will continue indefinitely into the future, or whether West African writers, for example, will continue to write in English rather than in their own mother tongues or in another African language that they have acquired, is fruitless to speculate upon, since history will decide. But the richness and variety of experience, and of the transmission of that experience in different kinds of English that are yet available to readers with multifarious cultural backgrounds, are what make the Commonwealth literatures (or whatever one calls them) exciting and rewarding and counteractive against provincialism. On the other hand, some hurdles already exist and in an article in the April 1977 issue of the *Journal of Commonwealth Literature*, Martin Jarrett-Kerr, C. R. questions our present levels of mutual accessibility, and points to Raja Rao's Vedantism in *The Serpent and the Rope* as a case in point.

Yet there is also some common *experience* right across the Commonwealth (even in the British Isles, as Scottish and Welsh nationalists would argue) — experience of colonialism in one form or another. In New Zealand between the world wars no less than in West Africa after the Second World War, the English language was used as an instrument of political nationalism and anti-imperialism, and the development of national literatures in the pre-1939 dominions, as well as in the Third World colonies after 1945, received considerable stimulus from national sentiment. No sooner does one make a general statement of this kind, than one is aware how it needs to be qualified for just about every Commonwealth country, which again underscores the dangers of the monolithic view of Commonwealth Literature. Broad similarity of experience there may well be, but one returns each time to the simple facts of particularity — that Achebe does not think of himself as a 'Commonwealth' writer but as first an Igbo, then a Nigerian, then an African; that with or without his Nobel Prize Patrick White is an Australian novelist; that Wilson Harris began writing as a Guyanese, interpreting human experience made manifest in the forests and rivers of Guyana; that Jewish (hence international in another sense) as his imagination is, A. M. Klein's poetry is also in a very real way Canadian.

Categorization of the kind that I have been bandying about has its uses, and may even be essential for such purposes as planning school and university syllabuses of literature in English. I have been dwelling quite deliberately upon the differences and divergences within 'Commonwealth Literature', because I believe that the more one reads in these areas the more one begins to realize that the common features are often beguiling and frequently lie on the surface only. What makes a literary work dynamic is the quality of the writer's imagination and his ability to transmute it into language — I mean as a single creative process, not as two separable faculties. Perhaps the only real service that categorizing in terms of monolithic 'Commonwealth' has done, is that it has brought to more readers' attention than otherwise might have come about, the work of non-metropolitan writers which deserves more than a merely national readership, though to have *that* on its own need not be inglorious. Whether in Elizabethan England or mid-twentieth-century Canada, nationalism can undoubtedly be a very valuable source of literary inspiration, and not necessarily in the obvious ways only. But once it has imparted its stimulating charge, it can too easily lead to the monotonous creaking of the parish pump. I think it is precisely here that those segments of the various national literatures of so many countries which are still written in generally accessible forms of English have a particular contribution to make. In theory at least (though some writers have undoubtedly demonstrated it in practice), it seems unlikely that even the most nationalist Sri Lankan or Kenyan writer can expunge from his consciousness an awareness that, even if only locally published, his writing is capable of being read and understood by many more millions beyond his national frontiers than within them. At this point, I find myself swinging somewhat from the advantages of the concept of single national literatures to those of a wider, more panoptic approach; yet the latter cannot be arrived at except through the former, just as African literature in English is a nonsense without the writings of novelists like Chinua Achebe (Nigeria), Nguigi wa Thiong'o (Kenya), Alex La Guma (South Africa), and the Nigerian dramatist, poet and novelist Wole Soyinka.

HISTORICAL AND ACADEMIC

My observations thus far have been general and perhaps theoretical, because I have wanted to show both the dangers and the potential rewards of the study of that very complex object, Commonwealth literatures. A brief résumé of its academic provenance is perhaps in order here. As a means of extending customary English Literature preoccupations and of examining more than one national literature in English at a time, it began to feature in university syllabuses independently, but almost simultaneously, in the late 1950s, under Professor Joseph Jones in the University of Texas, and Professor A.N. Jeffares in the University of Leeds, where an Annual Visiting Fellowship in Commonwealth Literature was established in 1959. Ironically, the first Chair of Commonwealth Literature was inaugurated not in an Anglo-Saxon country, but at the University of Venice, just a few weeks before the Chair at Leeds was set up in 1972.

In 1964 the first international conference on Commonwealth Literature took place at Leeds. Its effects were far-reaching and greatly stimulated the study of Commonwealth literatures in Britain and throughout the world. The book of selected papers delivered at this conference sold out within some seven months of publication, and the success of the meeting released funds via the British Council that made possible the appearance of the first issue of the *Journal of Commonwealth Literature (JCL)* in September 1965. It is just possible that these events have encouraged the actual amount of writing in the Commonwealth countries. Even allowing for the increasing efficiency of the compilers over the years, it is worth pointing out that the 'Annual Bibliography of Commonwealth Literature' occupied seventy-five pages in the first issue of *JCL*, whereas the 'Annual Bibliography' for 1975 ran to 181 pages set in a smaller size of type.

In 1966 a smaller meeting at Leeds resulted in the formation of the Association for Commonwealth Literature and Language Studies, with a world-wide membership; successive subventions from the Commonwealth Foundation made possible the holding of international conferences in Brisbane (1968), Kingston, Jamaica (1971), Kampala (1974), and New Delhi (1977). During these years the shift of emphasis I have remarked upon, from the monolithic to the national, has expressed itself in part in the formation of national and regional branches of the Assocation — the European branch with its Chairman at Aarhus, Denmark, its Secretary at Liège, Belgium, and its Treasurer at Stirling, Scotland; the Canadian branch; the South Pacific branch (Australia, New Zealand, Fiji and so on); and other branches in India, Sri Lanka, Malaysia and Singapore, West Africa and the West Indies. All these branches have held regional meetings and seminars, some more spectacularly and regularly than others, but the stimulation and the spirit of co-operation thus engendered have been immense. For instance, these more localized meetings have led to Australian scholars taking a fresh look at Indian writing in English and vice versa.

As the result of a week-end conference at Leeds early in 1970, a follow-up meeting was called a few months later at the Commonwealth Institute in London, which led to the setting up of the Working Party on Library Holdings of Commonwealth Literature (in United Kingdom libraries). In 1971 this Working Party produced a useful little reference book, *A Handbook of Library Holdings of Commonwealth Literature in the United Kingdom*, while a mimeographed supplement produced in 1974 extended its references to libraries in the rest of Europe; an extensively revised edition of the *Handbook* was produced in 1977.[2] The Working Party has also been responsible for the present volume on Commonwealth literature periodicals.

By no means all the attention given to the literatures of the Commonwealth countries in universities, polytechnics, colleges of education and some schools falls under the formal heading of 'Commonwealth Literature'. It does in the Universities of Leeds, Stirling and Hull, for instance, but in many institutions in Britain alone it appears under such headings as 'Third World Studies' (for example, African, Caribbean and Indian at Canterbury, Kent), 'African and Caribbean Studies' at Sussex and 'West African Studies' at Birmingham.

Not only in Britain but throughout the Commonwealth (indeed also in non-Commonwealth countries like the United States, France, Italy, Germany and, more recently, Japan) the study of the literatures of Commonwealth countries in one form or another has become an established part of tertiary education, and sometimes also of school activities.

HISTORICAL AND PERIODICAL

From the earliest days when literature was being practised in what were then the colonies, aspiring poets, novelists and dramatists sought to have their work accepted and published in London and/or New York. In 1881 Olive Schreiner arrived in London from the Cape Colony with at least one manuscript novel (perhaps two) in her portmanteau, and in 1883 her novel *The Story of an African Farm* was published by Chapman and Hall, probably the first 'colonial' novel to cause a real stir in the outside world and admit its author to the exclusiveness of literary London. But despite the pull of the metropolis (with its influential publishing houses), newspapers and literary journals in the colonies, dominions, and now independent countries of the Commonwealth have always existed, however unostentatiously, and provided outlets for local writers. Particular literary magazines like *Bim* and *Kyk-over-al* in the Caribbean and *Black Orpheus* in Nigeria have not only been outward signs of vigorous local creativity but have also stimulated further literary creativity. Most of the well-known writers from the Commonwealth have had their earliest work first published in such journals, as the researches of Bernth Lindfors and Reinhard W. Sander have shown very conclusively.[3]

As the study of Commonwealth literatures has tended to shift from a small number of outstanding writers to the total literary situations from which they have emerged, so the need for drilling into hitherto unknown historical strata has become more urgently felt. Certainly, the kind of discoveries that have begun to be made in the back files of both defunct and still existing literary journals has revealed a great wealth of historically interesting and intrinsically worthwhile submerged literature. One of the most dramatic recent discoveries made in the course of such delving has been the entirely new dimension given to the history of Black South African Literature in English by Tim Couzens's researches into the pre-1950 period,[4] reinforced by David Rabkin's thesis on the relationship between writing in *Drum* magazine and the work of the Black South African writers of the 1950s and early 1960s.[5] Mr. Couzens's labours have taken him well beyond literary journals *per se* into daily and weekly newspapers, revealing an unbroken history from the nineteenth century to the present day of black journalism carried on simultaneously with more 'serious' writing and political protest and involvement. His hunting has produced not only 'hidden' writings of real merit but has also led him to the discovery of unpublished texts in manuscript. His work still proceeds and will provide valuable material for any literary history of South Africa that may yet be compiled.

It was to assist in this kind of literary research that the Working Party on Library Holdings of Commonwealth Literature aimed from its very inception at producing a list of past and present literary magazines and of periodical publications that gave some space to literature and literary criticism. Work began almost immediately under the enthusiastic guidance of Alan Horne, then Librarian of the Commwealth Institute and Secretary of the Working Party. His successors Alan Evans and Michael Foster, especially the latter, continued to give the project encouragement and practical help. But it was not until a generous grant was made by the British Library and Ronald Warwick was appointed as Researcher/Bibliographer in 1975 that the present volume could become more than a gleam in the collective eye of the Working Party. I have no doubt whatever that this bibliography of Commonwealth Literature periodicals, together with the future supplements that will almost certainly be necessary, will prove an invaluable research tool.

Arthur Ravenscroft,
Senior Lecturer in English Literature,
University of Leeds;
Editor, *Journal of Commonwealth Literature*, 1965–1979.

NOTES

1. *Journal of Commonwealth Literature*, No. 4, 1967, pp. iv–vi.
2. Ronald Warwick (comp. and ed.), *A Handbook of Library Holdings of Commonwealth Literature: United Kingdom and Europe*, 2nd rev. ed., Boston Spa, British Library Lending Division for Working Party on Library Holdings of Commonwealth Literature, 1977.
3. See B. Lindfors, 'Wole Soyinka Talking Through His Hat' and R. W. Sander, 'The Impact of Literary Periodicals on the Development of West Indian Literature and Cultural Independence' in H. Maes-Jelinek (ed.), *Commonwealth Literature and the Modern World*, Brussels, 1975, pp. 115–25 and 25–32 respectively.
4. e.g. Tim Couzens, 'Black South African Literature in English, 1900–1950' in H. Maes-Jelinek (ed.), *Commonwealth Literature and the Modern World*, pp. 89–96; 'The Continuity of Black Literature in South Africa Before 1950', *English in Africa*, Vol. 1, No. 2, pp. 11–23; 'The Hidden Literature of Black South Africa', *New Society*, No. 35, pp. 272–3.
5. David Rabkin, '*Drum* Magazine (1951–1961) and the Black South African Writers Associated With It,' Ph.D. thesis, University of Leeds, 1975.

Introduction

The terms 'literary', 'periodicals' and 'Commonwealth' would seem self-explanatory but unfortunately there is no general agreement as to their exact meaning. A brief description of the scope of this bibliography is therefore necessary. In his Foreword, Arthur Ravenscroft has outlined the aims and development of the study of Commonwealth literature. It is for the benefit of the student of this subject that the present volume has been compiled Firstly, it aims to determine which periodicals falling within the scope of the subject have been published in the countries of the Commonwealth. Secondly, it aims to locate holdings of these periodicals in United Kingdom libraries.

COVERAGE

The bibliography lists periodical publications that give significant space to Commonwealth literature and related literary criticism. Periodicals specifically concerned with Commonwealth literature in general are in fact listed, but the intention has been to include periodicals from or about all countries of the Commonwealth (*excluding* the United Kingdom) together with former Commonwealth countries such as Pakistan, South Africa and the Sudan. The period covered is from the earliest colonial period to mid-1977.

The term 'literary' as used here covers not only specifically literary periodicals but also more general magazines likely to be of interest to the student of Commonwealth Literature, in the selection of which it has proved necessary to adopt a sliding scale. In the earlier period, in smaller countries, or in countries in which English is a minority language, periodicals tend to be less specialized so that a greater number of more general periodicals are listed. Similarly, in developing countries until quite recently, school and college magazines were an important source of creative literature so that a higher proportion of these has been included than would be appropriate in a more developed country. Periodicals written in languages other than English are not included, except for bilingual or multi-lingual publications with a significant English contribution. Neither are newspapers included; although almost all of them, particularly in the earlier period, contain poems, short stories and essays, these contributions are usually so incidental to the primary object of the dissemination of current intelligence that their inclusion would have created an imbalance in a work such as this.

Literary journals published in the Commonwealth, but which are devoted to non-Commonwealth Literatures (e.g. Classical or European) are not included, although the demarcation has sometimes been complicated by an unsuspected 'Commonwealth Literature' issue. Another complication arises when journals change the nature of their interest. A hitherto non-literary periodical may begin to include literary features, or a journal may cease to contain literary contributions. Consequently, journals have sometimes been listed, recent or earlier issues of which have scarcely any literary content.

ARRANGEMENT

Entries are arranged under geographical areas or countries and, when these divisions are unwieldy, are further arranged under broad subject headings, so that the user is advised to consult the alphabetical index of titles in order to locate a particular periodical. Of the geographical areas, particular mention should be made of Africa, which has been split into three broad regions. The reason for this arrangement is that it reflects the tendency of periodical literature to cross national boundaries in these areas. There is also a list of short titles arranged by country in this section to facilitate an alternative approach. For similar reasons a short-title list has been provided for the Caribbean section.

The recording of a periodical under a particular geographical area or country denotes its contents rather than its provenance. Most of the periodicals listed have a Commonwealth imprint. The exceptions are mostly journals concerned with Commonwealth literature generally, such as *Journal of Commonwealth Literature* (U.K.) or *WLWE (World Literature Written in English)* (U.S.A.), or with Afro-Asian literature such as *Conch* (U.S.A.), or *Journal of South Asian Literature* (U.S.A.).

The form of entry is as follows:

Title of periodical
Subtitle
Frequency. Volume, number and date of original and final issue
Place of publication. Statement of responsibility
Editor
International Standard Serial Number (ISSN)
Related title
Locations

For example:

LOTUS
Afro-Asian writings
q; no.1 1971–
Cairo, Egypt. Permanent Bureau of Afro-Asian Writers, 104 Kasr el Aini St.
ed. Youssef El Sabai
ISSN 0002–0664
Supersedes AFRO-ASIAN WRITINGS (q.v.)
LO/S26: no.1–16   LO/U14

Not all the elements listed above apply to every entry. In many instances the requisite information was not available or could not be ascertained. The absence of an ISSN is usually because the periodical is defunct and predates the assignment of these numbers. In other cases, especially if the ISSN is not printed on the periodical, this information has been impossible to obtain. A further difficulty is that the ISSN changes whenever the title of the periodical changes.

Entry is under successive title with a reference to previous and subsequent titles (described as 'related titles'). The title page has, wherever possible, been taken as the authority for the entry. Variants on covers and elsewhere are not recorded. Quite often the 'statement of responsibility' and the 'editor' amount to the same. Subtitles subject to frequent change are not included, except when they denote a substantial change in the nature of the periodical. In the same way the name of the editor is not supplied if this is liable to frequent change (as, for example, in the case of student magazines), nor are long lists of editors who constitute an editorial board, unless any of these is very well known. Editors' names are only supplied when intellectual responsibility for the publication may be reasonably attributed to them.

A location symbol without a following numerical designation denotes that the library held a complete file at the time this bibliography was compiled.

METHOD OF COMPILATION

The basis for this bibliography was a number of lists of Commonwealth literary periodicals compiled by Alan Horne who, when Librarian of the Commonwealth Institute, was the first Honorary Secretary of the Working Party. This information was supplemented by consulting bibliographies and union lists. As well as the national bibliographies for Commonwealth countries (see *Commonwealth National Bibliographies: An Annotated Directory*, Commonwealth Secretariat, 1977), national lists of current serials and union lists, numerous specialist lists of literary periodicals and indexes were consulted. Clearly much of this material is repetitive, and on the whole only the better known journals are recorded. In order to discover more fugitive items, it was necessary to distribute the lists resulting from the initial research to national and university libraries in Commonwealth countries for additions and amendments. In many instances, enquiries were directed to researchers compiling national lists of periodicals which led to the exchange of much useful information. Questionnaires were also sent to United Kingdom libraries in conjunction with preparing the revised edition of the *Handbook of Library Holdings of Commonwealth Literature: United Kingdom and Europe* (British Library Lending Division, for Working Party on Library Holdings of Commonwealth Literature, 1977). In this way, it was possible to determine the most important holdings of Commonwealth literary periodicals in the United Kingdom, and follow up with personal visits to record holdings and check bibliographical statements.

Any bibliography which deals with a subject not previously covered is, in a sense, an initial step. Despite the procedures adopted to collect this information, it would be rash to make any greater claim for this bibliography. The vagaries of periodical numbering (notorious in the case of literary magazines), irregularity of appearance, together with the reliance on secondary and frequently conflicting information for unlocated periodicals, inevitably creates doubt concerning the accuracy or completeness of many bibliographical statements and the comprehensiveness of coverage. It has been necessary in some cases to opt for the consensus that has emerged, even where this conflicts with a standard and usually reliable source. Another hazard that confronts the compiler of a work of this nature is the discovery of a chance reference to a periodical, and the failure to find any further information about it. Where the amount of information thus discovered has been minimal (e.g. simply a title), this has not been included. It is all too easy to generate a ghost periodical that owes its existence to the mistranscription of a similar title. Such ghosts can persist for many years in subsequent bibliographies. I hope, therefore, that as well as providing information, this bibliography will also stimulate it. Any corrections and new titles should be sent to the Secretary of the Working Party on Library Holdings of Commonwealth Literature, c/o The Commonwealth Institute Library and Resource Centre, Kensington High Street, London W8 6NQ.

Acknowledgements

This work has been carried out under the aegis of the Working Party on Library Holdings of Commonwealth Literature and has been made possible by a generous subvention from the British Library.

I wish to express my thanks to the special projects subcommittee of the Working Party; Mr. Donald Simpson (Chairman of the Working Party and Librarian of the Royal Commonwealth Society), Mr. Michael Foster (Secretary of the Working Party and Librarian of the Commonwealth Institute, London), and Mr. Peter Snow (of the Bodleian Library). The work of compilation has been carried out under their direction, and with their encouragement, assistance and unfailing kindness.

I would also like to thank the many academics, research workers and librarians who have been so generous with their time and expertise. In particular I would mention: Mr. Jonathan Barker (Arts Council Poetry Library), Mr. Robert Bateman (Micromedia Ltd., Oxford), Mr. Ulli Beier (Institute of Papua New Guinea Studies), Mr. B. C. Bloomfield (Librarian, School of Oriental and African Studies, London University), Miss M. M. Brennan (Brynmor Jones Library, Hull University), Miss June Cooling (Exeter University Library), Mr. D. S. Darlow (Librarian, Kent University), Miss Lesley Forbes (Librarian, Oriental Section, Durham University), Mr. Peter Freshwater (Birmingham University Library), Mrs. N. M. Gallimore (Canada House Library, London), Dr. L. Hallewell (Essex University Library), Mrs. Elizabeth Hammerton (Royal Commonwealth Society Library), Mr. Christopher Haywood (Dept. English, Sheffield University), Miss Vanessa Hinton (Brotherton Library, Leeds University), Mrs. Alexia Howe (National Library of Scotland), Mr. Peter Hughes (University of Auckland Library, New Zealand), Mrs. Christiane Keane (Commonwealth Institute Library, London), Mrs. M. A. Leitch (National Archives of Rhodesia), Mr. Clarke E. Leverette (bibliographer and little magazine editor), Mr. Cedric May (Dept. French, University of Birmingham), Miss Kathryn Mikoski (National Library of Canada), Miss Brenda Moon (Brynmor Jones Library, Hull University), Mr. Alan Moss (University of the West Indies, Jamaica), Mrs. Jeanie Moyo (for preparing a difficult typescript), Dr. Alastair Niven (Dept., English, Stirling University), Professor Anne Paolucci (St. John's University, New York), Mr. A. N. Peasgood (Sussex University Library), Mr. Arthur Ravenscroft (School of English, Leeds University), Mr. Reinhard Sander (Sussex University), Miss Ulla Schild (Mainz University, Germany), Mr. T. A. D. Smith (Sheffield University Library), Mrs. Vibeke Stenderup (State and University Library, Aarhus, Denmark), Mr. Tan Lai Wan (National Library of Singapore), Mr. Nick Toczek (Editor, *Little Word Review*), Mr. R. J. Townsend (Librarian, Institute of Commonwealth Studies, Oxford), Mrs. Carol Travis (Institute of Commonwealth Studies, London), Mr. Paul Xuereb (Librarian, University of Malta), Mr. Hans Zell (Editor, *African Book Publishing Record*).

Location Symbols

TEL = Telephone, EXT = Extension, TX = Telex

AB/N–1   National Library of Wales, Aberysthwyth, Cardiganshire, SY23 3BU.
TEL 0970–381617 TX 35165

AD/U–1   Aberdeen University Library, King's College, Aberdeen, AB9 2UB.
TEL 0224–40241 EXT 369

BH/U–1   Main Library, University of Birmingham, P.O. Box 363, Birmingham, BI5 2TT.
TEL 021–472 1301 EXT 171 TX 338160

BN/U–1   University College of North Wales, Bangor, Caernarvonshire. TEL 0248–25
TEL 0248–2501

BT/U–1   University of Sussex, Falmer, Brighton, BN1 9QL.
TEL 0273–66755 TX 87394

CA/U–1   Cambridge University, Cambridge, CB3 9DR. TEL 0223–61441 TX 81895

CB/U–1   The University of Kent, Canterbury, Kent, CT2 7NZ. TEL 0227–66822

CC/U–1   University of Essex, P.O. Box no.24, Wivenhoe Park, Colchester, Essex,
CC4 3UA. TEL 0206–44144 EXT 2063 TX 98440

DR/U–1   Durham University Library, Palace Green, Durham, DH1 3HP.
TEL 0385–61262/3 TX 537351

DR/U–4   Durham University Library, Oriental Section, School of Oriental Studies,
Elvet Hill, Durham, DH1 3TH. TEL 0385–64371

ED/N–1   National Library of Scotland, George IV Bridge, Edinburgh, EH1 1EW.
TEL 031–225 4104 TX 72638

ED/P–1   Edinburgh Public Library, George IV Bridge, Edinburgh, EH1 1EG.
TEL 031–225 5584/6

ED/U–1   Edinburgh University Library, George Square, Edinburgh, EH8 9LJ.
TEL 031–667 1011 EXT 6622

EX/U–1   The University of Exeter Library, Prince of Wales Drive, Exeter, Devon,
EX4 4PT. TEL 0392–77911 TX 42894

GL/U–1   University Library, Glasgow, G12 8QE. TEL 041–334 2122 TX 778421

HL/U–1   Brynmor Jones Library, The University of Hull, Cottingham Road, Hull,
Humberside, HU6 7RX. TEL 0482–408960

LA/U–1   Lancaster University Library, Bailrigg, Lancaster, LA1 4XX.
TEL 0524–65201 EXT 275 TX 6511

LD/P–1   Leeds City Libraries, Central Library, Leeds, West Yorkshire, LS1 3AB.
TEL 0532–31301 EXT 378

LD/U–1   Brotherton Library, Leeds University, Leeds, West Yorkshire, LS2 9JT.
TEL 0532–31751 EXT 6551

LO/N–1   British Library, Reference Division, The British Museum, London, WC1B 3DG.
TEL 01–636 1555 TX 21462

LO/N12   India Office Library, Foreign and Commonwealth Office, 197 Blackfriars
Road, London, SE1 8NG.
TEL 01–928 9531

LO/N17   Foreign and Commonwealth Office, 3 Sanctuary Buildings, Great Smith
Street, London, SW1P 3BZ. TEL 01–839 7010 EXT 251

LO/R98   Australian Reference Library, Australia House, Strand, London, WC2B 4LA.
TEL 01–836 2435

LO/S26   Commonwealth Institute, Kensington High Street, London, W8 6NQ.
TEL 01–602 3252

LO/S55   India House Library, High Commission for India, India House, Aldwych,
London, WC2B 4NA. TEL 01–836 8484 EXT 114

LO/S65   Royal Commonwealth Society, Northumberland Avenue, London,
WC2N 5BJ. TEL 01–930 6733

LO/T20   New Zealand High Commission, New Zealand House, Haymarket, London,
SW1Y 4TQ. TEL 01–930 8422 TX 24368

LO/T22   Office of the High Commissioner for Canada, Canada House, 5 Trafalgar
Square, London, SW1Y 5BJ. TEL 01–930 9741 EXT 235

LO/T83   West India Committee Library, c/o University of London, Institute of
Commonwealth Studies, 27 Russell Square, London, WC1B 5BS
TEL 01–580 5876

LO/U–1   University of London Library, Senate House, Malet Street, London,
WC1E 7HU. TEL 01–636 4514 EXT 22

LO/U–2   University College London, Gower Street, London, WC1E 6BT.
TEL 01–387 7050

LO/U–8   University of London, Institute of Commonwealth Studies, 27 Russell
Square, London, WC1B 5BS. TEL 01–580 5876

LO/U14   School of Oriental and African Studies, University of London, Malet Street,
London, WC1E 7HP. TEL 01–580 9021

LV/U–1   Liverpool University, P.O. Box 123, Liverpool, L69 3DA.
TEL 051–709 6022 TX 627095

MA/U–1   Manchester University, Oxford Road, Manchester, M13 9PL.
TEL 061–273 3333 TX 668932

NR/U–1   University of East Anglia, University Plain, Norwich, NR4 7TJ.
TEL 0603–56161 EXT 2427 TX 97154

NW/U–1   Newcastle University, Queen Victoria Road, Newcastle upon Tyne,
NE1 7RU. TEL 0632–28511 EXT 3773 TX 53654

OX/U–1   Bodleian Library, Oxford, OX1 3BG.
TEL 0865–44675 TX 83656

OX/U–9   Rhodes House, University of Oxford, South Parks Road, Oxford, OX1 3RG.
TEL 0865–55762

OX/U14   Institute of Commonwealth Studies, 21 St. Giles, Oxford, OX1 3LA.
TEL 0865–52952/4 EXT 24

QL/P–1   Manchester Public Libraries, St. Peter's Square, Manchester, M2 5PD.
TEL 061–236 7401 TX 66149

QL/P–2   Liverpool Public Library, William Brown Street, Liverpool, L3 8EW.
TEL 051–207 2147 TX 62500

QM/P−2	Birmingham Public Libraries, Reference Library, Ratcliffe Place, Birmingham B1 2AR. TEL 021−643 2948 TX 33455
QS/Q29	Westminster City Libraries, Marylebone Road, London, NW1 5PS. TEL 01−935 7766 EXT 131 TX 263305
SH/U−1	Sheffield University, Western Bank, Sheffield, Yorkshire, S10 2TN. TEL 0742−78555 EXT 332 TX 54348
ST/U−1	University of Stirling, Stirling, Scotland, FK9 4LA. TEL 0786−8171

Abbreviations

Assn.	Association
c.	about
Coll.	College
Dept.	Department
ed.	editor
ISSN	International Standard Serial Number
n.d.	no date
no.	number
P.	Press
q.v.	which see
U.	University
vol.	volume

Frequency Codes

a	annual
b	bimonthly
ƀ	irregular
c	semiweekly (twice a week)
e	biweekly (every two weeks)
f	semiannual
g	biennial (every two years)
m	monthly
q	quarterly
s	semimonthly
t	three times a year
w	weekly
z	other

The Bibliography

COMMONWEALTH

General

ACLALS BULLETIN
Bulletin of the Association for Commonwealth
Literature and Language Studies
f; 1st series no.1—5 1966—8(U. Leeds),no.6 1969
(Carleton U., Ottawa)   2nd series no.1—11
1971—2(Kampala, Uganda) and special issue un-
numbered   4th series no.3 1975— (Dept. of
English, U. Mysore, India) Numbering irregular
ISSN 0066—9083

LD/U—1: imperfect   LO/N—1: imperfect
LO/S26: imperfect   LO/S65: imperfect
LO/U—8: 1st series no.3—5; 4th series no.1—
ST/U—1: imperfect

CBCL NEWSLETTER
Conference on British Commonwealth Literature
∅; no.1—10 1962—7
Arlington, Texas. Dept. of English, U. Texas
Superseded by WLWE (q.v.)

LO/N—1   LO/S26: no.6—10   LO/S65

CENTRE FOR COMMONWEALTH LITERATURE
AND RESEARCH
∅; no.1 1976—
Mysore, Karnataka, India. U. Mysore

LO/N—1   LO/S26

COMMONWEALTH
Miscellanies, *mélanges*
a; no.1 1975—
Mont St. Aigan, France, Rodez (France) for the
Société d'Etudes des pays du Commonwealth,
37 rue Charles Lepneveu, 76130, Mont St. Aigan.
ed. J. Leclaire

LO/S65

COMMONWEALTH NEWSLETTER
f; no.1 1971—

Arhus, Denmark. ACLALS — European Branch.
Dept. of English, U. Arhus, 8000 Arhus C.

LD/U—1   LO/S26   LO/S65   ST/U—1

ECHOS DU COMMONWEALTH
Bulletin intérieur de la Société d'Etudes des Pays
du Commonwealth
∅; no.1 1973—
Mont St. Aigan, France. 35 rue Charles Lepneveu,
76130, Mont St. Aigan.

LO/S26   LO/S65   LO/U—8

JOURNAL OF COMMONWEALTH LITERATURE
t; vol.1,no.1 1965—
London, U.K. Oxford University P., Press Rd.,
London NW10
ed. Arthur Ravenscroft
ISSN 0021—9894

LD/U—1   LO/N—1   LO/S26
LO/S65   LO/U—1   LO/U—8
ST/U—1

MOKO NEWSLETTER
f; vol.1,no.1 1973—
Saskatoon, Sask. Canada. Canadian Association
for Commonwealth Literature and Language
Studies (CACLALS), Dept. of English, U. Sask-
katchewan, Saskatoon, Sask. S7N 0W0

LO/S26: vol.1,no.4 —   LO/S65

WLWE
f; no.11 1967—
Arlington, Texas, U.S.A. Dept. of English,
Arlington, Texas TX 76019
ed. Robert McDowell
ISSN 0042—9759
WORLD LITERATURE WRITTEN IN ENGLISH
Supersedes CBCL NEWSLETTER (q.v.)

LD/U—1   LO/S26   ST/U—1

AFRICA

Short-Title List by Country

Africa has been divided into four sections within which periodicals are arranged alphabetically by title. A list of short titles under individual countries is given for ease of reference

BOTSWANA

Bonesa
Bosele
Comment
Expression
Lesedi
Manang a lesedi

GAMBIA

Ndaanan

GHANA

Abuscondian
Achimota Review
Achimotan
Alector
Arts Council of Ghana Newsletter
Asemka
Atumpan
Bepowso bann
Clarion
Forum
Ghana Cultural Review
Ghana Library Journal
Kata School Magazine
Legacy
Legon Journal of the Humanities
Legonite
Literary and Social Guide
Mawulian
New Age
New Era
Northern Light
Okyeame
Owaria
Pleisure
Royal Gold Coast Gazette
Scroll
Siren
Talent for Tomorrow
Transition
Undergraduate
Universitas
University College of the Cape
    Coast workpapers
Voice of Aquinas
Voices of Youth

Workpapers
Writers' Workshop Notes

KENYA

Art
Busara
Chemichemi News
Dhana
Dialogue
Donovan Maule
East Africa Journal
Eastleigh School Magazine
Egertonian
Equator
Ghala
Happy Moments
Haroya
Indian voice
Joe
Joliso
Journal of the Language Association
Key
Maktaba
Nexus
Oddspot
On Stage
Pointer
Reveille
Upeo
Zuka

LESOTHO

Comment
Expression

MALAWI

Bits and Pieces
Change
Expression
Jacaranda
Likuni Boys' School Magazine
Likuni Girls' School Magazine
Odi
Reflection
Robert Blake School Magazine
University students' Magazine
University Vanguard

Vanguard
Voice of St. Patrick's

NIGERIA

Abadina
Aboki
Academician
Adventure
Africa
African Horizon
African Notes
African Writer
Afriscope
Afro Image
Afroculture
Agauda
Agboja
Agricola Ibadaniensis
Alfijir
Alfijir da nasiha
Amber
Anchor
Andrian
Anthonian
Anvil
Arbitrator
Aro
Awowerin
Ayangba Magazine
Barewa
Bauchi School Magazine
Beacon
Bende Progress
Benin Review
Black Orpheus
Blow
Bridge
Bronze
Buffalo
Bug
Call
Campus Opinion
Catalyst
Catholic Undergraduate
Ch'indaba
Christian Student
Cornelian
Criterion
Crown
Culvert
Down Randle Road
Eagle
Edo College Magazine
Egghead
Eggs
Eko
Ekorian

Eleiyele
Emerald
Enitonna
Epidemere
Everybody's Journal
Exit
Fiditian
Finbarria
Flamingo
Forerunner
Forward
Fresh Buds
Gamezaki
Gateway
Harmattan
Hill Man
Hoe
Horizon
Horn
Ibadan
Ibadan Studies in English
Ibonaco
Ideal Companion
Ife African Studies
Ife Writing
Igbarra Students' Magazine
Ijala
Ik il
Ikorok
Iksan
Journal of the Nigeria English
    Studies' Association
Key
Lagos Notes and Records
Lamp
Leader
Masque
Mbari Newsletter
Mellanbite
Muse
Nasiha
New Horn
Nigercol
Nigeria Magazine
Nigerian Student Verse
Norla News
Nsukkascope
Numo Torch
Odu
Oduma
Oke-ela
Okija Citizen
Olumo
Omaba
Omo egbado
Optimus
Penmag

People
Pioneer
Scorpion
Simbo
Sokoti
Spectator
Students' Echo
Tide
Tower
University Herald
Vanguard
Wasp
Work in progress

RHODESIA

Arundel School Magazine
Baines School Magazine
Borderer
Chirimo
Counterpoint
Electra
Illustrated Life
Literary Oscar
Mambo Review
Moto
Opus
Owl
Poetry Review
Review
Rhodesia Calls
Rhodesia Literature Bureau
Rhodesian Poetry
Rhodesiana
Two Tone

SIERRA
LEONE
Africana Research Bulletin
Aureol Mirror
Aureol Review
Bulletin of the Association for
    African Literature in English
Creole Boy
Gold Coast Youth
Negro
Saturday Ho
Zoom

SWAZILAND
Comment
Expression

TANZANIA
Darlite
Dawn
Journal of Modern African Studies
Maji maji
Mbioni

Umma

UGANDA
Makerere
Makerere Journal
Mawazo
Nanga
Penpoint
Roho
Transition

ZAMBIA
Beacon
Chickwakwa
Horizon
Jewel of Africa
New Writing from Zambia
News of African Writing
Northern Rhodesia Journal
Write
Young Zambians Writing
Zambezia

General

ABBIA
Revue culturelle Camerounaise
q; no.1−28 1963−74
Yaoundé, Cameroon. Centre de Littérature
Evangélique, B.P. 1501
ed. Bernard Fonlon
ISSN 0001−3102

BH/U−1	LO/N−1	LO/S65: no2−11
LO/U−2	LO/U14	OX/U14

AFRAM NEWSLETTER
q; no.1 1975−
Paris, France. Centre d'Etudes des Littératures
Afro-Américaine et du Tiers Monde Anglophone
de l'Université, Paris III, 5 rue de l'Ecole de
Médecine, 75006 Paris.

LO/S26: no.3−

AFRICAN ARTS
q; 1967−
Los Angeles, U.S.A. African Studies Center, U.
California

AFRICAN BOOK PUBLISHING RECORD
q; vol.1,no.1 1975−
Oxford, U.K. Hans Zell Ltd., P.O. Box 56,
Oxford OX1 3EI

ed. Hans Zell
ISSN 0306—0322

BH/U—1	LO/N—1	LO/S26
LO/U—8	LO/U14	MA/U—1
OX/U—1		

AFRICAN LITERATURE ASSOCIATION NEWSLETTER

ɤ; vol.1,no.1 1974—
Pennsylvania, U.S.A. 316 Burrowes Bldg., Pennsylvania State U., University Park, 16802
ed. Thomas A. Hale

AFRICAN LITERATURE TODAY

q/a; no.1 1968—
London, U.K. Heinemann Educational Books
Ltd., 48 Charles St., London W1
ed. Eldred D. Jones
ISSN 0065—4000

BH/U—1	LO/N—1	LO/S26
LO/U14	OX/U—1	

AFRO-ASIAN THEATRE BULLETIN

f; vol.1,no.1 1965—
Washington, D.C. American Educational Theatre
Assn., John F. Kennedy Center, 726 Jackson
Place, Washington D.C. 20566

AFRO-ASIAN WRITINGS

ɤ; vol.1,no.1—4 1967—70
Cairo, Egypt. Permanent Bureau of Afro-Asian
Writers, 104 Kasr el Aini St.
Superseded by LOTUS (q.v.)

LO/S26   LO/U14

BA SHIRU

f; no.1 1970—
Madison, Wisconsin, U.S.A. Department of
African Languages and Literature, University of
Wisconsin-Madison, 1456 Van Hise Hall, Madison,
WI 53706
ISSN 0045—1282

BLACK IMAGES

A critical quarterly on Black culture
ɤ; vol.1,no.1 1972—
Toronto, Canada. Box 280, Sta. F, Toronto,
Ont M4Y 2L7
ed. Lennox Brown
ISSN 0315—7784

LD/U—1: vol.1,no.2		LO/U—2
MA/U—1	OX/U—1: vol.1,no.2—4	

BULLETIN OF THE ASSOCIATION FOR AFRICAN LITERATURE IN ENGLISH

ɤ; no.1—4 1964—6
Freetown, Sierra Leone. Fourah Bay College
eds. T. R. M. Creighton and Eldred Jones
Superseded by AFRICAN LITERATURE
TODAY (q.v.)

BT/U—1: no.1,2,4		LD/U—1: no.1—2
LO/N—1: no.4	LO/S26	LO/U—14:
no.3—4		

CANADIAN JOURNAL OF AFRICAN STUDIES

t; no.1 1967—
Ottawa, Ont., Canada. Canadian Assn. of African
Studies, Carleton U., Ottawa, Ont K1S 5B6
eds. Michael Mason and Alfred Schwarz
ISSN 0008—3968

LO/U—8	LO/U14	ST/U—1: no.5—

CONCH

A sociological journal of African cultures and
literatures
ɤ; vol.1,no.1 1969—
Buffalo, N.Y., U.S.A. Conch Magazine Ltd., 102
Normal Ave., Buffalo, N.Y. 14213
ed. S. O. Anozie

BH/U—1	BT/U—1	CB/U—1
LO/N—1	LO/S26	LO/U14

CONCH REVIEW OF BOOKS

A literary supplement on Africa
ɤ; vol.1,no.1 1973—
Buffalo, N.Y., U.S.A. Conch Magazine Ltd., 102
Normal Ave., Buffalo, N.Y. 14213

LO/N—1   LO/U14

DRUM

(Separate editions for Nigeria, East Africa,
Central Africa and South Africa)
m; no.1 1952—
London, U.K. Drum Publications (U.K.) Ltd.,
40—43 Fleet St. London EC4
ed. O. Adetule
ISSN 0012—673X
See also DRUM (South Africa)

JOURNAL OF THE NEW AFRICAN LITERATURE AND THE ARTS

A quarterly international publication
ɤ; no.1—14 1966—73
New York. Third Press — Joseph Okpaku Publishing, 444 Central Park West, N.Y. 10025
ISSN 0022—5118

LO/N—1	LO/S26	LO/U14

LOTUS

Afro-Asian writings

q; no.1 1971—
Cairo, Egypt. Permanent Bureau of Afro-Asian
Writers, 104 Kasr el Aini St.
ed. Youssef El Sebai
ISSN 0002—0664
Supersedes AFRO-ASIAN WRITINGS (q.v.)

LO/S26: no.1—16   LO/U14

OKIKE
An African journal of new writing
t; no.1 1971—
Amherst, Mass., U.S.A. P.O. Box 597 or Nsukka,
Nigeria, P.O. Box 53
ed. Chinua Achebe

BT/U—1   LD/U—1: no.1   LO/S26:
no.4—   LO/S65   LO/U—2: no.7—
LO/U14   OX/U—1: no.3—   OX/U14

PRESENCE AFRICAINE
Revue culturelle du monde noir
q; vol.1,no.1 1947—
Paris, France. Nouvelle Société Présence Afri-
caine, 24 bis rue des Ecoles, Paris 5e
ISSN 0032—7638

LO/N—1   LO/S65: vol.5—   LO/U—8
LO/U14

RESEARCH IN AFRICAN LITERATURES
f; vol.1,no.1 1970—
Austin, Texas, U.S.A. African and Afro-American
Studies and Research Center, P.O. Box 7819,
Texas, TX 78712
ed. Bernth Lindfors
ISSN 0034—5210

LO/N—1   LO/S26   LO/S65
LO/U14

THIRD PRESS REVIEW
b; vol.1,no.1 1975—
New York. Joseph Okpaku Publishing, 444
Central Park West, N.Y. 10025

Central and Southern Africa

Botswana (formerly Bechuanaland)
Lesotho (formerly Basutoland)
Rhodesia
Swaziland
Zambia (formerly Northern Rhodesia)

ARUNDEL SCHOOL MAGAZINE
a; vol.1, 1960—
Salisbury, Rhodesia. Arundel School, Mount
Pleasant

BAINES SCHOOL MAGAZINE
a; 1958—67
Bulawayo, Rhodesia

BEACON
b; no.1 1970—
Lusaka, Zambia. Evelyn Hone College of Further
Education

BONESA
b; no.1 1969—
Gaberone, Botswana. National Library of
Botswana

LO/N—1; no.5—

BORDERER
a; no.1 1923—
Umtali, Rhodesia. Umtali Boys' High School

BORDERER
a; no.1 1954—
Umtali, Rhodesia. Umtali Girls' High School

BOSELE
b; 1969—
Mochudi, Botswana. Molefi Secondary School

CHICKWAKWA
a; 1971—
Lusaka, Zambia. U. Zambia

CHIRIMO
A thrice-yearly review of Rhodesian and international poetry
t; vol.1,no.1 1968—
Salisbury, Rhodesia. P.O. Box A294 Avondale
ed. C. T. E. Style
ISSN 0009—4684

LO/N—1   LO/S26   LO/U—2
LO/U14

COMMENT
b
Gaberone, Botswana. U. Botswana, Lesotho and
Swaziland

COUNTERPOINT
b; vol.1,no.1—3 1963
Bulawayo, Rhodesia. 63 Group M

ELECTRA
♭; no.1—2 1968
Salisbury, Rhodesia. 56 Monica Road
ed. Alex Israel

EXPRESSION
Magazine of the literary circle, University of
Basutoland, Bechuanaland and Swaziland
♭; no.1—3 1965—8
Gaberone, Botswana
ed. S. Shana

EXPRESSION
f; no.1 1970—
Roma, Lesotho. English Society, U. Botswana,
Lesotho and Swaziland
ed. Njabulo S. Ndebele
ISSN 0014—5343

HORIZON
♭; 1969—
Ndola, Zambia. R.S.T. Group, P.O. Box 1505
ed. R. P. Furniss

ILLUSTRATED LIFE RHODESIA
e; vol.1,no.1 1968—
Salisbury, Rhodesia. Graham Publishing Co.,
P.O. Box 2931
ed. P. Joyce
vol.5,no.11 1972 contains loose supplement
LITERARY OSCAR (q.v.)

JEWEL OF AFRICA
A literary and cultural magazine from Zambia
m; vol.1,no.1 1968—
Lusaka, Zambia. Mphala Creative Society, c/o
International House 5—13, U. Zambia, P.O. Box
2379, Lusaka
ed. Stephen P. C. Moyo
ISSN 0021—6259

LO/U14: vol.2,no.1—

LESEDI
a
Palapye, Botswana. Moeng College

LITERARY OSCAR
z(1 issue); 1972
Salisbury, Rhodesia. Graham Publishing Co.,
P.O. Box 2931 being a loose supplement to vol.5,
no.11 of ILLUSTRATED LIFE RHODESIA (q.v.)

MAMBO REVIEW OF CONTEMPORARY
LITERATURE
Gwelo, Rhodesia
see REVIEW

MANANG A LESEDI
♭; no.1 1972—
Francistown, Botswana. Setlabekgosi Secondary
School

MOTO
w; vol.1,no.1— vol.16,no.9 1959—74
Gwelo, Rhodesia. Mambo P., P.O. Box 779
ISSN 0027—1675

NEW WRITING FROM ZAMBIA
q; vol.1,no.1 1964—
Lusaka, Zambia. New Writers Group, P.O. Box
1889
ISSN 0028—7083

CB/U—1: vol.8,no.1—   ED/U—1
LD/U—1: vol.2,4   LO/S26: vol.6,no.1—
LO/U—2   LO/U14: vol.6,no.2—
OX/U—1: vol.9,no.3—

NEWS OF AFRICAN WRITING
♭
Lusaka, Zambia. English Dept., U. Zambia,
P.O. Box 2379
ed. Alison Love

NORTHERN RHODESIA JOURNAL
m; vol.1,no.1—6 1909
Fort Jameson, Northern Rhodesia
ed. Revd. W. J. Bell

LO/N—1: vol.1,no.1—2   OX/U—1
OX/U—9

OPUS
t; no.1 1969—
Salisbury, Rhodesia. Dept. of English, U.
Rhodesia, P.O. Box 167, Mount Pleasant

OWL
z(1 issue); vol.1,no.1 1897
Bulawayo, Rhodesia
ed. Lionel Goldsmid

POETRY REVIEW SALISBURY
♭; 1952—4
Salisbury, Rhodesia. Salisbury Poetry Society
Supersedes RHODESIAN POETRY (q.v.)
Superseded by RHODESIAN POETRY (q.v.)
ed. Monty Bennett

LO/S65: no.2   LO/U—2: no.1

REVIEW
A supplement to the Mambo Magazine
♭; no.1—2 1974
Gwelo, Rhodesia. Mambo P., P.O. Box 779
ed. L. B. Rix

RHODESIA CALLS
ƥ; *c.* 1970s
Salisbury, Rhodesia. P.O. Box 8045
ed. A. G. Aberman

RHODESIA LITERATURE BUREAU BULLETIN
ƥ; no.1 1960—
Salisbury, Rhodesia. Rhodesia Literature Bureau

LO/N—1: no.4

RHODESIAN POETRY
ƥ; no.1 1950—
Salisbury, Rhodesia. Poetry Society of Rhodesia,
22 Bradfield Rd., Hillside, Salisbury E61
From 1952—4 called POETRY REVIEW
SALISBURY (q.v.)

LO/S26: no.8

RHODESIANA
f; no.1 1956—
Salisbury, Rhodesia. Rhodesiana Society, P.O.
Box 8268, Causeway, Salisbury
ed. W. V. Brelsford

LO/N—1   LO/S65

TWO TONE
A quarterly of Rhodesian poetry
q; vol.1,no.1 1964—
Salisbury, Rhodesia. P.O. Box 79, Mount Pleasant
e.d. Olive H.Robertson
ISSN 0049—4917

LO/U—2: vol.3,no.3

WRITE
ƥ; no.1 1965—
Kitwe, Zambia. Africa Literature Centre,
P.O. Box 1319

YOUNG ZAMBIANS WRITING
ƥ; no.1—6 1967—8
Lusaka, Zambia. Chalimbana Secondary School
ed. Robert McDonald

LO/S26

ZAMBEZIA
a; vol.1,no.1 1971—
Salisbury, Rhodesia. P.O. Box MP45, Mount
Pleasant
ed. R. S. Roberts

East Africa

Kenya
Malawi (formerly Nyasaland)
Tanzania (formerly Tanganyika, Zanzibar and
Pemba)
Uganda

ART
b; no.1 1965—
Nairobi, Kenya, P.O. Box 392

BITS AND PIECES
ƥ; no.1 1965—
Kasupe, Malawi. Malosa Secondary School

BUSARA
t; vol. 1, no.1. 1968—
vol.1,no.2 wrongly numbered as vol.2,no.1
Nairobi, Kenya. East African Publishing House,
P.O. Box 30571
ISSN 0007—6376
eds. E. Osoti and Richard Gacheche
Supersedes NEXUS

BT/U—1	CA/U—1	CB/U—1
LD/U—1; vol.2,no.1		LO/S26; vol.1,no.2—
LO/U—2	LO/U14	OX/U—1

CHANGE
a
Dowa, Malawi. Kongwe Secondary School

CHEMICHEMI NEWS
m; no.1—9
Nairobi, Kenya. Chemichemi Cultural Centre

DARLITE
A magazine of original writing from University
College, Dar es Salaam
ƥ; vol.1,no.1— vol.5,no.1 1966—70
Dar es Salaam, Tanzania. Literature Dept., U.
College, P.O. Box 35041
ISSN 0011—6696
Superseded by UMMA (q.v.)

BH/U—1	BT/U—1	ED/U—1
LD/U—1	LO/N—1	LO/N17
LO/S65	LO/U—2	LO/U14
OX/U—1		

DAWN
a
Kibaha, Tanzania. Kibaha Secondary School

DHANA
f; vol.1,no.1 1971—
Nairobi, Kenya. East African Literature Bureau,

P.O. Box 30022
ed. Cliff P'Chong
Supersedes PENPOINT (q.v.)

CB/U−1: vol.1,no.2−	LD/U−1	
LO/S26: vol.4,no.1−	LO/U−2	
LO/U14	OX/U−1: vol.3,no.1	OX/U14

DIALOGUE
ɓ; no.1 1965−
Nairobi, Kenya

DONOVAN MAULE THEATRE MAGAZINE
m
Nairobi, Kenya. P.O. Box 2333
Superseded by ON STAGE (q.v.)

EAST AFRICA JOURNAL
m; vol. 1−9 1964−72
Nairobi, Kenya. East African Institute of Social
and Cultural Affairs, P.O. Box 30571
ISSN 0012−8309
From 1968, contains literary issues called GHALA
(q.v.)

BH/U−1	ED/U−1	LO/S65: (incomplete)
LO/U−2	LO/U−8	LO/U14: vol.5−9
OX/U14	SH/U−1: vol.9	ST/U−1:
vol.6−9		

EASTLEIGH SECONDARY SCHOOL MAGAZINE
a; 1964−
Nairobi, Kenya

LO/N−1

EGERTONIAN
a; 1962−
Njoro, Kenya. Egerton College

EQUATOR
A magazine of East African writing
z(1 issue); vol.1,no.1 1945
Mombasa, Kenya. The Club

LO/S65

EXPRESSION
ɓ; no.1−4 1968−72
Limbe, Malawi. Limbe U.
Superseded by ODI (q.v.)

LO/U14

GHALA
ɓ; vol.5,no.7 1968, vol.6,no.1 1969, vol.6, no.8
1970, vol.7,no.1 1970
Nairobi, Kenya, East African Publishing House,
P.O. Box 30571
ISSN 0046−5895

being the name of literary issues of EAST
AFRICA JOURNAL (q.v.)

BH/U−1	ED/U−1	LO/S65
LO/U−2	LO/U−8	LO/U14
OX/U14	ST/U−1: 1969−70	

HAPPY MOMENTS
m
Eldoret, Kenya. P.O. Box 55

HAROYA
w
Nairobi, Kenya

**INDIAN VOICE OF BRITISH EAST AFRICA,
UGANDA AND ZANZIBAR**
m; vol.1,no.1− vol.3,no.155 1911−3
Nairobi, Kenya

LO/N−1: vol.1,no.6− vol.3,no.155 (imperfect)

JACARANDA
a; vol.1,no.1 1966−
Limbe, Malawi. Soche Hill College

JOE
Africa's entertainment monthly
m; no.1 1975−
Nairobi, Kenya. Joe Publications Ltd., P.O. Box
30362

JOLISO
East African journal of literature and society
f; vol.1,no.1 1973−
Nairobi, Kenya. East African Literature Bureau,
P.O. Box 30022
ed. Chris Lukorito Wanjala

LD/U−1	LO/U14	OX/U−9

**JOURNAL OF THE LANGUAGE ASSOCIATION
OF EASTERN AFRICA**
f; vol.1,no.1 1970−
Nairobi, Kenya. East African Publishing House,
P.O. Box 30571
ed. Tom Gorman

LO/U14	OX/U−1: vol.3,no.1−

JOURNAL OF MODERN AFRICAN STUDIES
q; vol.1,no.1 1963−
Dar es Salaam, Tanzania. Cambridge University P.
for U. College

LO/S26

KEY
ɓ; no.1 1958−?

Nairobi, Kenya. East African Literature Bureau, P.O. Box 30022

LO/N—1: no.2

LIKUNI BOYS' SECONDARY SCHOOL MAGAZINE
a
Likuni, Malawi. Lilongwe Likuni P.

LIKUNI GIRLS' SECONDARY SCHOOL MAGAZINE
a
Likuni, Malawi. Lilongwe Likuni P.

MAJI MAJI
ƥ
Dar es Salaam, Tanzania. Tanu Youth League, U. Dar es Salaam, P.O. Box 35054

BT/U—1: no.17   LO/U—8: vol.6,no.14—

MAKERERE
ƥ; vol.1,no.1 1946—
Kampala, Uganda. Makerere U., P.O. Box 262

BH/U—1: vol.1,no.1— vol.3,no.3   BT/U—1: vol.1,no.1—2, vol.3,no.2—3   LO/N17
LO/S65: vol.1,no.1— vol.4,no.1   LO/U14: vol.1,no.2— vol.2,no.5   OX/U—9: vol.1,no.1— vol.3,no.3

MAKERERE JOURNAL
f; no.1—12 1958—66
Kampala, Uganda. Makerere U., P.O. Box 262
Superseded by MAWAZO (q.v.)

BH/U—1   BT/U—1   LO/S65
LO/U—1   LO/U—8   LO/U14
OX/U—9

MAKTABA
Official journal of the Kenya Library Association
f; vol.1,no.1 1974—
Nairobi, Kenya
ed. Johnston L. Abakutsa

LO/U—8   LO/U14   OX/U—9

MAWAZO
The Makerere journal of the arts and social sciences
f; vol.1,no.1 1967—?
Kampala, Uganda. Makerere U.
eds. Geoffrey Rugege and Ocaya Lakidi
Supersedes MAKERERE JOURNAL (q.v.)

BH/U—1   BT/U—1: vol.1,no.1—2,4, vol.3,
no.2—   CB/U—1: vol.2,no.1—   EX/U—1
LD/U—1   LO/N—1   LO/S26: vol.1,no.1—

vol.4,no.2   LO/S65: vol.2,no.1   LO/U—1
LO/U—8   LO/U14   MA/U—1
OX/U—9   ST/U—1: vol.2,no.1—

MBIONI
The journal of Kivukoni College
m; no.1 1964—
Dar es Salaam, Tanzania. Nuta P., P.O. Box 2982

LO/U—8: (lacks no.2,4—5,11)

NANGA
f; vol.1,no.1 1969—
Kampala, Uganda. National Teachers' College, Kyambago, P.O. Box 20012.
eds. E. I. Karebaliirwe and F. I. Ika

NEXUS
ƥ; vol.1,no.1— vol.2,no.4 1966—8
Nairobi, Kenya. Dept. of English, U. College, Nairobi
ed. Leonard Kibera
Superseded by BUSARA (q.v.)

LD/U—1: vol.1,no.1   LO/U14   OX/U—1: vol.2,no.1—4

ODDSPOT
m
Nairobi, Kenya. East Africa Literary Agency

ODI
Bilingual quarterly of Malawian writing
q; vol.1,no.1 1974—
Limbe, Malawi. Limbe U.
Supersedes EXPRESSION (q.v.)

LO/U14   MA/U—1

ON STAGE
ƥ
Nairobi, Kenya
Supersedes DONOVAN MAULE THEATRE MAGAZINE (q.v.)

PENPOINT
ƥ; no.1—25 1958—70
Kampala, Uganda. Dept. of English, Makerere U.
Superseded by DHANA (q.v.)

BH/U—1: no.17—21,24   BT/U—1: no.17—22
LO/U—2: no.17—24   LO/U14: no.16—19,
21—25   OX/U—1: no.16—25

POINTER
ƥ; vol.1,no.1 1966—
Nairobi, Kenya. National Union of Kenya Students

REFLECTION
Journal of Students' Union, Soche Hill College
e; no.1 1972–
Limbe, Malawi

REVEILLE
m; vol.1,no.1– vol.5,no.7 1916–19
Nairobi, Kenya. Swift P.

LO/S65

ROBERT BLAKE SECONDARY SCHOOL
MAGAZINE
a
Dowa, Malawi

ROHO
Journal of the visual arts in East Africa
f; no.1–2 1961–2
Kampala, Uganda. School of Art, Makerere U.

BH/U–1   LO/N17   LO/S65

TRANSITION
b; vol.1,no.1– vol.7,no.37 1961–8
Kampala, Uganda
Suspended after vol.7,no.37 Resumed publication
in Accra (see WEST AFRICA)

BH/U–1   BT/U–1   CA/U–1
CB/U–1   EX/U–1: no.26–   LD/U–1:
no.1–6   LO/N17: no.11–37   LO/S26:
no.18–   LO/S65   LO/U–1: no.8–34
LO/U–2: no.17–   LO/U–8   LO/U14
NR/U–1: no.6–   OX/U14   ST/U–1:
no.6–

UMMA
f; vol.1,no.1 1970–
Dar es Salaam, Tanzania. U. College of Tanzania,
P.O. Box 35041
ed. Edwin Semzaba
ISSN 0011–6696
Supersedes DARLITE (q.v.)

BT/U–1   LD/U–1   LO/S26
LO/S65: vol.1,no.1– vol.2,no.2   LO/U14
OX/U–1: vol.1,no.1– vol.2,no.2

UNIVERSITY STUDENTS' MAGAZINE
ϕ; vol.1,no.1 1970–
Limbe, Malawi. Malawi U.

UNIVERSITY VANGUARD
z(1 issue); vol.1,no.1 1967
Limbe, Malawi. Chancellor College
Superseded by VANGUARD (q.v.)

UPEO
z(1 issue); vol.1,no.1 1972
Nairobi, Kenya. Dept. of Literature, Kenyatta
U.C.

VANGUARD
ϕ; no.1 1967–
Limbe, Malawi. Chancellor College
Supersedes UNIVERSITY VANGUARD (q.v.)

VOICE OF ST. PATRICK'S
ϕ; no.1 1968–
Limbe, Malawi. St. Patrick's Secondary School

ZUKA
A journal of East Africa creative writing
ϕ; no.1–6 1967–72
Nairobi, Kenya. Oxford University P.,
P.O. Box 72532 ed. Jonathan Kariara
ISSN 0044–5444

CB/U–1: no.2–6   LD/U–1: no.1–2
LO/S26   LO/S65   LO/U–2   LO/U14

West Africa

Gambia
Ghana (formerly Gold Coast)
Nigeria
Sierra Leone

ABADINA
ϕ; vol.1,no.1–2 1964
Ibadan, Nigeria. Official organ of the Students'
Union, U. Ibadan

ABOKI
q; no.1–8 1957–8
Zaria, Nigeria. Northern Regional Literature
Agency, Gaskiya Corp.

ABUSCONDIAN
a; 1961–
Kibi, Ghana. Abuakwa State College

ACADEMICIAN
a; vol.1,no.1 1952–
Ibadan, Nigeria. Ibadan City Academy

ACHIMOTA REVIEW
a; 1927–47
Achimota, Ghana. Achimota College P.

LO/S65: 1927–37

ACHIMOTAN
a; 1971–
Ghana

ADVENTURE
f; 1957–62
Nigeria. Ijebu Igbo Girls' Secondary School

AFRICA
ϕ; no. 1–3 1960–5
Lagos, Nigeria. African Printing and Publishing
Co. Ltd.

AFRICAN HORIZON
ϕ; no. 1–3 1960–1
Zaria, Nigeria. Gaskiya Corp.

AFRICAN NOTES
Bulletin of the Institute of African Studies
t; vol. 1, no. 1 1963–
Ibadan, Nigeria. U. Ibadan, Institute of African
Studies

LO/U–8

AFRICAN WRITER
z(1 issue); no. 1 1963
Onitsha, Nigeria. African Authors' Association of
Nigeria

AFRICANA RESEARCH BULLETIN
q; vol. 1, no. 1 1970–
Freetown, Sierra Leone. Institute of African
Studies
ed. J. G. Edowu Hyde

LD/U–1   LO/U14: vol. 3, no. 2–

AFRISCOPE
Your monthly brief on Africa
m; vol. 1, no. 1 1971–
Yaba, Nigeria. Pan Afriscope (Nigeria) Ltd.
ed. Uche Chukwumeriji

LO/S26: vol. 4, no. 1–   LO/U–8: vol. 2, no. 1–

AFRO IMAGE
m; 1972–
Ogwashi Uku, Nigeria. African Cultures Publications Ltd., Mile 2 Ubulunor Rd., P.O. Box 20

AFROCULTURE
A magazine of the society for the study and promotion of African culture
a; no. 1–3 1956–8
Ibadan, Nigeria. U. College

AGAUDA
The magazine of the Kano Provincial Secondary
School
a; 1963–
Kano, Nigeria

AGBOJA
The magazine of the Ijebu Ijesha Grammar Scho
a; 1966–
Nigeria

AGRICOLA IBADANIENSIS
The annual magazine of the Society of Agricul-
tural Students
a; vol. 1, no. 1–2 1959–60
Ibadan, Nigeria. U. College

ALECTOR
a; 1959–
Legon, Ghana. U. Ghana

ALFIJIR
m; no. 1–6 1953–4
Zaria, Nigeria. Northern Regional Literature
Agency, Gaskiya Corp.
Superseded by ALFIJIR DA NASIHA (q.v.)

ALFIJIR DA NASIHA
m; vol. 2, no. 1– vol. 5, no. 6 1958
Zaria, Nigeria. Northern Regional Literature
Agency, Gaskiya Corp.
Supersedes ALFIJIR (q.v.) and NASIHA (q.v.)

AMBER
Nigeria women's magazine
m; vol. 1, no. 1– vol. 2, no. 10 1963–5
Lagos, Nigeria. Sun Publishing Co.

ANCHOR
a; 1959–
Ovon, Nigeria. Methodist Boys' High School

ANDRIAN
a; 1953–
Oyo, Nigeria. St. Andrew's College

ANTHONIAN
a; 1964–
Esure, Nigeria. St. Anthony's Grammar School

ANVIL
ϕ; vol. 1, no. 1 1970–
Ibadan, Nigeria. Students' Union, Ibadan U.
ed. Yakubu Abdulazeeg
ISSN 0003–6226

MA/U–1

ARBITRATOR
ϕ; vol.1,no.1—2 1953—5
Ilesha, Nigeria. Ilesha Grammar School

ARO
z(1 issue); no.1 1958
Ibadan, Nigeria. Ibadan Students' Association

ARTS COUNCIL OF GHANA NEWSLETTER
m; vol.1,no.1 1975—
Accra, Ghana

ASEMKA
A literary journal of the University of the Cape
Coast
f; vol.1,no.1 1974—
Cape Coast, Ghana. U. Cape Coast
ed. Atta Britwum

LD/U—1

ATUMPAN
a; 1964—
Tweneboa, Ghana. Tweneboa Kodua Secondary
School

AUREOL MIRROR
ϕ; vol.1,no.1 1958—
Freetown, Sierra Leone. Fourah Bay College

LO/N—1: vol.1,no.4, vol.9,no.1

AUREOL REVIEW
z(8 p.a.); vol.1,no.1 1969—
Freetown, Sierra Leone. Fourah Bay College
LO/N—1

AWOWERIN
q; 1952—?
Ibadan, Nigeria. Western Region Literature
Committee

AYANGBA MAGAZINE
a; no.1 1964—
Ayangba, Nigeria

BAREWA
a; vol.1,no.1 1956—
Zaria, Nigeria. Government College

BAUCHI PROVINCIAL SECONDARY SCHOOL
MAGAZINE
a; 1957—9
Bauchi, Nigeria.

BEACON
a; vol.1,no.1 1956—
Ibadan, Nigeria

Supersedes UNIVERSITY HERALD (q.v.)

BENDE PROGRESS
z(1 issue); vol.1,no.1 1961
Umuahia, Nigeria. Chuks Publishing Enterprise

BENIN REVIEW
f; no.1 1974—
Benin City, Nigeria. Ethiope Publishing Corp.,
P.O. Box 1192
eds. Abio la Irele and Pius Oleghe

LO/S26   LO/U14

BEPOWSO BANN
a; 1963—
Aburi, Ghana. Aburi Girls' Secondary School

BLACK ORPHEUS
f; no.1—22, vol.2,no.1 1957—
Lagos, Nigeria. Longman 1st series. *Times of
Nigeria* vol.2,no.1—
ed. J. P. Clarke
ISSN 0067—9100

BH/U—1: no.5—   HL/U—1: no.5—
LO/S26: no.3—18   LO/S65   LO/U—2:
imperfect   LO/U—8: no.2—   LO/U14
OX/U—1   OX/U—9: no.2—   SH/U—1:
lacks no.8—9   ST/U—1: no.2—

BLOW
ϕ; no.1 1970—
Ibadan, Nigeria

BRIDGE
a; 1965—
Okeigbo, Nigeria. Okeigbo Ifetedo Grammar
School

BRONZE
m; no.1 1967—
Ile Ife, Nigeria. Students' Union, U. Ife
ed. Olapade Ajeigbe
ISSN 0007—2281

BUFFALO
a; 1958—
Ile Oluji, Nigeria. Gboluji Anglican Grammar
School

BUG
ϕ; vol.1,no.1 1950—
Ibadan, Nigeria

BULLETIN OF THE ASSOCIATION FOR
AFRICAN LITERATURE IN ENGLISH
ϕ; no.1—4 1964—6

Freetown, Sierra Leone. Fourah Bay College
eds. T. R. M. Creighton and Eldred Jones
Superseded by AFRICAN LITERATURE TODAY
(q.v.)

BT/U—1: no.1,2,4   LD/U—1: no.1—2
LO/N—1: no.4   LO/S26   LO/U—14: no.3—4

CALL
a; 1965—
Calabar, Nigeria. St. Patrick's College

CAMPUS OPINION
A bi-monthly publication of the University of
Ibadan Press Club
b; vol.1,no.1—5 1966—7
Ibadan, Nigeria

CATALYST
b; no.1 1962—
Enugu, Nigeria. U. Nigeria
ed. E. O. Ogbo

CATHOLIC UNDERGRADUATE
b; vol.1,no.1 1964—
Ibadan, Nigeria. Nigerian Federation of Catholic
Students

CH'INDABA
q; no.1 1976—
Ile Ife, Nigeria. Ife U.P.
ed. Wole Soyinka
Supersedes TRANSITION (q.v.)

BH/U—1	BT/U—1	CA/U—1
CB/U—1	EX/U—1	LO/N—1
LO/S26	LO/S65	LO/U—2
LO/U—8	LO/U14	NR/U—1
OX/U—9	ST/U—1	

CHRISTIAN STUDENT
m; vol.1,no.1— vol.10,no.3 1954—63
Ibadan, Nigeria. Student Christian Movement

CLARION
A magazine of the University College of the Cape
Coast
b; vol.1,no.1 1967—
Cape Coast, Ghana. Cape Coast U.P.

EX/U—1: vol.1,no.1

CORNELIAN
a; 1963—
Uyo, Nigeria. Cornelia Connelly Secondary School

CREOLE BOY
A monthly magazine of West African stories

m; vol.1,no.1—4 1901—2
Freetown, Sierra Leone

CRITERION
Or Le Pyratica, the University's most readable
newspaper
a; no.1—4 1954—8
Ibadan, Nigeria. Pirates' Fraternity

CROWN
a; 1964—
Ohafia, Nigeria. Coronata Secondary School

CULVERT
m; vol.1,no.1 1969—
Nigeria. Literary and Debating Society of Okeigto
Ifekedo Grammar School

DOWN RANDLE ROAD
m; vol.1,no.1 1961—
Lagos, Nigeria. Ahmadiya Boys' High School

EAGLE
a; no.1 1955—
Port Harcourt, Nigeria. Port Harcourt Literary
and Debating Society, St. John's College

EAGLE
m; 1963—6
Onitsha, Nigeria. Etudo Ltd.

EDO COLLEGE MAGAZINE
a; 1949—66
Benin City, Nigeria

EGGHEAD
a; no.1 1963—
Ahmadu Bello, Nigeria. Fine Arts Dept., Northern
U.
ed. Nelson Olawaiye

LO/S65: no.1—3

EGGS
The voice of Ernest Gems Grammar School
a; no.1 1960—
Orlu, Nigeria

EKO
z(1 issue); 1959
Mushin, Nigeria. Eko Boys' High School

EKORIAN
a; 1965—
Nigeria

ELEIYELE
a; no.1 1958—
Ibadan, Nigeria. Ahmadiyya Grammar School

EMERALD
a; no.1 1961–
Calabar, Nigeria. Duke Town Secondary School

ENITONNA
z(1 issue); 1958
Port Harcourt, Nigeria. Enitonna High School

EPIDEMERE
♭; vol.1,no.1 1961–
Uyo, Nigeria. Ubium Students' League

EVERYBODY'S JOURNAL
m; vol.1,no.1– vol.4,no.36 1961–5
Lagos, Nigeria. International Educational Publications' Ass.

EXIT
♭
Ibadan, Nigeria. Claverianum P.

FIDITIAN
a; vol.1,no.1 1958–
Fiditi, Nigeria. Fiditi Grammar School

FINBARRIA
Students' magazine of St. Finbarr's College
a
Akoko, Yaba, Nigeria

FLAMINGO
m; vol.1,no.1 1961–
Lagos, Nigeria. Book & Press Distributors

FORERUNNER
The newsletter of the Eastern Nigeria Library
Board Staff Association
q; vol.1,no.1– vol.3,no.1 1964–6
Enugu, Nigeria

FORUM
Journal of the students of the University of
Ghana
a; vol.1,no.1 1970–
Legon, Ghana

FORWARD
a; 1954–6
Calabar, Nigeria. Duke Town School

FRESH BUDS
Verse by students of the Nigerian College of
Technology
q; vol.1,no.1–4 1959–60
Enugu, Nigeria

GAMEZAKI
m; 1954–
Zaria, Nigeria. Northern Regional Literature
Agency, Gaskiya Corp.

GATEWAY
a
Calabar, Nigeria. Hope Waddell Training Institution

GHANA CULTURAL REVIEW
q; vol.1,no.1– vol.2,no.2 1965–6
Accra, Ghana. Ministry of Art and Culture

GHANA LIBRARY JOURNAL
q; vol.1,no.1 1963–
Accra, Ghana. Library Association of Ghana,
P.O. Box 663
ed. A. N. de Heer

| BH/U–1 | LO/N–1 | LO/U–2 |
| LO/U14 | OX/U–9 | SH/U–1 |

GOLD COAST YOUTH
z(1 issue); no.1 1948
Freetown, Sierra Leone. Fourah Bay College

LO/N–1

HARMATTAN
A cool dry wind
q; vol.1,no.1–5 1956–8
Ibadan, Nigeria. U. College Hospital

HILL MAN
♭; vol.1,no.1–4 1955–8   new series vol.1,no.1
1959
Oshogbo, Nigeria. Oshogbo Grammar School
Literary and Debating Society

HOE
Quarterly literary magazine of the writers' workshop
q; vol.1,no.1 1973–
Enugu, Nigeria
ed. Obi Egbuna

HORIZON
Journal of the Ibadan Renaissance Society
♭; vol.1,no.1– vol.3,no.6 1961–8
Ibadan, Nigeria.
ed. Kayode Iwakun

HORN
♭; vol.1,no.1– vol.7,no.3 1958–64
Ibadan, Nigeria. U. College, Ibadan
ed. F. Onyema Iheme

Superseded by NIGERIAN STUDENT VERSE
(q.v.)

IBADAN
t; no.1 1957—
Ibadan, Nigeria. U. Ibadan
ed. T. Adesanya Ige Grillo
ISSN 0019—0969

BH/U—1: no.1—5,13—   CB/U—1: no.11,13,
15—16,20,22,24—   LD/U—1: no.2—3, 19—20
LO/U—8   LO/U14: no.2—   OX/U14:
lacks no.6,8—9,11—12

IBADAN STUDIES IN ENGLISH
f; vol.1,no.1 1969—
Ibadan, Nigeria. Dept. of English, U. Ibadan
eds. P. Young and J. McVeagh

IBONACO
a; 1965—7
Aba, Nigeria. Ibo National High School

IDEAL COMPANION
m; vol.1,no.1 1967—
Ibadan, Nigeria. Prospect P.
ed. Bola Olaniram
ISSN 0019—1345

IFE AFRICAN STUDIES
Research bulletin of the University of Ife
f; vol.1,no.1 1974—
Ife, Nigeria. U. Ife
ed. Babatunde Lawal

LO/S65   LO/U—8   LO/U14

IFE WRITING
ƥ; no.1 1967—
Ife, Nigeria. Ile—Ife Writers' Circle

IGBARRA STUDENTS' MAGAZINE
a; 1959—
Ibadan, Nigeria

IJALA
Unife poetry magazine
ƥ; vol.1,no.1—2 1975
Ife, Nigeria. Dept. of English, U. Ife
ed. Charles Okigbo

IK IL
a; vol.1,no.1— vol.3,no.2 1954—9
Okitipupa, Nigeria. Manuwa Memorial Grammar
School

IKOROK
Bulletin of the African Studies' Institute

q; vol.1,no.1 1971—
Nsukka, Nigeria. African Studies' Institute
ed. C. O. Okoriaffia

BH/U—1; vol.1,no.2—   LO/U—8   LO/U14

IKSAN
ƥ; 1947—50
Ibadan, Nigeria. Kamerun Students' Assn.

**JOURNAL OF THE NIGERIA ENGLISH
STUDIES' ASSOCIATION**
q; vol.1,no.1 1968—
Ibadan, Nigeria. British Council
ed. B. Smith

KATA SECONDARY SCHOOL MAGAZINE
a; 1963—
Accra, Ghana. Graphic P.

KEY
a; 1959—
Akure, Nigeria. St. Peter's College

LAGOS NOTES AND RECORDS
A journal of African studies
q; vol.1,no.1 1967—
Lagos, Nigeria. U. Lagos
ed. Rebecca N. Agheyisi

LO/S65: vol.5,no.1—   LO/U—8   LO/U14

LAMP
The monthly magazine
m; no.1 1969—
Ibadan , Nigeria

LEADER
m; vol.1,no.1— vol.5,no.12 1953—7
Zaria, Nigeria. Northern Regional Literature
Agency, Gaskiya Corp.

LEGACY
A literary magazine
ƥ; vol.1,no.1 1972—
Legon, Ghana. U. Ghana

LEGON JOURNAL OF THE HUMANITIES
f; no.1 1974—
Accra, Ghana. U. Ghana
ed. L. A. Boadi

EX/U—1   LO/U14

LEGONITE
Annual students' publication
a; vol.1,no.1 1964—
Accra, Ghana

LO/N17: vol.3,no.1—   LO/U—2: vol.3,no.3
OX/U—9: vol.3,no.3—

LITERARY AND SOCIAL GUIDE
m; 1919—22
Accra, Ghana

MASQUE
Official organ of the Association of Theatre Arts
Students
ƥ; vol.1,no.1 1973—
Ibadan, Nigeria
ed. Emeka Pat Idoye

MAWULIAN
a; 1962—
Mawali, Ghana. Mawali Secondary School

MBARI NEWSLETTER
m; no.1—13 1966—7
Ibadan, Nigeria. Mbari Club

MELLANBITE
Magazine of Mellanby Hall, University of Ibadan
a; vol.1,no.1 1961—
Ibadan, Nigeria

MUSE
Literary magazine of the University of Nigeria
a; no.1 1963—
Nsukka, Nigeria
ed. Emeka Nwabueze

NASIHA
m; no.1—9 1955—6
Zaria, Nigeria. Northern Regional Literature
Agency, Gaskiya Corp.
Superseded by ALFIJIR DA NASIHA (q.v.)

NDAANAN
The Gambia writers' club
f; vol.1,no.1 1971—
Bathurst, Gambia. P.O. Box 248
ed. Swaebou Conateh

LO/S26: vol.2,no.1—

NEGRO
m; 1872—3
Freetown, Sierra Leone

NEW AGE
ƥ; vol.1,no.1 1967—
Accra, Ghana. New Age Pubs.

NEW ERA
m; vol.1,no.1 1968—
Cape Coast, Ghana. Insight Pubs.

NEW HORN
ƥ; no.1 1974—   no.2=vol.1,no.2
Ibadan, Nigeria, Ibadan U.P.
ed. Kole Omotoso

NIGERCOL
The magazine of the students of Zaria branch of
the Nigerian College of Art, Science and Technology
ƥ; no.1—2 1958—61
Zaria, Nigeria.

NIGERIA MAGAZINE
q; no.1 1934—
Lagos, Nigeria. Cultural Division, Ministry of
Information
eds. Garba Ashiwaju and Onuora Nzekwu
ISSN 0029—0033

BH/U—1   BT/U—1: no.88—   LO/N—1
LO/S26: no.9—112   LO/U14: no.14—21,47—
MA/U—1: 1970—

NIGERIAN STUDENT VERSE
ƥ; 1959—?
Ibadan, Nigeria. Ibadan U.P.
ed. Martin Banham
Supersedes HORN (q.v.)

NORLA NEWS
q; 1955—
Zaria, Nigeria. Northern Regional Literature
Agency

NORTHERN LIGHT
Tamale, Ghana. Government Secondary School

NSUKKASCOPE
q; no.1 1972—
Nsukka, Nigeria. Institute of African Studies
ed. Chinua Achebe

LO/S26: [3-year temporary file]

NUMO TORCH
Journal of the Umunumo Social Circle
ƥ
Ibadan, Nigeria

ODU
A journal of West African studies
ƥ; no.1—9 1955—63   new series vol.1,no.1—
vol.4,no.2 1964—8   3rd series no.1 1969—
Lagos, Nigeria. Western Regional Literature
Committee, Oxford University P.

BT/U—1   CA/U—1   CB/U—1
LD/U—1   LO/N—1   LO/U—8; n.s.vol.1,
no.1— vol.4,no.2; 3rd series no.1—   LO/U14

OX/U—1: no.1—4   OX/U—9   OX/U14
SH/U—1: 3rd series no.9—   ST/U—1: 3rd
series no.9—

ODUMA
f; vol.1,no.1 1973—
Port Harcourt, Nigeria. Rivers State Council for
Arts and Culture
ed. Theo Vincent

LD/U—1: vol.2,no.1—   LO/U14
OX/U—1

OKE-ELA
The official magazine of the literary society
b; no.1 1957—
Ilaro, Nigeria. Ilaro Teachers' Training College

OKIJA CITIZEN
q; vol.1,no.1 1965—
Umuatuogwu-Okija, Nigeria

OKYEAME
Ghana's literary magazine
f; vol.1,no.1— vol.4,no.1 1964—8
Legon, Ghana. Institute of African Studies
ed. Efua Sutherland
ISSN 0048—1629

BT/U—1: vol.1,no.1, vol.2,no.1— vol.3,no.1,
vol.4,no.1—   EX/U—1: vol.3,no.1—
LO/N17   LO/U—2: vol.1,no.1— vol.5,no.1
LO/U14   MA/U—1: vol.2,no.1—
OX/U14

OLUMO
a; no.1—2 1954—5
Abeokuta, Nigeria. Abeokuta Grammar School

OMABA
A monthly poetry magazine
b; no.1 1972—
Nsukka, Nigeria. Dept. of English, Nigeria U.
ed. Nnadozie Inyama
Variant title: OMABE

LO/S26: no.9—

OMO EGBADO
a; no.1 1961—
Egbado, Nigeria. Egbado Students' Assn.

OPTIMUS
a; 1963—
Ibadan, Nigeria. Lagebu Grammar School

OWARIA
a; 1964—5
Kumasi, Ghana. Opoku Ware Secondary School

PENMAG
m; no.1 1967—
Nigeria. Kaduna Pen Club Magazine

PEOPLE
m; vol.1,no.1 1969—
Lagos, Nigeria. People's Publishing Co.

PIONEER
a; vol.1,no.1 1961—
Nsukka, Nigeria. Students' Union, U. Nigeria

PIONEER
a; 1965—
Irrua, Nigeria. Annunciation College

PLEISURE
Ghana's sunshine magazine
z(8 p.a.); 1973—
Accra, Ghana. P.O. Box M160
ed. Roland James Moxon

**ROYAL GOLD COAST GAZETTE AND
COMMERCIAL INTELLIGENCER**
w; no.1—52 1822—3
Cape Coast Castle, Ghana
ed. W. M. Cooling

LO/S65: no.1—3,6—8,10—41,44—52

SATURDAY HO
m; 1891—6
Freetown, Sierra Leone

SCORPION
b; vol.1,no.1 1962—
Ibadan, Nigeria. Pyrates Confraternity

SCROLL
a
Nunqua, Ghana. Nunqua Secondary School

SIMBO
The magazine of the poelpe
m; vol.1,no.1— vol.3,no.8 1963—5
Port Harcourt, Nigeria. Goodwill P.

SIREN
1964—?
Accra, Ghana. Ghana U.

SOKOTI
Magazine of the Ife writers' workshop
z(1 issue); vol.1,no.1 1972
Ife, Nigeria
ed. Chris Awonuga

SPECTATOR
Everybody's magazine
m; vol.1,no.1 – vol.2,no.15 1965–6
Aba, Nigeria. International P.

STUDENTS' ECHO
A magazine of the students' union
a; no.1–4 1957–61
Ibadan, Nigeria. Nigerian College of Technology

TALENT FOR TOMORROW
a
Accra, Ghana. Ministry of Education

TIDE
Ø; no.1 1968–
Lagos, Nigeria. Group Pubs. Ltd.

TOWER
z(1 issue); vol.1,no.1 1960
Enugu, Nigeria. Nigerian College of Art, Science
and Technology

TRANSITION
b; no.38–50 1968–76
Accra, Ghana
ISSN 0041–1191
Supersedes TRANSITION (East Africa) (q.v.)
Superseded by CH'INDABA (q.v.)

BH/U–1	BT/U–1	CA/U–1
CB/U–1	EX/U–1	LO/N–1
LO/S26	LO/S65	LO/U–2
LO/U–8	LO/U14	NR/U–1
OX/U–9	ST/U–1	

UNDERGRADUATE
t; no.1 1954–?
Ghana. U. College of Gold Coast

LO/N–1: vol.1,no.2

UNIVERSITAS
An inter-faculty journal
q; vol.1,no.1 – vol.5,no.2 1953–62   new series
vol.1,no.1 1969–
Legon, Ghana. U. Ghana

CB/U–1: new series vol.1,no.1–   ED/U–1:
vol.3,no.2–   LO/U–1   LO/U–8

UNIVERSITY COLLEGE OF THE CAPE COAST
DEPARTMENT OF ENGLISH WORKPAPERS
Ø; no.1 1969–
Cape Coast, Ghana

UNIVERSITY HERALD
t; vol.1,no.1 – vol.5,no.2 1948–53
Ibadan, Nigeria

VANGUARD
Ø; vol.1,no.1 – vol.2,no.9 1960–1
Port Harcourt, Nigeria

VOICE OF AQUINAS
a; 1961–
Accra, Ghana. Aquinas Secondary School

VOICES OF YOUTH
The literary magazine of the Young African
Writers' Club
q; vol.1,no.1 1957–
Akropong, Ghana. Young African Writers' Club

WASP
m; vol.1,no.1 1969–
Ibadan, Nigeria. Alpha Club

WORK IN PROGRESS
a; no.1–2 1972–3
Zaria, Nigeria. Ahmadu Bello U.
ed. Keith Allan

LD/U–1   LO/U14

WORKPAPERS
Cape Coast, Ghana. Cape Coast U. of Ghana
ed. Sam K. Opoku

WRITERS' WORKSHOP NOTES
Ø; vol.1,no.1 1954–
Legon, Ghana. Institute of African Studies,
U. Ghana

ZOOM
m; vol.1,no.1 1966–
Freetown, Sierra Leone. Zoom Publications,
P.O. Box 868
ed. Chesterton D. Ekpo

LO/N–1

AUSTRALIA

General

AARDVARK
A blood transfusion in print
ƀ; no.1—3 1968
Box Hill, S. Victoria. No.3 publ. in Christchurch, N.Z.
eds. J. Jenkins and others

LO/U—2: no.1,3

ADAM
m; 1946—
Sydney. Murray Organization, 142 Clarence St.,
Sydney 2000
ISSN 0001—8023

LO/N—1: vol.1,no.6, vol.2,no.1

ADAM AND EVE
The big Australian national monthly
m; vol.1,no.1— vol.16,no.1 1926—41
Melbourne. 64 Elizabeth St.
ed. Charles E. Taylor
Incorporates PLAYBILL (q.v.)

ADELAIDE MISCELLANY
A journal of news, literature, music, etc.
1869
Adelaide. Simms and Elliot

ADELAIDE PUNCH
w; 1868—1884
Adelaide
ed. Herbert J. Woodhouse
Incorporated in LANTERN (q.v.)

ALEPH
ƀ; 3 issues — 1963, 1964 and 1966
Brisbane. Junior Poets', Essayists' and Novelists'
Society of Queensland

ALLEN'S TWOPENNY TRASH
ƀ; vol.1,no.1—3 1858
Adelaide

LO/N—1

ANGRY PENGUINS
ƀ; no.1—9 1940—6
Adelaide
eds. Max Harris and John Reed

First 2 nos. temporarily supersede PHOENIX
(q.v.) Supplemented by ANGRY PENGUINS
BROADSHEET (q.v.)

LO/U—2

ANGRY PENGUINS BROADSHEET
m; no.1—10 1946
Melbourne
eds. Max Harris and others
Supplements ANGRY PENGUINS (q.v.)

LO/N—1: no.3—10

ANOTHER ONE FOR MARY
m; vol.1,no.1 1976—
Cumberland Park, S.A. 34 Mathia Ave., Cumberland Park, S.A. 5041
ISSN 0313—4644

ANTHOLOGY
The arts magazine of Armidale Teachers' College
a; 1956—
Armidale, N.S.W. Armidale Teachers' College

ANTIPODEAN
An illustrated annual
ƀ; no.1—3 1893, 1894, 1897
Melbourne. George Robertson & Co.

ED/N—1: no.2   ED/P—1   LO/N—1
LO/S65   OX/U—1

ARCA
a; 1959—72
Adelaide. Wattle Park Teachers' College

ARDEN'S SYDNEY MAGAZINE
no.1—2 1843
Sydney

LO/N—1: no.2

ARETE
z(1 issue); vol.1,no.1 1967
Melbourne. Arts Faculty Assn., Monash U.

ARK
ƀ; 1973—

North Ryde, N.S.W. 2/158 Herring Rd., North Ryde
N.S.W. 2113
eds. Sue and Ronald Clarke
ISSN 0311–2926
Supersedes MENTOR (q.v.)

ARNA
♭; 1918–
Sydney. Arts Society of the U. Sydney

ARROW
♭; no.1–2 1954–5
Brisbane.
Arts-Commerce faculties, U. Queensland

ART IN AUSTRALIA
A magazine devoted to art, music, literature and
architecture
q; 1st series no.1–11 1916–21   2nd series
vol.1,no.1–2 1922   3rd series no.1–81 1922–40
4th series no.1–6 1941–2
Sydney. Ure Smith

ED/N–1: 3rd series no.1–6,9, 15–80
LO/N–1: 3rd series no.1–5   OX/U–1: 1st
series no.10–   3rd series no.9

ARTALIVE
♭; vol.1,no.1 1975–
Sydney. Renaissance Artists & Writers Assn.,
209 Walker St., N. Sydney, N.S.W.
ISSN 0312–5785

ARTS
♭; vol.1,no.1 1958–
Sydney. Arts Assn., Sydney U.

LD/U–1: vol.1,no.3, vol.2,no.1–3, vol.3,no.1,
vol.4–

ASPECT
♭; 1955–63
Adelaide. English Dept., U. Adelaide
Superseded by SOUTHERN REVIEW (q.v.)

ED/N–1   LO/N–1

ASPECT
Art and literature
q; no.1 1975–
Paddington, N.S.W. 9 Cambridge St., Paddington,
N.S.W. 2021
ed. Rudi Krausman

ATLAS
The Sydney weekly journal of politics, commerce
and literature

w; 1844–8
Sydney

LO/N–1: vol.1,no.1– vol.2,no.109

AURORA AUSTRALIS
New Australian literary, scientific and social
monthly
m; vol.1,no.1–6/7 1951–2
Melbourne. Hungarian Literary Society of
Australia

AUSSIE
The cheerful monthly
m; no.1–154 1918–31
Sydney. New Century P.

LO/N–1

AUSTRALASIAN
A quarterly reprint of articles selected from lead-
ing periodicals of the United Kingdom with
original contributions, chiefly on subjects of
colonial interest
q; no.1–4 1850–1   New Series no.1–4329 and
1851–1931 Melbourne.

CA/U–1: n.s. no.2–3,6–27   LO/N–1: no.1–3
OX/U–1: n.s. no.40–70,2075–2282,2388–4329

**AUSTRALASIAN BOOK NEWS AND LITERARY
JOURNAL**
m; vol.1,no.1– vol.2,no.10 1946–8
Sydney. F. H. Johnson Publishing Co.

LO/S65: vol.1,no.7– vol.2,no.10   LO/U–1

AUSTRALASIAN CRITIC
A monthly review of literature, science and art
m; vol.1,no.1–12 1890–1
Melbourne. Melville, Mullen & Slade
eds. Prof. T. G. Tucker and W. Baldwin Spencer

LO/N–1

AUSTRALASIAN MONTHLY REVIEW
m; vol.1,no.1–2 1866
Melbourne
ed. G. A. Walstab

LO/N–1

AUSTRALASIAN SMALL PRESS REVIEW
t; 1975–
Sydney, N.S.W. Second Back Row P., P.O. Box
197, North Sydney, N.S.W. 2095
eds. Tom and Wendy Whitton
ISSN 0312–0112

AUSTRALIA
For liberty of the individual
m; vol.1,no.1— vol.4,no.6 1923—5
Sydney
ed. Fred Davison

AUSTRALIA
m; vol.1,no.1—vol.9,no.11 1939—47
Sydney. Ure Smith
eds. S. U. Smith and G. M. Spencer

AUSTRALIA KAT
w; vol.1,no.1—7 1902—3
Sydney. Ure Smith
Supersedes KAT (q.v.)

AUSTRALIA WEEK-END BOOK
a; no.1—5 1942—6
Sydney. Ure Smith
eds. S. U. Smith and G. M. Spencer

CA/U—1: no.4   LO/N—1: no.4—5

AUSTRALIAN
A monthly magazine
m; vol.1,no.1— vol.5,no.4 1878—81
Sydney

LO/N—1: vol.2,no.1—12

AUSTRALIAN ARGOSY
z(1 issue); vol.1,no.1 1888
Brisbane. F. Crawford

AUSTRALIAN BOYS AND GIRLS
An illustrated annual of stories by Australian
writers
z(1 issue); no.1 1895
Sydney. Gordon & Gotch

AUSTRALIAN CAVALCADE
m
Sydney

LO/N—1: n.s. vol.4,no.3—5

AUSTRALIAN COMPOSER AND WRITERS'
MONTHLY
m; vol.1,no.1— vol.2,no.7 1933—4
Sydney. Australian Publ. Service
Incorporated in GUARDIAN OF AUSTRALIAN
ART (q.v.)

AUSTRALIAN EX-LIBRIS SOCIETY JOURNAL
z(1 issue); no.1 1930
Sydney

LO/N—1

AUSTRALIAN FAMILY JOURNAL
A weekly magazine of literature, science, arts, etc.
w; 1852—?
Sydney

LO/N—1: no.1—3

AUSTRALIAN FAMILY JOURNAL
A magazine dedicated to fiction, literature, poetry,
art, science, amusements, etc.
vol.1,no.1 1864—?
Melbourne. H. S. Ward

AUSTRALIAN GOLD-DIGGER'S MONTHLY
MAGAZINE AND COLONIAL FAMILY VISITOR
m; 1852—3
Melbourne

BN/U—1: 1853

AUSTRALIAN HOME COMPANION AND BAND
OF HOPE JOURNAL
e; vol.1,no.1— vol.6,no.147 1856—61
Sydney. H. B. Lee

AUSTRALIAN HOME COMPANION AND
ILLUSTRATED WEEKLY MAGAZINE
w; vol.1,no.1 1856—?
Melbourne. Calvert Bros.

AUSTRALIAN JOURNAL
Australia's national monthly magazine
m; 1865—1962
Melbourne

LO/N—1: vol.2,no.70— vol.3,no.123, vol.7,no.1—
vol.12,no.147

AUSTRALIAN KANGAROO
þ; no.1—12 1892—4
Melbourne
ed. Hal E. Stone
Superseded by VICTORIAN KANGAROO (q.v.)

AUSTRALIAN LETTERS
A quarterly review of writing and criticism
q; vol.1,no.1— vol.8,no.1 1957—66
Melbourne. Sun Books, 44 Latrobe St.

LD/U—1: incomplete   LO/N—1: vol.1,no.2—
LO/R98   QL/P—2: vol.2,no.1—

AUSTRALIAN MAGAZINE
Or compendium of religious, literary and miscellaneous intelligence
m; 1821—2
Sydney
ed. Revd. Ralph Mansfield

LO/N—1: vol.1,no.1— vol.2,no.9

AUSTRALIAN MAGAZINE
m; 1859–65
Melbourne
Superseded by AUSTRALIAN MONTHLY
MAGAZINE (q.v.)

LO/N–1: vol.1,no.1–2

AUSTRALIAN MAGAZINE
m; 1886
Melbourne. Sands & McDougall Ltd., 46 Collins
St. W.

LO/S65: 1886

AUSTRALIAN MAGAZINE
m; vol.1,no.1– vol.11,no.117 1901–11
Sydney. A.A.A. Publishing Co.

AUSTRALIAN MERCURY
z(1 issue); vol.1,no.1 1935
Sydney. Waite and Bull, 24 Bond Street
ed. P. R. Stephensen

LO/U–2

AUSTRALIAN MONTHLY MAGAZINE
m; vol.1,no.1– vol.4,no.24 1865–7
Melbourne. W. H. Williams, 23 Little Bourke St. E.
Superseded by COLONIAL MONTHLY (q.v.)

LO/N–1   LO/S65: vol.1,no.1– vol.3,no.12

AUSTRALIAN NATIONAL REVIEW
m; vol.1,no.1– vol.6,no.32 1937–9
Canberra. Canberra Publ. Co.
eds. R. J. Tillyard and W. Farmer Whyte

ED/N–1: vol.2,no.12   LO/N–1   LO/S65:
lacks vol.2,no.2, vol.4,no.23, vol.6,no.32

AUSTRALIAN ONCE A WEEK
w; vol.1,no.1–5 1878
Sydney
ed. C. H. Barlee
Supersedes SYDNEY ONCE A WEEK (q.v.)

AUSTRALIAN OUTLINE
Books, authors, music, art, stories and the theatre
ƥ; no.1–2 1933–4
Sydney

AUSTRALIAN QUARTERLY
q; vol.1,no.1 1929–
Sydney. Australian Institute of Political Science

EX/U–1: vol.10,12–19,22–23   LO/U–8:
vol.9,no.1–   OX/U–9

AUSTRALIAN QUARTERLY JOURNAL
ƥ; vol.1,no.1–4 1828
Sydney
ed. C. P. N. Wilson

CA/U–1   LO/S65

AUSTRALIAN TIT-BITS
Original and selected
w; vol.1,no.1– vol.2,no.10 1899–1900
Sydney
ed. Nat J. Barnet

AUSTRALIAN TRADITION
ƥ; vol.1,no.1 1964–
Melbourne. Folklore Society of Victoria and
Victorian Folk Music Club
Supersedes GUMSUCKERS' GAZETTE (q.v.)

AUSTRALIAN WEEK-END REVIEW
e; vol.1,no.1–21 1950–1
Melbourne. Allan & Higgins

AUSTRALIAN WITNESS
vol.1–2 1853–4
Sydney

LO/N–1: vol.1,no.1–2

AUSTRALIAN WOMEN'S DIGEST
m; vol.1,no.1– vol.4,no.2 1944–8
Sydney. United Associations of Women
ed. Vivienne Newson

AUSTRALIA'S PROGRESS
w/m; vol.1,no.1–33 1945–6
Sydney. R. Chiplin & R. Smith

AUSTROVERT
An occasional journal devoted mainly to Australian
literature
ƥ; no.1–10 1950–3
Melbourne and Darwin
ed. B. W. Muirden

B. P. MAGAZINE
q; vol.1,no.1– vol.14,no.3 1928–42
Sydney. Burns Philp
ed. Dora Payter

BACKGROUND TO COLLECTING
b; 1958–63   New series vol.1,no.1– vol.3,no.2
1963–5
Melbourne. Melbourne Branch of the Book
Collectors' Society of Australia

BALCONY
The Sydney review

q; no.1–6 1965–7
Sydney. Dept. of English, Sydney U.
eds. L. N. Cantrell and others

LO/N–1   LO/U–2

BARINGA
a; 1958–
Wagga Wagga, N.S.W. Wagga Teachers' College

BARJAI
A meeting place for youth
b; no.1–23 1943–7
Brisbane. Barjai Publishing Service

BIALA
A journal of creative writing
a; vol.1 1976–
Prahran, Victoria. Dept. of General Studies,
Prahran College of Advanced Education, 142 High
St., Prahran, Vic. 3181.
eds. Julian Glitzen and John Powers

LO/S26

BIBLIONEWS AND AUSTRALIAN NOTES AND
QUERIES
A journal for book collectors
q; vol.1,no.1– vol.17,no.3 1947–64   2nd series
vol.1,no.1 1966–
Sydney. Book Collectors' Society of Australia

LO/R98: vol.14,no.1–

BIG AUS
A periodical of plain horse sense and patriotism
ƥ; vol.1,no.1–3 1913–14
Brisbane. Gordon & Gotch
ed. E. S. Emerson

BLACK SWAN
The magazine of undergraduates of the University
of Western Australia
ƥ; vol.1,no.1– vol.13,no.1 1917–49
Perth. Guild of Undergraduates at U. W. Australia.

BLACKSMITH
a; no.1 1973–
Wollongong, N.S.W. Wollongong U. College
ed. Gary Hayes

BLOSSOM
z(1 issue); no.1 1828
Sydney
ed. J. W. Fulton

LO/N–1

BOHEMIA
ƥ; no.1–16 1939–40   New series vol.1,no.1–

vol.15,no.11 1945–67
Melbourne. Bread and Cheese Club

BONFIRE
t; vol.1,no.1–3 1960
Sydney. Sydney Eagle Publications
eds. Sydney Dorne, Roy Ravenscroft and Ingram
Smith

BOOK LOVER
m; vol.1,no.1– vol.24,no.249 1899–1921
Melbourne
ed. H. H. Champion

BOOK NEWS
An Australian magazine for the book lover
m; vol.1,no.1–5 1933
Sydney. Bookstall Co.

BOOK NEWS
Official organ of the Australian Book Society
z(1 issue); no.1 1945
Sydney. Australian Book Society
Superseded by AUSTRALIAN BOOKS (q.v.)

BOOK OF THE OPAL
See HEART OF THE ROSE

BOOKS OF TODAY
A readers' review
m; vol.1,no.1–5 1940–1
Melbourne

BOOKSHELF MISCELLANY
z(1 issue); no.1 1933–4
Hobart. W. E. Fuller (ed. and publisher)

BOOKWORM
Monthly magazine of the book clubs of the
Southern District
m; no.1–87 1950–7
Toowoomba, Queensland. Queensland Board of
Adult Education

BOOKWORM
q; no.1 1975–
Carlingford, N.S.W. P.O. Box 156, Carlingford,
N.S.W. 2118
ISSN 0313–1173

BOOMERANG
w; vol.1,no.1 1887–92
Brisbane

BRIDGE
q; c. 1970s

Sydney. Australian Jewish Quarterly Foundation,
P.O. Box 4074, Sydney 2001

BRISBANE WRITERS' GROUP ANTHOLOGY
a; 1954—63
Brisbane

BROGLA
National arts magazine
♭; no.1—2 1951—7
Sydney. Sydney Arts Faculty Bureau, National
Union of Australian U. Students

LO/N—1

BROKEN HILL GRAPHIC
a; 1892—3
Broken Hill, N.S.W. Gold & Attkins

BROWN'S MONTHLY
A humorous, literary and critical journal
m; c. 1870s
Melbourne

LO/N—1: 1879

BULLETIN
w; vol.1,no.1 1880—
Sydney. P.O. Box 4088, Sydney, N.S.W. 2001
ed. Trevor Kennedy
ISSN 0007—4039

CAT
z(1 issue); 1969
Beaconsfield, Victoria. Cat Productions, Box 49

LO/U—2

CENTENNIAL MAGAZINE
An Australian monthly
m; vol.1,no.1— vol.3,no.2 1888—90
Sydney. A. Hutchinson & Sons

CHAPBOOK
a; no.1—2 1935—6
Adelaide. Chapbook Committee
eds. Allan Francis and Noel Wood

CHIRON
a; 1946—69
Perth. Claremont Teachers' College

CLARION
m; 1907—9
Melbourne
ed. Randolph Bedford

COLONIAL ADVOCATE AND TASMANIAN
MONTHLY REVIEW AND REGISTER
m; no.1—8 1828
Hobart

LO/N—1

COLONIAL LITERARY JOURNAL AND
WEEKLY MISCELLANY OF USEFUL INFORM—
ATION
w; vol.1,no.1— vol.2,no.40 1844—5
Sydney
eds. James Reading and Francis Sandoe

COLONIAL LITERARY JOURNAL
And weekly miscellany of useful information
w; 1844—5
Sydney

COLONIAL MONTHLY
m; vol.1,no.1— vol.5,no.29 1867—70
Melbourne. Clarson, Massina & Co.
Supersedes AUSTRALIAN MONTHLY
MAGAZINE (q.v.)

LO/N—1: vol.1—4

COLONIAL SOCIETY
w; vol.1,no.1—8 1868—9   New series no.1—15
1869
Sydney
ed. Walter J. Greenup

COLONIST
A weekly journal of politics for the colony of
New South Wales
w; vol.1—3 1835—7
Sydney

LO/N—1   LO/S65: vol.3,no.115

COMMENT
♭; no.1—26 1940—7
Melbourne
ed. Cecily Crozier

COMMENT
a; no.1—5 1953—8
Bathurst, N.S.W.

COMMENTS
z(1 issue); vol.1,no.1 1908
Melbourne
ed. Arthur F. Doyle

COMMON SENSE
♭; vol.1,no.1—3 1879
Adelaide. Paul W. Ward

COMMONWEALTH
m; vol.1,no.1−2 1899
Melbourne. Echo Publishing Co.

COMMONWEALTH ANNUAL
∮; no.1−2 1901−3
Sydney. N.S.W. Bookstall Co.
Superseded by ROWLANDSON'S SUCCESS (q.v.)

COMPASS
∮; no.1−14 1956−63
Melbourne. Literature Club, Melbourne U.

CONTEMPA
q; 1972−
Armadale, Victoria. Contempa Pubs., P.O. Box
115, Armadale, Vic. 3143
ed. Phillip Edmonds
ISSN 0310−2017

LO/U−2

COO-EE
Official magazine of the Australian Amateur
Press Association
∮; no.1−3 1948−52
Sydney. Australian Amateur Press Assn.
ed. Hal E. Stone

COPY
The annual shriek of the Australian Journalists'
Association
a; 1913
Sydney
ed. Frank Bignold

CORROBOREE
The journal of the Australian Literature Society
m; vol.1,no.1−12 1921−2
Melbourne. Australian Literature Society

COSMOS MAGAZINE
m; vol.1,no.1− vol.5,no.11 1894−9
Sydney. Cosmos Publishing Co.

CROSSBEAT
∮; no.1−7 1962−5   New series vol.1,no.1−
vol.2,no.4 1965−7
Sydney
ed. Revd. Ted Naffs

CRUMPET
A literary magazine
z(1 issue); no.1 1957
Melbourne. Aesthetic Club, Melbourne U.

DAISY
1907
Melbourne. Wayside P.

DAWN
A journal for Australian women
vol.1,no.1− vol.19,no.3 1888−1905
Sydney

DESCANT
∮; no.1−2 1948−50
Sydney. Sydney Teachers' College Literary Club

DESIDERATA
A guide to good books
q; no.1−41 1929−39
Sydney
ed. F. W. Preece

DHARMA
∮; no.1 1971−
Prospect, S.A. P.O. Box 5, Prospect, S.A. 5082
eds. Stephen Measday and Larry Buttrose

LO/U−2

DIAFAN 4
A magazine of original literature
z(1 issue); no.1 1966
Sydney
ed. David Ellis

DIOGENES
A literary annual
a; no.1−11 1955−65
Hobart. Literary Society of U. Tasmania
Supersedes PLATYPUS (q.v.)

DIRECTION
New literature in Australia
∮; vol.1,no.1−4 1952−5
Melbourne
ed. C. H. Davison

DISCONTENT
z(1 issue); no.1 1925
Brisbane
ed. R. Dash

DJAMAGA
A review of the creative arts at Mitchell College
of Advanced Education
∮; no.1−2 1970−2
Bathurst, N.S.W. Mitchell College of Advanced
Education

DODO
The questionable quarterly

♭; 1975–
Sydney
ed. Tom Thompson
ISSN 0313–3230

DRYLIGHT
Literary journal of the Sydney Teachers' College
a; 1934–
Sydney. Students' Representative Council,
Sydney Teachers' College

EASY CHAIR AND MELBOURNE ADVERTISER
m; vol.1,no.1 1895–?
Melbourne. Drakard & Fraser

EDGE
♭; no.1–8 1956–7
Melbourne. 436 Nepean Rd., East Brighton St.
ed. Noel Stock

ED/N–1   EX/U–1   LO/N–1
LO/U–2

ENDEAVOUR
Magazine of the Sunshine Coast Literary Society
♭; vol.1,no.1 1971–
Buderim, Queensland. 19 Tindale Ave., Buderim,
Qld. 4556
ed. Alf Wood

LO/U–2

ENIGMA
q; c. 1970s
Sydney. Dept. of English, U. Sydney

ERN MALLEY'S JOURNAL
♭; vol.1,no.1– vol.2,no.2 1952–5
Heidelberg, Victoria
eds. Max Harris, John Reed and Barrie Reid

LD/U–1: vol.1,no.3

EXPRESSION
Australasia
b; vol.1,no.1– vol.12,no.6 1963–73
Adelaide, S.A. G P.O. Box 755
eds. Nancy Gordon and others

LO/U–2: vol.9,no.1– vol.12,no.6   OX/U–1:
vol.3,no.1– vol.11,no.1

EXPRESSION
a; 1964–
Wollongong, N.S.W. Literary Club, Wollongong
Teachers' College
ISSN 0085–039X

FELLOWSHIP
Official organ of the Fellowship of Australian
Writers
t; vol.1,no.1– vol.4,no.1 1944–8
Sydney. Pinnacle P.
ed. G. Farwell

LO/R98: vol.1,no.2, vol.2,no.2

FIELDS
♭; no.1–4 1971
Rostrevor, S.A. 3 Radnor Ave.
ed. Adrian Flavell

LO/U–2

FIGARO
♭; no.1–40 1883–1936
Brisbane

FIRE O' THE FLAME
see HEART OF THE ROSE

FITZROT
♭; c. 1970s
Collingwood, Victoria. 11 Johnson St.

FLAGSTONES
♭; vol.1,no.1–4 1969
Burwood, Victoria. 23 Fairview Ave.
ed. Ian Robertson

LO/U–2

FOCUS
m; vol.1,no.1– vol.3,no.5 1946–8
Melbourne. Millward

FOOLSCAP
♭; no.1–3 1932
Adelaide

FORERUNNER
q; no.1–8 1930–8
Adelaide. Printing Trade School

FORERUNNER QUARTERLY
q; no.1 1975–
Warrimoo, N.S.W. 32 Spurwood Rd., Warrimoo,
N.S.W. 2775
ed. S. Clarke

FOUNDATION
♭; c, 1970s
Footscray, Victoria. 87a Ballarat Rd., Footscray,
Vic. 3011

FREELANCER
m; vol.1,no.1−22 1930−1
Sydney

FRIENDS OF THE GLENAEON LIBRARY
ϸ; 1961−3
Sydney
Superseded by VISION (q.v.)

GADFLY
w; 1906−9
Adelaide

GALADRIEL
ϸ; *c.* 1970s
Adelaide. 18 Kate Court

GARNET WALCH'S ILLUSTRATED
AUSTRALIAN ANNUAL
a; no.1−8 1874−83
Adelaide. Cameron Laing & Co.

LO/N−1: no.8

GARTRONIAN ECHO
a; vol.1,no.1−3 1926−8
Adelaide. Gartrell Memorial Literary Society

GERALDTON GRAPHIC
a; no.1 1969−
Geraldton, W.A. Geraldton Branch of the Fellowship of Australian Writers

GLEAM
An illustrated monthly magazine for young men
and maidens
m; vol.1,no.1−6 1900
Adelaide. A. F. Pearson

GOLD MINER
Australian journal of general literature
ϸ; no.1−3 1853
Melbourne. John Hetherington

GOODWILL
Journal of the New Australian Cultural Association
a; 1950−1
Sydney. New Australian Cultural Assn.

GREAT AUK
ϸ; vol.1,no.1− vol.10 1968−9
Parkville, Victoria. Gruyere P.O. Box 3770
ed. Charles Buckmaster

LO/U−2

GRIST
z(1 issue); no.1 1944
Adelaide
ed. D. A. Dunstan

GUARDIAN OF AUSTRALIAN ART
m; vol.1,no.1− vol.2,no.10 1933−5
Sydney. Australian Publishing Service
Incorporates AUSTRALIAN COMPOSER
AND WRITERS' MONTHLY (q.v.)

GUM
Magazine of the Guild of Undergraduates of the
University of Western Australia
z(1 issue); no.1 1963
Perth. Guild of Undergraduates of the U. Western
Australia

GUMSUCKERS' GAZETTE
m; vol.1,no.1− vol.4,no.11 1960−3
Prahran, Victoria. Folklore Society of Victoria
and Victoria Bush Music Club
Superseded by AUSTRALIAN TRADITION (q.v.)

HAT
z(1 issue); no.1 1965
Canberra. Arts Society, Australian National U.
eds. J. D. Whelen and R. M. Mackay

HEADS OF THE PEOPLE
An illustrated journal of literature, whims and
oddities
w; vol.1,no.1− vol.2,no.24 1847−8
Sydney
ed. William Baker

LO/N−1   LO/S65

HEART OF THE ROSE
A quarterly magazine
q; vol.1,no.1−4 1907−8
Melbourne
ed. Thomas C. Lothian
Title varies: no.2: BARK OF THE OPAL
no.3: SHADOW OF THE HILL   no.4: FIRE O' TH
FLAME

HECATE
A women's interdisciplinary journal
ϸ; vol.1,no.1 1975−
St. Lucia, Queensland
ed. Carole Ferrier
ISSN 0311−4198

LO/R98

HEMISPHERE
An Asian-Australian monthly

m; vol.1,no.1 1957–
Woden, ACT. P.O. Box 826
ed. K. J. R. Henderson
ISSN 0018–0300

HENSLOWE'S ANNUAL
An artistic and literary annual
a; no.1–6 1900–4
Sydney. Henslowe Publishing Syndicate

HERMES
a; vol.1,no.1– vol.10,no.7 1886–94   New series
vol.1 1895–
Sydney. Students' Representative Council,
U. Sydney

HOBART TOWN MONTHLY MAGAZINE
m; vol.1,no.1– vol.3,no.18 1833–4
Hobart, Tasmania. H. Melville

LO/N–1: vol.1,no.3

HOBART TOWN PUNCH
e; vol.1,no.1–13 1866–7   New series vol.1,no.1–
vol.2,no.13 1867–8
Hobart, Tasmania
ed. Major L. Hood

LO/N–1: n.s. vol.1,no.2,4,7, vol.2,no.6,8–13

HUMBUG
A weekly illustrated journal of satire
w; vol.1,no.1– vol.2,no.19 1869–70
Melbourne. Clarson, Massina & Co.

LO/N–1

IDENTITY
q; c. 1970s
Perth. Aboriginal Publications Foundation

IF REVIVED
f; vol.1,no.1– vol.7,no.2 1949–55
Geelong,,Victoria. Geelong Grammar School

ILLUSTRATED AUSTRALIAN MAGAZINE
m; vol.1,no.1– vol.4,no.12 1850–2
Melbourne. Ham Bros.

LO/N–1   LO/S65: vol.1,no.1,6–14

ILLUSTRATED JOURNAL OF AUSTRALASIA
Monthly magazine
m; vol.1,no.1– vol.4,no.24 1856–8
Melbourne. George Slater
vol.1 entitled JOURNAL OF AUSTRALASIA

LO/N–1   LO/S65   OX/U–1: vol.1–2

IMAGE
z(1 issue); no.1 1962
Brisbane. Kedron Park and Kelvin Grove
Teachers' Colleges

IMP
Imagination, motivation and perseverance
b; vol.1,no.1 1975–
Rockhampton, Queensland. Rockhampton
Writers' Club, P.O. Box 616, Rockhampton,
Qld. 4700
ISSN 0311–7308

IMPERIAL REVIEW
q; no.1–60 1879–1919
Melbourne. McKinley, 59 Queen St.

LO/N–1: no.4–60   LO/S65: no.6–58
OX/U–9: no.9–57

IN PRINT
a; 1972–
Townsville, Queensland. 6 First St., Railway
Estate, Townsville, Qld. 4810
ISSN 0310–3048

INK
b; no.1 1932–?
Sydney. Society of Women Writers of N.S.W.
ed. Constance Robertson

INTELLIGENTSIA
m; no.1–5 1943–4
Brisbane
eds. Noel Burnett, Charles Osborne and M.
Atherton

INTERPRETER
An Australian monthly magazine
m; no.1 1861–?
Melbourne

LO/N–1: no.1–2

JARGON
a; no.1 1936–
Melbourne. Students' Representative Council of
the Royal Melbourne Institute of Technology

JARRAH LEAVES
A literary and artistic annual wholly written and
illustrated by Western Australians
z(1 issue); no.1 1933
Perth. Imperial Printing Co.
ed. John L. Glascock

JINDYWOROBAK ANTHOLOGY
a; 1938–53

Melbourne. Jindyworobak Pubs.
ed. Rex Ingamells

LO/N–1: 1951–3

JINDYWOROBAK REVIEW
z(1 issue); no.1 1948
Melbourne. Jindyworobak Pubs.

JOURNAL OF AUSTRALASIA
see ILLUSTRATED JOURNAL OF
AUSTRALASIA

JOURNEY
A selection of writings from the Canberra
Grammar School
ɓ; 1968–
Canberra. Canberra Grammar School

JUDGMENT
q; vol.1,no.1–2 1920
Melbourne. Melbourne Literary Club
vol.1,no.1 issued as DAY OF JUDGMENT

KALEIDOSCOPE
ɓ; no.1–2 1960–2
Melbourne. Oldfort Publications
eds. C. E. Goode and P. B. Cox

KAT
e/m; vol.1,no.1– vol.4,no.2 1901–2
Sydney
ed. Ure Smith
Superseded by AUSTRALIA KAT (q.v.)

KOOLINDA
ɓ; no.1–10 1943–55
Sydney. Australian Library of Amateur Journalism,
Wayside P.

KOORAKA
ɓ; vol.1,no.1– vol.3,no.1 1923–9
Sydney. Australian Amateur Press Assn.

KOOROORA
a; vol.1,no.1–5 1932–7
Sydney. Kooroora Literary and Debating Society

LANTERN
w; 1874–90
Adelaide
Incorporates ADELAIDE PUNCH (q.v.)

LEATHERJACKET
c. 1970s
Sydney. Box N110, Grosvenor St. P.O., Sydney,
N.S.W. 2000

LEEUWIN
m; vol.1,no.1–6 1910–11
Perth. E. S. Wigg & Son

LEFT TO WRITE
t; 1972–
Perth. Education Dept., Board of Secondary
Education, 3 Ord St., West Perth, W.A. 6005
ed. B. Bennetts
ISSN 0310–3250

LIFE
A record for busy folk
m; vol.1,no.1– vol.52,no.4 1904–38
Melbourne. Fitchett Bros.

LO/N–1: vol.1–12,34–54   LO/S65: vol.1,
no.8– vol.23,no.3

LILLEY'S MAGAZINE
m; vol.1,no.1–5 1911
Sydney. Norman Lilley (ed. and publisher)

LINES
ɓ; no.1 1975–
Toowoomba, Queensland. Darling Downs In-
stitute of Advanced Education, School of Arts,
P.O. Box 128, Toowoomba, Qld. 4350
ISSN 0312–5866

LITERARY INTELLIGENCER AND GENERAL
ADVERTISER
m. 1859–1916
Hobart, Tasmania. J. Walch & Sons
Also called WALCH'S LITERARY INTELLI-
GENCER AND GENERAL ADVERTISER

LO/N–1: n.s. vol.1–52

LITERARY LETTER
m; no.1–44 1966–7
Canberra. Australian News and Information
Bureau

LITERARY NEWS
A review of fact and fiction, the arts, sciences
and *belles-lettres*
w; vol.1,no.1–26 1837–8
Sydney. Tegg

LONE HAND
m; vol.1,no.1– vol.13,no.7 1907–13   New
series vol.1,no.1– vol.11,no.2 1913–21
Sydney. *The Bulletin*

LO/S65

LUNA
A literary publication edited by women
♭; vol.1,no.1 1975–
Kew, Victoria. 101 Edgevale Rd., Kew, Vic. 3101
ed. Barbara Giles
ISSN 0312–9888

LYCEUM LITERARY CIRCLE MAGAZINE
z(1 issue); no.1 1932
Hobart, Tasmania

MAGIC SAM
c. 1970s
Glebe, N.S.W. 9 Arcadia Rd., Glebe, N.S.W. 2037

MAKAR
A magazine of new writing
q; no.1 1960–
St. Lucia, Queensland. Makar P., P.O. Box 71,
St. Lucia, Qld. 4067
ed. Martin Dudwell

ED/N–1: 1975–   LD/U–1: vol.10,no.2–3,
vol.11,no.1–2   LO/U–2; vol.10,no.1–

MANA REVIEW
see under PACIFIC ISLANDS section

MANUSCRIPTS
A miscellany of art and letters
♭; no.1–13 1931–5
Geelong, Victoria
ed. H. Tatlock Miller

MELBOURNE MONTHLY MAGAZINE OF
ORIGINAL COLONIAL LITERATURE
m; vol.1,no.1– vol.2,no.7 1855
Melbourne

LO/N–1: vol.1,no.1– vol.2,no.1

MELBOURNE PARTISAN
♭; no.1–3 1965
Melbourne. Melbourne Partisan Publ. Co.
eds. Lauric Clancy and John Timlin

MELBOURNE QUARTERLY
no.1–4 1882–3
Melbourne

LO/N–1: no.1,4

MELBOURNE REVIEW
q; vol.1,no.1– vol.10,no.40 1876–85
Melbourne. Robertson & Co.

LO/N–1   LO/S65   LO/U–1: no.15

MENTOR
♭; no.1 1962–
Sydney
ed. Ron L. Clarke
Superseded by ARK (q.v.)

MERE ANARCHY
♭; c. 1970s
Adelaide, S.A. Chaotic P., 51 Main Terrace,
ed. Alexander Chaos

MERRINGEK
For an understanding of Australia's history and
traditions, primeval, colonial and modern
z(1 issue); no.1 1953
Melbourne. Jindyworobak Publications
ed. Rex Ingamells

MICROBE
A journal published in the interests of amateur
writers
m; no.1–8 1901–2
Melbourne
eds. Albert and Frank Wilmot

MIRRABOOKA
A Catholic literary quarterly
f; no.1–2 1946
Bendigo, Victoria. Mirrabooka Writers' Group

MOK
♭; no.1–5 1968–9
Adelaide
eds. R. J. O. Tipping and R. H. Tillett

LO/U–2

MONTH
A literary and critical journal
m; vol.1,no.1– vol.3,no.6 1857–8
Sydney. J. L. Cole & Co.
eds. Frank Fowler and J. Sheridan Moore

MOONABOOLA QUILL
The magazine of the Hervey Bay writers' work-
shop
♭; no.1 1959–
Maryborough, Queensland. Maryborough Adult
Education Centre, P.O. Box 65, Maryborough,
Qld. 4650
ed. A. Crawfoot

MOPE HAWK
m; vol.1,no.1 1868–?
Hobart, Tasmania

LO/N–1: vol.1,no.1–11

MORPETH REVIEW
A review of life and work
q; vol.1,no.1– vol.3,no.27 1927–34
Morpeth, N.S.W. St. John's College P.
vol.1,no.1 called REVIEW OF LIFE AND WORK

MS
ϸ; 1950–1
Sydney

MUNDANE EGG
ϸ; c. 1970s
Beecroft, N.S.W. 39 Hill Rd.

MUSES MAGAZINE
A monthly magazine of the musical, artistic,
literary, scientific and intellectual life of Queensland
m; vol.1,no.1– vol.2,no.3 1927–9
Brisbane
ed. Luis Amadeo Pares

NADIRIAN
z(1 issue); no.1 1894
Brisbane. Edwards, Dunlop & Co.

NATIVE COMPANION
An Australian monthly magazine of literature
and life
m; vol.1,no.1– vol.2,no.5 1907
Melbourne
ed. Thomas C. Lothian

LO/S65: vol.1,no.1– vol.2,no.2

NEPEAN REVIEW
a; 1975–
Wentworthville, N.S.W. Nepean College of
Advanced Education
ISSN 0312–7559

NEW NATION
An Australian review
m; vol.1,no.1– vol.2,no.2 1955–6
Adelaide. Twentieth Century Arts Group

NEW SIGNATURES IN AUSTRALIAN LITERA-
TURE
z(1 issue); no.1 1944
Melbourne. View Publishing Co.
ed. J. M. Stevenson

NEW SOUTH WALES MAGAZINE
m; vol.1 1833
Sydney

LO/N–1

NEW SOUTH WALES MAGAZINE
Or journal of general politics, literature, science
and the arts
m; vol.1,no.1–11 1843
Sydney. James Reading, King St. E.

LO/N–1   LO/S65

NEW TRIAD
m; vol.1,no.1– vol.2,no.7 1927–8
Sydney
eds. Hugh McCrae and Ernest Watt
Supersedes TRIAD (q.v.)

NIMROD
ϸ; vol.1,no.1 1962–
Shortland, N.S.W. Students' Assn., U. Newcastle,
Shortland, N.S.W. 2308
ISSN 0085–4204

NOBIS
An anthology of creative work
a; no.1 1955–
Perth. Graylands Teachers' College

NOISE
a; 1963–
Sydney. Arts Faculty Society, U. N.S.W.

NORTH
ϸ; no.1 1963–
Townsville, Queensland. Townsville Branch of
the English Assn.

NUDE DODO
q; no.1 1975–
Hunter's Hill, N.S.W. 6 Mount St.
eds. K. Shadwick and T. Thompson

NUMBER ONE
ϸ; no.1–3 1943–8
Sydney
ed. Garry Lyle
A magazine with no title, but only issue numbering, viz., NUMBER ONE, NUMBER TWO,
NUMBER THREE

NUMBER THREE
see NUMBER ONE

NUMBER TWO
See NUMBER ONE

OBSERVER
e; vol.1,no.1– vol.4,no.6 1958–61
Sydney. Australian Consolidated P.

OBSERVER MISCELLANY
w; no.1—261 1875—9
Adelaide
Supplement to ADELAIDE OBSERVER

LO/S65: no.106—157,210—261

ONCE A MONTH
A magazine for Australasia
m; vol.1,no.1— vol.4,no.6 1884—6
Melbourne
ed. Peter Mercer

LO/N—1   LO/S65: vol.1   OX/U—1: vol.2

OPINION
m; vol.1,no.1—4 1935
Sydney. Paternoster P.

OPINION
t; 1955—
Adelaide. South Australia English Teachers' Assn.,
64 Pennington Terrace, N. Adelaide, S.A. 5000

ORARA
m; no.1—2 1941
Brisbane
eds. J. B. Davenport and H. Robinson

ORION
q; vol.1,no.1— vol.2,no.4 1919—21
Adelaide
eds. Margaret Cheadle and Rex Boundy

ORPHEUS
a; 1963—4
Melbourne.
Students' Representative Council, Monash U.,
Monash University Magazine

OSIRIS
♭; vol.1,no.1 1974—
Albion, Queensland. P.O. Box 235, Albion, Qld.
4010
ed. D. Stocks

OUR SWAG
♭; vol.1,no.1— vol.3,no.4 1903—6
Sydney

OUTLAW
♭; c. 1973
Fitzroy, Victoria. P.O. Box 159, Fitzroy, Vic.
3065

OVERLAND
Incorporating *Realist Writer*
q; no. 1 1954—

Melbourne. P.O. Box 98a, Melbourne, Vic. 3001
ed. Dr. Stephen Murray-Smith
ISSN 0030—7416
Supersedes REALIST WRITER (q.v.)

ED/N—1   LD/U—1: no.3—   LO/N—1:
no.25—   LO/R98: no.3—   LO/S26: no.40—
LO/U—2: no.5—   QL/P—2: no.25—

PARTHENON
m; vol.1,no.1— vol.4,no.3 1889—92
Sydney
eds. Lily and Ethel Turner

PASTON'S MELBOURNE QUARTERLY
A journal of literary pleasantry
z(1 issue); no.1 1958
Melbourne

PEN
The newsletter of the Sydney Centre of International P.E.N.
♭; no.1 1966—
Sydney. P.E.N. Sydney Centre

PERRY
♭; c. 1970s
Mooroopna, Vic. 2 Lenne St.

PERTINENT
♭; vol.1,no.1— vol.5,no.2 1940—7
Sydney. Pertinent Publishing Co.

PHOENIX
a; 1935—67
Adelaide. Students' Representative Council,
Adelaide U.
Supersedes ADELAIDE UNIVERSITY
MAGAZINE (q.v.) In 1940 temporarily super-
seded by ANGRY PENGUINS (q.v.)

PHOENIX AUSTRALIA
q; no.1 1975—
Nambour, Queensland. Dulong Road, Nambour,
Qld. 4560
ed. Les Alcorn
ISSN 0312—7672

PLATYPUS
♭; 1914—52
Hobart. U. Tasmania
Superseded by DIOGENES (q.v.)

PLOUGHMAN
q; 1973—
Sydney. Fragment P., P.O. Box 2217 Royal
Exchange, Sydney, N.S.W. 2000
ed. Gary Oliver

ISSN 0310–6837
supersedes PLOUGHMAN'S LUNCH

POETRY AND PROSE BROADSHEET
ƅ; no.1 1969–
Sydney
ed. Jurgis Janavicius

POINT
An Australian quarterly of independent expression
q; vol.1,no.1–2 1938
Melbourne. Point Writers' Group
ed. Alan Marshall

PORT PHILLIP GAZETTE
ƅ; vol.1,no.1– vol.2,no.3 1952–6
Melbourne. Rising Sun P.
ed. Desmond Fennessy

PRAHRAN LITERARY SOCIETIES' UNION
RECORD
z(1 issue); vol.1,no.1 1890
Melbourne

PRESS NEWS
w; no.1–5 1899
Sydney
ed. Lady Mary Lygon

PROSPECT
A quarterly review
q; vol.1,no.1– vol.7,no.4 1958–64
Melbourne. Universities' Catholic Publishing
Cooperative

PUBLICIST
The paper loyal to Australia first
m; no.1–69 1936–42
Sydney. Publicist Publishing Co.

PURGE
t; vol.1,no.1– vol.2,no.3 1964–5
Canberra. Arts Society, National U.

QUANTUM
ƅ; no.1–? 1959–60   New series no.1 1961–?
Bowral, N.S.W.
ed. J. M. Baxter

QUEENSLAND WRITING
ƅ; 1954, 1957
Brisbane. Queensland Authors' & Artists' Assn.

RAMBLER
w; vol.1,no.1–11 1899

Melbourne
ed. Heinrich Lauritz Nielson

RATAPLAN
The magazine of the arts
ƅ; no.1–2 1968
Melbourne
ed. Leigh Edmonds

READERS AND WRITERS
Australasian Book Society news
ƅ; no.1–23 1962–7
Sydney

READERS' AND WRITERS' WEEKLY
w; vol.1,no.1–9 1937
Sydney. Assn. of Modern Writers of Australia in
conjunction with the Lovejoy Lending Library

REALIST
q; vol.1,no.1 1958–
Northbridge, N.S.W. National Council of the
Realist Writers' Group, P.O. Box 12, Northbridge,
N.S.W. 2063
ISSN 0048–6884

REALIST WRITER
q; no.1–9 1952–4
Melbourne. Realist Writers' Group
Superseded by OVERLAND (q.v.)
eds. Bill Wannan and S. Murray-Smith

RED ANT
An Australian magazine
ƅ; 1912
Sydney
ed. Hal E. Stone

REFRACTORY GIRL
A women's studies journal
q; no.1 1972–
Sydney. 25 Alberta St.

LO/R98

REVIEW OF LIFE AND WORK
See MORPETH REVIEW

RIGMAROLE OF THE HOURS
ƅ; c. 1970s
Fitzroy, Victoria. 166 Napier St., Fitzroy, Vic.
3065

RIVERRUN
A magazine
ƅ; no.1 1976–

Cook's Hill, N.S.W. Riverrun P., 107 Laman St.

LO/S26

ROWLANDSON'S SUCCESS
a; 1907–8
Sydney. N.S.W. Bookstall Co.
Supersedes COMMONWEALTH ANNUAL (q.v.)

S.L.S. MAGAZINE
♭; no.1–2 1934–5
Sydney. Sydney Literary Society
ed. Jean M. Cooper

SALIENT
A literary magazine (mainly for women)
q; vol.1,no.1– vol.2,no.1 1959–61
Geelong, Victoria
eds. J. Alston and K. Titze

SCOPE
m; 1956–
Eagle Junction, Queensland. Fellowship of
Australian Writers, Queensland Division, 15 Howie
St.
ed. Margaret Connah

SCRIBBLER
a; 1974
Crawley, West Australia. Arts and Literature Club,
St. George's College, U. of W.A.
ed. John Webb
ISSN 0313–5233

SHADOW ON THE HILL
See HEART OF THE ROSE

SILVER WATTLE
a; vol.1,no.1–2 1925–6
Sydney. Australian Amateur Press Assn.
ed. Hal E. Stone

SINGABOUT
♭; vol.1no.1– vol.6,no.2 1956–67
Sydney. Bush Music Club, Box 433, G.P.O.
Sydney, N.S.W. 2001

SMITH'S WEEKLY
w; vol.1,no.1– vol.32,no.35 1919–50
Sydney

SO THIS IS ADELAIDE
m; no.1–4 1931–2
Adelaide

SOUTH AUSTRALIAN MAGAZINE
♭; 1841–3
Adelaide.

ed. J. Allen

LO/N–1: no.1,2

SOUTH BRITON
Or Tasmanian literary journal
m; no.1–2 1843
Hobart, Tasmania. William Pratt

LO/N–1: no.1

SOUTHERN CROSS
A weekly journal of politics, literature and social
progress
w; vol.1,no.1–46 1859–60
Sydney. Francis Smith

SOUTHERN SPECTATOR
m; no.1–3 1957–9
Melbourne
ed. R. Fletcher

SOUTHERN SPHERE
The Australian illustrated journal
m; 1910–2
Melbourne. Osboldstone & Co.

SPECTATOR
w; 1846–7
Sydney

SPECTRUM
♭; 1962–
Sydney. Balmain Teachers' College
Supersedes WORDS (q.v.)

SPECTRUM
♭; vol.1,no.1 1967–
Brisbane. Queensland Writers' Workshop

SPIRIT OF THE AGE
m; vol.1,no.1–12 1856
Sydney

LO/N–1

STEAD'S REVIEW
m; vol.1,no.1– vol.68,no.3 1897–1931
Melbourne. 241 William St.
Superseded by TO-DAY (q.v.)

LO/S65: vol.10,no.5– vol.68,no.1

STEELE RUDD'S ANNUAL
a; 1917–24
Brisbane
ed. Arthur Hoey Davis ('Steele Rudd')

STEELE RUDD'S MAGAZINE
m; vol.1,no.1— vol.4,no.9 1904—7   New series
vol.1,no.1—? 1923—5   3rd series vol.1,no.1—?
1926—?
Brisbane
ed. Arthur Hoey Davis ('Steele Rudd')

STREAM
m; vol.1,no.1—3 1931
Melbourne
ed. Cyril Altson Pearl

STRIFE
z(1 issue); vol.1,no.1 1930
Melbourne

STRIVINGS
A quarterly magazine trying to encourage and to
give others our strivings after beauty
q; no.1—4 1931—2
Melbourne

SYDNEY MAGAZINE
m; 1878
Sydney
ed. G. R. Maclean

SYDNEY ONCE A WEEK
w; vol.1,no.1—24 1878
Sydney
ed. C. H. Barlee
Superseded by AUSTRALIAN ONCE A WEEK
(q.v.)

LO/N—1

SYDNEY QUARTERLY MAGAZINE
q; vol.1,no.1— vol.9,no.4 1883—92
Sydney

TABLE TALK ANNUAL
a; 1904—37
Melbourne. Edgerton & Moore

TALISMAN
Newcastle's own magazine
ϸ; vol.1,no.1—2 1947
Newcastle, N.S.W. Newcastle Writers' Club
ed. Eric Sparke

TASMANIAN ATHENAEUM
Or journal of science, literature and art
m; vol.1,no.1— vol.6,no.6 1853—4
Hobart. Huxtable & Deakin
eds. Richard Lee and William Coote

LO/N—1: vol.1

TATLER
Art, literature, music and the drama
w; vol.1,no.1— vol.2,no.60 1897—8
Melbourne. George Robertson & Co.

TEGG'S MONTHLY MAGAZINE
m; vol.1,no.1—5 1836
Sydney
ed. James Tegg

LO/N—1

THYRSUS
b; no.1—2 1935
Newcastle, N.S.W.
ed. Bert Birtles

TIMES TALES
Being a collection from the files of the Sydney
Sunday Times
z(1 issue); no.1 1898
Sydney. *Sunday Times* Office

TIMESTREAM
b; 1971—
Sydney S. P.O. Box A360, N.S.W. 2000
ed. Richard Coady

TINKER
ϸ; no.1 1970—
Melbourne
ed. Glenn Moore

TO-DAY
m; vol.68,no.4— vol.71,no.16 1931—4
Sydney. 321 Pitt St.
Supersedes STEAD'S REVIEW (q.v.)

LO/S65

TRANSIT
ϸ; no.1 1968—
Paddington, N.S.W. 112 Lawson St., Paddington
N.S.W. 2021
ed. John Tranter

TRIAD
m; vol.1,no.1— vol.13,no.6 1915—27
Sydney. Triad Magazine Ltd.
Superseded by NEW TRIAD (q.v.)

TWEED
q; 1972—
Murwillumbah, N.S.W. P.O. Box 304, N.S.W. 24
eds. Janice M. Bostok and S. L. Poulter
ISSN 0310—0200

TWENTIETH CENTURY
An Australian quarterly review
q; vol.1.no.1 1946–
Kew, Victoria. Institute of Social Order, 12
Sackville St., Kew, Vic. 3101
ed. W. G. Smith

LO/R98: vol.18–

21st CENTURY
The magazine of a creative civilization
b; no.1–2 1955–7
Sydney. 21st Century Art Group
ed. Harry Hooton

UNDER CAPRICORN
b; 1954   New series no.1–2 1955
Sydney
ed. James Gidley

UNDERGROWTH
A magazine of youth and ideals
b; 1925–9
Sydney
eds. Nancy A. Hall and D. Hawthorne

UNITED AUSTRALIA
A monthly review for thinking men and women
b; vol.1,no.1– vol.2,no.13 1900–2
Melbourne. 243 Collins St.

VENTURE
An Australian literary quarterly
z(1 issue); vol.1,no.1 1937
Adelaide. Hassell P.
ed. Rex Ingamells
Superseded by VENTURE: Jindyworobak
quarterly pamphlet (q.v.)

VENTURE
Jindyworobak quarterly pamphlet
q; vol.1,no.1– vol.2,no.3 1939–40
Adelaide. Jindyworobak Pubs.
eds. F. W. Preece and Rex Ingamells
Supersedes VENTURE: An Australian literary
quarterly (q.v.)

VENTURE
z(1 issue); no.1 1961
Hobart. Literary Society, U. Tasmania

VERVE
b; vol.1,no.1–5 1957–60
Adelaide. Literary Society, U. Adelaide

VICTORIAN KANGAROO
b; vol.1,no.1 1894–1902

Melbourne
ed. Hal E. Stone
Supersedes AUSTRALIAN KANGAROO (q.v.)
Superseded by YE KANGAROO (q.v.)

VICTORIAN MONTHLY MAGAZINE
m; vol.1,no.1–12 1859
Melbourne

LO/N–1: no.1–2

VICTORIAN REVIEW
m; vol.1,no.1– vol.13,no.76 1879–86
Melbourne. Victorian Review Publishing Co.
ed. H. Mortimer Franklyn

VISION
A literary quarterly
q; no.1–4 1923–4
Sydney
eds. F. C. Johnson, Jack Lindsay and Kenneth
Slessor

LO/N–1: no.1,3

VISION
A magazine of the arts, science and Australiana
b; no.1 1963–
Sydney. Adelphi Students' Library, P.O. Box
5155
Supersedes FRIENDS OF THE GLENAEON
LIBRARY (q.v.)

LO/U–2: no.20–27

VISTA
A magazine of literature and art
b; vol.1,no.1–2 1946
Brisbane. Catholic Writers' Movement

VOID
q; no.1 1975–
St. Kilda, Victoria. P.O. Box 66, St. Kilda, Vic.
3182
ed. P. Collins

WADDY
With which is incorporated the salami
z(1 issue): vol.1,no.1 c. 1909
Melbourne. Brown Prior & Co.

WALCH'S LITERARY INTELLIGENCER AND
GENERAL ADVERTISER
m; 1859–1916
Hobart, Tasmania. J. Walch & Sons
also called LITERARY INTELLIGENCER

LO/N–1: n.s. vol.1–52

WALLET
w; no.1−30 1864−5
Adelaide. Arthur Coventry
Supplement to WEEKLY MAIL

WANDERER
A monthly periodical of original literature
m; no.1−7 1853
Sydney
ed. Timothy Short

WAYFELLOW
þ; vol.1−4 1915−43
Adelaide. Koolinda P.
ed. Hal E. Stone

WAYSIDE GOOSE
m; vol.1,no.1−? 1904−5   New series vol.1,
no.1−10 1906
Sydney
eds. Hal E. Stone, M. C. Brennan and Sydney
Partridge

WESTERN WRITING
þ; no.1−2 1939−40
Perth. Western Australian section of the Fellowship of Australian Writers

WILLIAMS'S ILLUSTRATED ANNUAL
a; no.1−3 1868−71
Melbourne
ed. Henry Kendall

WINTHROP REVIEW
t; vol.1,no.1 1953−?
Perth. Arts Union of the U. Western Australia

WOOMERA
þ; no.1−4 1951−3
Sydney
ed. Nick Solnsteff

WORDS
a; no.1 1954−?
Melbourne. Writers' Group, Adult Education Assn.

WORDS
Literary expressions
a; no.1−16 1946−61
Sydney. Balmain Teachers' College
Superseded by SPECTRUM (q.v.)

WREATH
A journal of literature, drama, etc.
e; c. 1835
Hobart, Tasmania
ed. M. Olding

WRITER
m; no.1−24 1944−6   New series vol.3,no.1−
vol.4,no.5 1946−8
Melbourne. Writer Publishing Co.

WRITERS' WORLD
b; no.1 1953−
Melbourne. Australian Writers' Professional
Service, P.O. Box 28, Collins St., Melbourne,
Vic. 3001
ed. Gordon R. Pittaway
ISSN 0043−9576

LO/U−2: no.98

YE KANGAROO
þ; vol.1,no.1− vol.7,no.1 1902−5
Melbourne
ed. Hal E. Stone
Supersedes VICTORIAN KANGAROO (q.v.)

YESTERDAY AND MOST OF TODAY
m; no.1−14 1932−4
Sydney
eds. Will Alfredo and C. William

YOUR FRIENDLY FASCIST
þ; no.1 1970−
Darlington, N.S.W. Pig's Arse P. P.O. Box 164,
Wentworth Bldg., City Rd., Darlington, N.S.W.
2008
eds. John Edwards and Rae Desmond Jones

LO/U−2: no.5,9−

YOUTH ANNUAL
z(1 issue); 1930
Sydney
ed. W. H. Honey

YR YMWELYDD
m; vol.1,no.1− vol.2,no.12 1875−6
Melbourne. Walker, May & Co.

ZEST
A magazine for living Australians
m; vol.1,no.1−2 1932
Sydney
ed. L. L. Woolacott

Academic and Critical

A.L.S. MONTHLY
m; vol.1,no.1−5 1938
Melbourne. Australian Literary Society,
Hawthorn P.

ADELAIDE LITERARY SOCIETY JOURNAL
m; no.1–99 1877–85
Adelaide. Adelaide Literary Society

ADELAIDE UNIVERSITY MAGAZINE
t; vol.1,no.1– vol.6,no.1 1918–34
Adelaide
Superseded by PHOENIX (q.v.)

ADELAIDE UNIVERSITY MAGAZINE
a; 1953–67 None issued 1955,1957
Adelaide, Students' Representative Council,
U. Adelaide
1958 issue as VARSITY

ADULT EDUCATION
q; vol.1,no.1– vol.12,no.4 1956–68
Melbourne. Council of Adult Education

ALL ABOUT BOOKS
For Australian and New Zealand readers
m; vol.1,no.1– vol.10,no.3 1928–38
Melbourne
ed. D. W. Thorpe

ALL ABOUT BOOKS
m; vol.10,no.1–20 1961–3
Melbourne
ed. D. W. Thorpe
Supersedes previous ALL ABOUT BOOKS (q.v.)
Superseded by IDEAS

LO/N–1: vol.10,no.4–20

ARENA
A Marxist journal of criticism and discussion
c.1960s
Victoria. Box 36, Greensborough P.O., Vic. 3088
eds. Geoff Sharp and Doug White

LD/U–1: no.26

AUMLA
A journal of literary criticism, philology and
linguistics
f; no.1 1953–
Townsville, Queensland. Australasian Universities
Language and Literature Assn., James Cook U.,
Townsville, Qld. 4810
ed. R. T. Sussex
ISSN 0001–2793

BH/U–1	CA/U–1	CB/U–1
DR/U–1	ED/N–1	ED/U–1
EX/U–1: no.21–	GL/U–1	HL/U–1
LD/U–1: lacks no.6	LO/N–1	LO/U–1
LO/U–2	MA/U–1: no.29–	NR/U–1:
no.25–	SH/U–1: no.3–	ST/U–1

AUSTRALASIAN AND PACIFIC SOCIETY FOR
18th-CENTURY STUDIES
b; 1971–
Canberra. Dept. of English, School of General
Studies, Australian National U., P.O. Box 4,
Canberra, A.C.T. 2601
ed. J. C. Eade

AUSTRALIAN AUTHOR
q; vol.1,no.1 1969–
Sydney. Australian Society of Authors, 252
George St., Sydney, N.S.W., 2000
ed. Gavin Souter
ISSN 0045–026X

LO/R98

AUSTRALIAN BOOK REVIEW
m/q; vol.1,no.1 1961–
Kensington Park, S.A. 27 Park Rd., Kensington
Park, S.A. 5068
eds. Max Harris and Rosemary Wighton

ED/N–1   LO/N–1: vol.1,no.3–
LO/R98   LO/S65: vol.1,no.11–12, vol.2,no.1,
vol.3–6, vol.8,no.3,9   OX/U–1: vol.10,no.4,
vol.11,no.9, vol.12   QL/P–2

AUSTRALIAN BOOKMAN
An illustrated magazine of literature and life
m; vol.1,no.1–2 1905–6
Sydney. Angus & Robertson

AUSTRALIAN BOOKS
Official journal of the Australian Book Society
b; vol.1,no.1– vol.2,no.9 1946–8
Sydney. Australian Book Society
Supersedes BOOK NEWS (q.v.)

AUSTRALIAN ENGLISH ASSOCIATION,
SYDNEY: BULLETIN
b; vol.1,no.1–10 1936–9
Sydney. Australian English Assn.
Superseded by SOUTHERLY (q.v.)

AUSTRALIAN ENGLISH ASSOCIATION,
SYDNEY: LEAFLET
b; no.1–19 1923–34
Sydney. Australian English Assn.

LO/N–1: no.5,8,16,18–19

AUSTRALIAN ENGLISH ASSOCIATION,
SYDNEY: OFFPRINT
b; no.1–29 1930–7
Sydney. Australian English Assn.

AUSTRALIAN LITERARY STUDIES
f; vol.1,no.1 1963–

St. Lucia, Queensland. Dept. of English, U.
Queensland, St. Lucia, Qld. 4067
ISSN 0004—9697
eds. L. T. Hergenhan and E. Stokes

CA/U—1	CB/U—1: vol.5,no.3—4, vol.7,no.1—	
DR/U—1: vol.3,no.1—		ED/N—1
EX/U—1	HL/U—1	LD/U—1
LO/R98	LO/S26: vol.2,no.1—	LO/U—1
LO/U—2	OX/U—1	

AUSTRALIAN MODERN LANGUAGE REVIEW
see MODERN LANGUAGE REVIEW OF NEW
SOUTH WALES

AUSTRALIAN RHODES REVIEW
ϸ; no.1—5 1934—46
Carlton, Victoria. Assn. of Rhodes Scholars in
Australia, 372—4 Drummond St.

CA/U—1	LD/U—1: no.1—2	LO/N—1
LO/S65: no.1—2,5	LO/U—1	OX/U—9
QL/P—1		

CHAUNTECLEER
t; no.1 1970—
Parkville, Victoria. P.O. Box 49, Parkville,
Vic. 3052

CRITIC
ϸ; vol.1,no.1— vol.11,no.2 1961—70
Perth. Literary Society, Guild of Undergraduates,
U. Western Australia

CRITIC
vol.1,no.1 1883—?
Melbourne
ed. S. Myth

CRITICAL REVIEW
a; no.1 1958—
Melbourne. Dept. of English, U. Melbourne,
Parkville, Vic. 3052
ed. Prof. S. L. Goldberg
ISSN 0070—1548
from no.3—7 as MELBOURNE CRITICAL
REVIEW

BH/U—1: no.8—	ED/N—1	ED/U—1
HL/U—1	LD/U—1	LO/S26: no.1—9
LO/U—1: no.3—	NR/U—1	

DESIGN
An Australian review of critical thought
ϸ; no.1—3 1940
Melbourne. Hawthorn P.
ed. P. I. O'Leary

ENGLISH ASSOCIATION ADELAIDE BRANCH
PAMPHLET
ϸ; no.1—3 1932—7
Adelaide
ed. F. W. Preece

ENGLISH ASSOCIATION ADELAIDE BRANCH
PAMPHLET (EXTRA SERIES)
z(1 issue); no.1 1935
Adelaide
ed. F. W. Preece

ENGLISH IN AUSTRALIA
q; 1965—
Parkside, S.A. Australian Assn. for the Teaching
of English, 163 Greenhill Rd. Parkside, S.A. 5063
ed. Warwick Goodenough
ISSN 0046—208X

ENGLISH TEACHER
ϸ; no.1 1959—
Sydney. English Teachers' Group

ENGLISH TEACHERS' ASSOCIATION
JOURNAL
q; vol.1,no.1— vol.4,no.2 1965—8   New series
vol.1,no.1 1968—
Perth. English Teachers' Assn. of W. Australia

ESPRIT AND GEIST
A bulletin for teachers of modern languages
ϸ; no.1—5 1958—64
Sydney. N.S.W. Dept. of Education in association
with Modern Language Teachers' Assn. of N.S.W.

FELLOWSHIP
A monthly magazine of undogmatic religion and
social and literary criticism
m; vol.1,no.1— vol.8,no.12 1914—22
Melbourne. Fraser & Jenkinson
ed. Revd. F. Sinclaire

FOREWARD
An Australian review
b; vol.1,no.1— vol.2,no.11 1937—41
Sydney. Liberal Magazine Co.

GALMAHRA
Magazine of the University of Queensland Union
t; vol.1,no.1 1921—
Brisbane. Union, U. Queensland
Supersedes QUEENSLAND UNIVERSITY
MAGAZINE (q.v.)

IDIOM
z(8 p.a.); no.1 1963—
Carlton, Victoria. Victorian Assn. for the Teach-

ing of English, 49a Rathdowne St., Carlton, Vic.
3053
ed. Veni Scoborio
Incorporates VATE JOURNAL (q.v.)

JANUS
f; vol.1,no.1 1975–
Bathurst, N.S.W. Mitchell College of Advanced
Education, Bathurst, N.S.W. 2795
ISSN 0312–2727

LANGUAGE
A literary journal
b; vol.1,no.1–2 1952
Sydney. Athenian Publishing Co.
ed. G. A. Mill

LAWSONIAN
m; no.1 1960–
Chadstone, Victoria. Henry Lawson Memorial
and Literary Society, 2 Paringa Court, Chadstone,
Vic. 3148
ed. Harry H. Pearce

LINQ
q; no.1 1971–
Townsville, Queensland. Dept. of English, James
Cook U., Townsville, Qld. 4811

MEANJIN QUARTERLY
A magazine of literature, art and discussion
q; vol.1,no.1 1940–
Parkville, Victoria. U. Melbourne, Parkville,
Vic. 3052
eds. C. B. Christensen and J. H. Davidson
ISSN 0025–6293
Also called MEANJIN PAPERS and MEANJIN
See also MEANJIN BROADSHEET and WORK-
SHOP

BH/U–1: vol.23–   CA/U–1: vol.2,5,8–
ED/N–1: 1954–   EX/U–1: vol.19,no.2–4,
vol.20,no.2–4, vol.21,no.3–4, vol.22,no.1–4,
vol.23,no.1–2,4, vol.24–   HL/U–1: vol.16,
no.1–3, vol.20,no.2–4, vol.21–26, vol.27,no.1–2
LD/U–1: vol.5–6,no.2, vol.7–   LO/N–1:
vol.2,no.2–   LO/R98: vol.7–   LO/S26:
1963–   LO/S65: vol.3–8,12,15–16,18–
LO/U–1: vol.7,no.2–   LO/U–2: vol.7,no.2–
OX/U–1: vol.2–   QL/P–2: vol.7–
ST/U–1: vol.33–

MELBOURNE CRITICAL REVIEW
see CRITICAL REVIEW

MELBOURNE UNIVERSITY MAGAZINE
a; vol.1,no.1 1907–
Parkville, Victoria. Students' Representative
Council, Melbourne U.
ISSN 0085–3283

MELBOURNE UNIVERSITY REVIEW
ƅ; vol.1,no.1– vol.8,no.4 1884–91
Melbourne

MENS EADEM
a; no.1 1958–?
Sydney. College Group of the Newman Society
at the U. Sydney

MODERN LANGUAGE REVIEW OF NEW
SOUTH WALES
t; vol.1,no.1– vol.2,no.2 1920   New Series
vol.1,no.1 1921 Sydney. Modern Language Assn.
of N.S.W. vol.1,no.1 called AUSTRALIAN
MODERN LANGUAGE REVIEW

NEW LITERATURE REVIEW
ƅ; no.1 1975–
Sydney. Dept. of English, U. Sydney
ed. M. Griffith

PANDEMONIUM
A critical Australian monthly
m; vol.1,no.1–12 1934–5
Melbourne. Pandemonium P.
ed. Mervyn Skipper

PLURALIST
A journal of social and literary criticism
ƅ; no.1 1962–
Sydney
ed. Richard Appleton

PRESENT OPINION
t; vol.1,no.1– vol.4,no.1 1946–9
Melbourne. Arts Assn., Melbourne U.

QUADRANT
An Australian quarterly review
b; vol.1,no.1 1956–
Sydney. Australian Assn. for Cultural Freedom,
P.O. Box C344, Clarence St., Sydney, N.S.W. 2000
eds. Peter Coleman and Vivian Smith
ISSN 0033–5002

ED/N–1: 1976–   LD/U–1: lacks vol.8,no.1
LO/R98   LO/S26: 1971–   LO/S65:
vol.11,no.5–   OX/U–1

QUEENSLAND UNIVERSITY MAGAZINE
ɸ; vol.1,no.1– vol.6,no.1 1911–20
Brisbane. Union, U. Queensland
Superseded by GALMAHRA (q.v.)

SOUTHERLY
A review of Australian literature
q; vol.1,no.1 1939–
Surrey Hills, N.S.W. English Assn., Sydney
Branch, Wentworth P., 48 Cooper St. Surrey
Hills, N.S.W. 2010
ed. G. A. Wilkes
ISSN 0038–3732

ED/N–1: 1975–   HL/U–1: vol.29–
LD/U–1: vol.1–6, vol.15,no.2–   LO/N–1:
vol.5,no.4,vol.6,no.3,vol.7,no.3,vol.8–
LO/R98   LO/S26: 1971–   LO/S65
LO/U–1: vol.15–   LO/U–2: vol.26–
OX/U–1: vol.1,11–   QL/P–2: vol.19–

SOUTHERN REVIEW
An Australian journal of literary studies
f; vol.1,no.1 1963–
Adelaide and Sydney. English Dept., U. Adelaide,
and School of English Studies, Macquarie U.
eds. Ed Le Mire, Kevin Magarey and Manfred
Mackenzie
ISSN 0038–4526
Supersedes ASPECT (q.v.)

BH/U–1   CA/U–1   CB/U–1
ED/N–1: 1976–   EX/U–1   HL/U–1
LD/U–1   LO/R98   LO/U–1
LO/U–2: vol.1,no.2–   MA/U–1
NR/U–1: vol.1, no.3–   SH/U–1

SPAN
Newsletter of the South Pacific Association for
Commonwealth Literature and Language Studies
f; no.1 1975–
Brisbane. South Pacific Assn. for Commonwealth
Literature and Language Studies, U. Queensland
ed. Chris Tiffen
ISSN 0313–1459

LO/S26

SYDNEY STUDIES IN ENGLISH
a; no.1 1975–
Dept. of English, U. Sydney
eds. G. A. Wilkes and A. P. Riemer

SYDNEY UNIVERSITY MAGAZINE
q; no.1–3 1855
Sydney. Waugh & Cox

LO/S65

SYDNEY UNIVERSITY MAGAZINE
A literary, scientific and educational journal
m; vol.1,no.1– vol.2,no.6 1878–9
Sydney. Kindersley, 41 Market St.

LO/S65: vol.1,no.1–4

TOUCHSTONE
A Saturday journal of criticism, commentary and
satire
w; vol.1,no.1– vol.3,no.63 1869–70
Melbourne. C. Chapman & Co.

LO/N–1: lacks vol.2,no.25–27

V.A.T.E. JOURNAL
ɸ; vol.1,no.1– vol.4,no.8 1963–9
Melbourne. Victorian Assn. for the Teaching of
English
Incorporated in IDIOM (q.v.)

WESTERLY
A quarterly review
q; no.1 1956–
Nedlands, Western Australia. English Dept.,
Western Australia U., Nedlands, W.A. 6009
ed. Peter Cowan
ISSN 0043–342X

CB/U–1: 1968–   ED/N–1: 1975–
LD/U–1   LO/R98   LO/S26: no.4–
LO/U–2

Drama

AUSTRALASIAN STAGE ANNUAL
An annual devoted to the interests of the
theatrical and musical professions
a; no.1–7 1900–6
Melbourne. J. J. Miller
ed. William A. Crawley

DRAMA AND THE SCHOOL
f; 1948–
Sydney. Whitehall Productions
ed. C. Fenton

KOMOS
A quarterly of drama and arts of the theatre
q; vol.1,no.1 1967–
Clayton, Victoria. English Dept., Monash U.
ed. Margery M. Morgan

CB/U–1: vol.1,no.3–   LO/R98
LO/U–1

MASQUE
A magazine of performing arts
ƀ; vol.1,no.1 1967–
Sydney, N.S.W. Masque Publications, P.O. Box
3504, Sydney, N.S.W. 2001

PLAYBILL
m; 1935
Melbourne. Playbill Publishing Co.
eds. Lesley Williams and George Walton
Incorporated in ADAM AND EVE (q.v.)

THEATRE
ƀ; no.1–5 1962–4
Melbourne. Marlowe Society

Fiction

ALBANY WRITES
a; 1966–
Albany, W.A. Albany Branch of the Fellowship
of Australian Writers

AUSTRALIAN NEW WRITING
ƀ; no.1–4 1943–6
Sydney. Current Book Distributors, Rawson
Chambers, Rawson Place
eds. Katherine Susannah Prichard, George Farwell
and Bernard Smith

LO/U–2: no.2

AUSTRALIAN SCIENCE FICTION ASSOCI-
ATION JOURNAL
ƀ; vol.1,no.1 1965–
Canberra. Australian Science Fiction Assn.,
P.O. Box 852, Canberra, A.C.T. 2601
ISSN 0084–7585

AUSTRALIAN SCIENCE FICTION MONTHLY
m; no.1 1970–
Melbourne. Australian Science Fiction Commun-
ications Organization
Supersedes AUSTRALIAN SCIENCE FICTION
REVIEW (q.v.)

AUSTRALIAN SCIENCE FICTION REVIEW
ƀ; no.1–21 1955–69
Melbourne. John Bangsund (ed. and publisher)
Superseded by AUSTRALIAN SCIENCE FICTION
MONTHLY (q.v.)

AUSTRALIAN WRITERS' ANNUAL
a; no.1 1936
Sydney. Fellowship of Australian Writers
ed. Flora S. Eldershaw

CHAO
A science fiction magazine
ƀ; no.1 1970–
Maryborough, Victoria. Clanalder P.
ed. John J. Alderson

COAST TO COAST
Australian stories
a/f; 1941–
Sydney. Angus & Robertson

LO/N–1

COR SERPENTIS
ƀ; 1971–
Clayton, Victoria. Monash U. Science Fiction
Assn., Clayton, Vic. 3168
ISSN 0311–1248

DROLL
Variegated stories
ƀ; vol.1,no.1– vol.2,no.8 1948–50
Melbourne. Droll Publications

DROLL STORIES MAGAZINE
ƀ; vol.1,no.1–2 1930
Sydney

FAMOUS DETECTIVE STORIES
m; vol.1,no.1– vol.8,no.1 1946–54
Sydney. Frank Johnson

FLAME
A magazine of fiction
m; vol.1,no.1–4 1936
Sydney. Australian Industry Ltd.
ed. L. L. Woolacott

FORERUNNER
Science fiction and fantasy quarterly
q; no.1–2 1952–3
Sydney
ed. R. D. Nicholson

GEGENSCHEIN
ƀ; c.1960s
Faulconbridge, N.S.W. 6 Hillcrest Ave.,
Faulconbridge, N.S.W. 2776
ed. Eric B. Lindsay
ISSN 0310–9968

LO/U–2: no.3

JOURNAL OF OMPHALISTIC EPISTEMOLOGY
ƀ; no.1 1969–
Mulgrave, Victoria
ed. John Foyster

LING
t; no.1 1973—
Townsville, Queensland. Dept. of English, James
Cook U. of N. Qld., P.O. Box 999, Townsville,
Qld. 4810
ed. Peter Bell

NEW MILLENIAL HARBINGER
ϸ; no.1 1968—
Melbourne
ed. John Bangsund

PLAIN TURKEY
ϸ; 1973—
Mount Isa, Queensland. Mount Isa Writers'
Workshop, 97 Trainor St., Mount Isa, Qld. 4825
ed. Mrs. R. Algie
ISSN 0311—0753

PREDATOR OF THE MARVELOUS
ϸ; no.1 1976—
Sydney
ed. Te Rea Nolan

LO/S26

QUESTION MARK
ϸ; no.1—5 1953—4
Melbourne. Amateur Fantasy Publications of
Australia

ROMANCE
The Australian fiction magazine
m; vol.1,no.1—5 1922—3
Melbourne. Osboldstone & Co.

SCIENCE FICTION NEWS
m; no.1 1953—
Sydney. Australian Science Fiction Assn., P.O.
Box 4440, Sydney, N.S.W. 2001
ed. Graham B. Stone

SCIENCE FICTION REVIEW
z(1 issue); no.1 1954
Sydney. Australasian Science Fiction Society
ed. Graham B. Stone

SF COMMENTARY
ϸ; no.1 1969—
Melbourne. P.O. Box 5195AA Melbourne,
Vic. 3001
ed. Bruce Gillespie
ISSN 0036—1348

SF REVIEW
Comments on recent science fiction
m; no.1—10 1952—3

Sydney
ed. G. R. Meyer

SLITHY TOVE
ϸ; no.1 1970—
Melbourne. Science Fiction Assn., Melbourne U.
ed. David Griggs
incorporates YGGDRASIL (q.v.)

SOMERSET GAZETTE
ϸ; no.1 1970—
Melbourne. Melbourne Science Fiction Club

TABLOID STORY
ϸ; 1972—
Glebe, N.S.W. P.O. Box 41
eds. Michael Wilding, Colin Talbot and Brien
Kiernan

TEN SHORT STORIES
Selected by the Tasmanian Fellowship of
Australian Writers
a; 1965—9
Hobart. Tasmanian Fellowship of Australian
Writers, Fullers Bookshop

YGGDRASIL
z(1 issue); no.1 1970
Melbourne. Science Fiction Assn., Melbourne U.
ed. David Griggs
Incorporated in SLITHY TOVE (q.v.)

Poetry

AUSTRALIAN POETRY
a; 1941—
Sydney. Angus & Robertson, 102 Glover St.,
Sydney, N.S.W. 2090
ed. Richard Walsh
ISSN 0084—7550

CA/U—1: 1949—50   HL/U—1: 1962, 1966
LO/N—1   LO/R98   LO/S26: 1962—
LO/U—2: 1965—71   OX/U—1: 1943—

AUSTRALIAN POETRY ANNUAL
a; 1920—1
Melbourne. Melbourne Literary Club
Composed of selections from BIRTH (q.v.)

AUSTRALIAN POETRY LOVER
m; 1955—9
Melbourne. Australian Poetry Lovers' Society
Superseded by POETRY LOVER (q.v.)

BEYOND POETRY
Brooklyn, N.S.W. 66 Brooklyn Rd., Brooklyn,
N.S.W. 2253

BIRTH
A little journal of Australian poetry
m; no.1—72 1916—22
Melbourne. Melbourne Literary Club

BROADSHEET
♭; c.1970s
Canberra. Open Door P., P.O. Box 26, O'Connor,
A.C.T. 2601

BRONZE SWAGMAN BOOK OF BUSH VERSE
a; 1973—
Winton, Queensland. Winton Tourist Promotion
Assn., P.O. Box 44, Winton, Qld. 4735
ISSN 0310—2467

CANBERRA POETRY
f; c.1972—
Canberra. Poetry Society, Australian National U.,
S.R.C. Office, G.P.O. Box 4, Canberra, A.C.T.
2600
ISSN 0310—6241

CROSS CURRENTS
Recent Australian poetry
♭; vol.1,no.1 — vol.2,no.2 1968—9
Heidelberg West, Victoria
ed. Michael Dugan

LO/U—2

EAR IN A WHEATFIELD
♭; 1973—
Westgarth, Victoria. 24 Urquhart St., Westgarth,
Vic. 3070
ed. Kris Hemensley
Supersedes EARTHSHIP (q.v.)

EARTHSHIP
♭; Series 1, no.1—13 1971—2
Southampton, U.K.
Superseded by EAR IN A WHEATFIELD (q.v.)

FREE GRASS
z(1 issue); no.1 1974
Adelaide.
ed. R. Tillett

FREE POETRY
♭; no.1—8 1968—70
East Balmain, N.S.W. 2041 Clift St.

GARGOYLE POETS
b; 1972—
St. Lucia, Queensland. Makar P., P.O. Box 71,
St. Lucia, Qld. 4067
ed. Martin Dudwell

GENTLE FOLK AND OTHER CREATURES
♭; 1972—
Canberra. Union Bldg., Australian National U.,
P.O. Box 4, Canberra, A.C.T. 2601
ISSN 0310—639X

HEART
♭; 1972—
Adelaide. P.O. Box 401, Adelaide, S.A. 5001
ed. J. P. Horsam and others
ISSN 0311—0354

KHASMIK POETS
q; no.1 1974—
Annandale, N.S.W. 26 Breillat St., Annandale,
N.S.W. 2038
ISSN 0311—1814
Also called KHASMIK POETRY QUARTERLY

MEANJIN BROADSHEET
♭; vol.1,no.1—3 1945—6
Melbourne
ed. Elizabeth Hamill
Produced as a supplement to MEANJIN
QUARTERLY (q.v.) Superseded by WORK-
SHOP (q.v.)

NEW POETRY
q; vol.1,no.1 1954—
Sydney. Poetry Society of Australia, Box No. 110
Grosvenor St. P.O., Sydney, N.S.W. 2000
ed. Cheryl Adamson
ISSN 0028—6478
Incorporates POETRY MAGAZINE (q.v.)

LO/R98   LO/S26: vol.19,no.1—
LO/U—2   OX/U—1: vol.20,no.5—6, vol.21,
no.1

OUR GLASS
A poetry magazine
b; no.1—5 1968—9
Carlton, Victoria. 21 Queensbury St., Carlton,
Vic. 3052
ed. Kris Hemensley

PARACHUTE POEMS
♭; 1975—

Melbourne. 523 Elizabeth St., Melbourne,
Vic. 3000

PATTERNS
∅; no.1 1974–
Fremantle, Western Australia. Fremantle
Arts Centre
ISSN 0312–049X

PEOPLE'S POETRY
Clarity, reality, sincerity
∅; no.1–4 1939–40
Sydney. People's poetry group of the Left Book
Club
eds. H. Collingwood and Peter Green

POEM
∅; no.1–2 1969
Melbourne
eds. Ross Thompson and John Tozer

POETRY
m; no.1–3 1928
Sydney
ed. R. A. Broinowski
Supersedes SPINNER (q.v.)

POETRY
A quarterly of Australian and New Zealand verse
q; vol.1,no.1–25 1941–7
Adelaide. P.O. Box 1219K
ed. Flexmore Hudson and others

LO/N–1: vol.1,no.11–12,16,18   LO/U–2
OX/U–1: vol.1,no.7–25

POETRY AUSTRALIA
q; no.1 1964–
Sydney. South Head P., 350 Lyons Rd., Five
Dock, Sydney, N.S.W. 2046
ed. Grace Perry
ISSN 0032–2059

DR/U–1   ED/N–1   EX/U–1: no.5–
HL/U–1   LD/U–1   LO/N–1
LO/R98   LO/S26: no.39–   LO/U–1:
no.4–   LO/U–2   OX/U–1
SH/U–1: no.8–   ST/U–1: no.45–

POETRY IN AUSTRALASIA
a; no.1–3 1925–7
Melbourne
Annual cumulation of SPINNER (q.v.)

POETRY LOVER
m; 1959–
Melbourne. Australian Poetry Lovers' Society
Supersedes AUSTRALIAN POETRY LOVER (q.v.)

POETRY MAGAZINE
∅; vol.1,no.1– vol.18,no.6 1964–71
Sydney. Poetry Society of Australia, Box 110,
George St. N., Sydney, N.S.W. 2001
eds. Roland Robinson and others
Supersedes PRISM (q.v.) Incorporated in NEW
POETRY (q.v.)

LD/U–1: 1963–9 (incomplete)   LO/R98
LO/U–2

PRISM
m; 1954–64
Sydney. Poetry Society of Australia, 217a George
St.
Superseded by POETRY MAGAZINE (q.v.)

LO/R98

PROMETHEUS
∅; 1933–
Canberra. Australian National U.

LO/R98: 1956–

SALT
∅; 1941–6
Melbourne

SATURDAY CLUB BOOK OF POETRY
q; vol.1,no.1– vol.4,no.3 1972–6
Newtown, N.S.W. 61 Newman St., Newtown,
N.S.W. 3042
ed. Patricia Laird
ISSN 0310–4272
Superseded by SCOP (q.v.) and SCOPP (q.v.)

SCOP
Saturday Centre of Poetry and Prose
z(1 issue); no.1 1977
Cammeray, N.S.W. P.O. Box 140, Cammeray,
N.S.W. 2062
ed. Patricia Laird
Supersedes SATURDAY CLUB BOOK OF
POETRY (q.v.) Superseded by SCOPP (q.v.)

LO/S26   LO/U–2

SCOPP
Saturday Centre of Prose and Poetry
t; Issue 1, vol.1,no.1 1977–
Cammeray, N.S.W. Saturday Centre of Prose and
Poetry, Saturday Centre, P.O. Box 140,
Cammeray, N.S.W. 2062
ed. Patricia Laird
ISSN 0313–685X
Supersedes SCOP (q.v.) and SATURDAY CLUB
BOOK OF POETRY (q.v.)

LO/S26   LO/U–2

SHEET
An occasional sheet of concrete poetry
z(1 issue); no. 1 1969
Heidelberg W., Victoria
ed. Michael Dugan

LO/U−2

SOUTHWELLIAN
z(1 issue); no. 1 1938
Brisbane. Catholic Poetry Society of Queensland
ed. Paul Grano

SPINNER
An Australasian magazine of verse
m; vol. 1,no. 1− vol. 3,no. 11 1924−7
Melbourne
ed. R. A. Broinowski
Superseded by POETRY (q.v.) Issues cumulated
annually and published as POETRY IN
AUSTRALASIA (q.v.)

SWAN
a; 1969−
Nedlands, Western Australia. West Australian
Secondary Teachers' Training College, Nedlands,
W. A. 6009

UNKNOWN POETS
♭; vol. 1 1974−
Prahran, Victoria. P. O. Box 410, Prahran, Vic.
3181
ed. Richard Summers
ISSN 0311−7049

VERSE
b; vol. 1,no. 1− vol. 4,no. 24 1929−33
Melbourne. The Old Book Shop
ed. Louis Lavater
Supersedes POETRY (q.v.)

OX/U−1

VERSE IN AUSTRALIA
a; 1958−61
Adelaide. Australian Letters

LO/N−1   LO/R98

WORKSHOP
Poetry and practical criticism
♭; vol. 1,no. 1− vol. 2,no. 1 1946−8
Melbourne
ed. Elizabeth Hamill
Produced as a supplement to MEANJIN
(q.v.) Supersedes MEANJIN BROADSHEET (q.v.)

CANADA

General

ABBEY
♭; 1969
Quebec. White Urp P., 55 Tudor Court, Pointe
Clare

ABEGWEIT REVIEW
♭; no. 1 1974−
Charlottetown, P.E.I.

ACADIAN MAGAZINE
Or literary mirror, consisting of original and
selected matter on literary and other subjects
m; vol. 1,no. 1− vol. 2,no. 20 1826−8
Halifax, N.S. J. S. Cunabell

Superseded by HALIFAX MONTHLY
MAGAZINE (q.v.)

ACADIAN RECORDER
1813−1930
Halifax, N.S.
ed. Anthony Henry Holland

ACADIE
T. G. R.'s magazine reflecting the life and literature of the Atlantic seaboard of Canada
m; vol. 1,no. 1−7 1930
Fredericton, N.B.

ACADIENSIS
A quarterly devoted to the interests of the
Maritime Provinces of Canada
q; vol.1,no.1 – vol.8,no.4 1901–8
St. John, N.B.
ed. David Russell Jack

CA/U–1: vol.1,no.1 – vol.3,no.1   ED/N–1
LO/N–1   LO/S65

ADDER
♭; vol.1–2,no.1 1961–2   3 numbers only
Vancouver, B.C. 3492 West 12th Ave.
ISSN 0380–6200

AGRICULTURALIST
And Canadian journal, devoted to agriculture,
literature, education, useful improvement, science
and general news
m/s; vol.1,no.1–15 1848
Toronto

AISLING
♭; no.1 1970
Mackenzie, B.C.

ALBERTA WRITERS SPEAK OVERLAND TO
KLONDIKE
g; 1957–
Edmonton, Alberta. Words Unlimited Writers'
Group, 11575 University Ave.
ed. Gladys Willison
ISSN 0065–6089

ALCHEMIST
q; 1974–
Quebec. Box 123, La Salle
ed. Marco Fraticelli
ISSN 0384–8523

ALCOOL
q; 1970
Montreal. Students of McGill U., 3587 University
St., Montreal 110
ed. Seymour Mayne and others

ALL ABOUT US/NOUS AUTRES
♭; no.1 1975–
Ottawa

ALPHABET
A semi-annual devoted to the iconography of the
imagination
f; no.1–19 1960–71
London, Ont. English Dept., U. Western Ontario
ed. James Reaney
ISSN 0002–6425

Supersedes WATERLOO REVIEW (q.v.)

LD/U–1: no.13–18/19   LO/U–1: no.2–17

ALTERNATE SOCIETY
b; 1970–?
Toronto. P.O. Box 5819, Station A
ed. Gary Moffatt

LO/U–2: vol.3,no.4,6–7, vol.4,no.1

AMARANTH
A monthly magazine of new and popular tales,
poetry, history and biography
m; vol.1,no.1 – vol.3,no.12 1841–3
St. John, N.B.
ed. Robert Ghives

AMBER
q; no.1 1973–
Dartmouth, N.S. Scotian Pen Guild
ed. and published by Hazel Firth Goddard, P.O.
Box 173, Dartmouth, N.S. B2Y 3Y3
Supersedes INNOVATOR (q.v.) and PEGASUS
(q.v.)

AMETHYST
q; vol.1,no.1 – vol.4,no.1 1962–4
Wolfville, N.S. Students' Union, Acadia University
ISSN 0569–9290
Superseded by EITHER/OR (q.v.)

AMPHORA
♭; no.1 1967–
Richmond, B.C. Alcuin Society, P.O. Box 94108,
Richmond, B.C. V6Y 2A2
ISSN 0003–200X

ANACHRONISM
z(1 issue); 1968
Hamilton, Ont. McMaster U.

ANGLO-AMERICAN MAGAZINE
b; vol.,no.1 – vol.7,no.6 1852–5
Toronto

ANTENNAE
m; vol.4 1968
Edmonton, Alberta. Undergraduate newspaper of
U. Alberta
Supersedes PULPINSIDE (q.v.)

ANTIDOTE
w; vol.1,no.1–50 1892–3
Montreal

ANTS FOREFOOT
♭; no.1–11 1967–72

Toronto. Coach House P., 401 Huron St. (rear),
Toronto 181, Ont.
eds. D. Rosenberg and others
ISSN 0003—6153

EX/U—1: no.1—5,7—9,11   LO/S26: no.7/8
LO/U—2: no.11   OX/U—1: no.1—4,6,9

ANVIL
z(1 issue); no.1 1931
Vancouver

APPLEGARTH'S FOLLY
♭; no.1 1973—
London, Ont. P.O. Box 40, Station B, London,
Ont. N6A 1M1
eds. Jill Jamieson, MacLean Jamieson and
Michael Niederman
ISSN 0316—1412

LO/U—2: no.1

ARBOR
a; vol.1—4 1910—3
Toronto. Toronto U.P.

ARCADIA
A semi-monthly journal devoted exclusively to
music, art and literature
s; vol.1,no.1—21 1892—3
Montreal

LO/N—1

ARCHAI
♭; no.1 1973—
Coquitlam, B.C. Archai Publications,
743 Gauthier Ave.
eds. Tom Grieve and Henry Hoekema

LO/U—2

ARCTURUS
A Canadian journal of literature and life
w; vol.1,no.1—24 1887
Toronto

ARKANEM
♭; no.1 1972—
Ottawa

ART AND LITERARY DIGEST
q; no.1 1967—1969
Tweed, Ont. Madoc-Tweed Art and Writing Centre,
Canada Publishing Co., Tweed, Ont. KOK 3JO
ed. Roy Cadwell
ISSN 0317—6509
Superseded by CANADA PUBLISHING
COMPANY (q.v.)

ARTISAN
Vancouver, B.C. U. British Columbia
ed. Greydon Moore

ARTS
A creative magazine
a; no.1 1952—
Sackville, N.B. English Dept., Mount Allison U.
ISSN 0518—8164

ASPEN GROVE
z(1 issue); no.1 1972
Manitoba. Dept. of English, Brandon U.
ISSN 0316—9022

ATHENAEUM
An advocate and exponent of educational,
literary and social progress
z(1 issue); vol.1,no.1 1883
Toronto

ATHENEUM
w; no.1—53 1855—6
Halifax, N.S.

ATLANTIC ADVOCATE
m; 1910—
Fredericton, N.B. New Brunswick U.P.
ISSN 0004—6744
Incorporates ATLANTIC GUARDIAN from
1958 (q.v.)

ATLANTIC GUARDIAN
The magazine of Newfoundland
m; vol.1—14 1945—57
Montreal
Superseded by ATLANTIC ADVOCATE (q.v.)

ATLANTIC MIRROR
The voice of the maritime writer
q; 1967—
Glace Bay, N.S. Atlantic Literary Alliance,
4 Hector St.
ed. Norman Lipschitz
ISSN 0004—6787

ATLANTIC PROVINCES BOOK REVIEW
q; no.1 1974—
Halifax, N.S. Division of Continuing Education
St. Mary's U., N.S., B3H 3C3
ed. John H. Battye

AUGURIES
♭; 1975—
Ottawa. 432 Rideau St., Ottawa, Ont. K1N 5ZI

AURICLE
z(5 p.a.); vol.1,no.1— vol.2,no.4 1969—71
Saskatoon, Sask. Students' Union, U. Saskatchewan

AURORA
Ᵽ; vol.1,no.1 1968—
Vancouver

AXIOM
Atlantic Canada's Magazine
b; no.1 1974
Halifax, N.S. P.O. Box 1525, Halifax, N.S. B3J 2Y3
ed. D. T. Murphy
ISSN 0316—7747

BALLSOUT
A magazine of unpleasant verse and impolite prose
Ᵽ; vol.1,no.1—2 1969
Vancouver. B.C. Pendejo P., 3358 West 1st Ave.,
Vancouver 8
ed. Bertram Maird
ISSN 0005—4399

BANTER
m; vol.1,no.1 1853—?
Halifax, N.S.

BARKER'S CANADIAN MONTHLY MAGAZINE
m; vol.1,no.1—12 1846—7
Kingston, Ont. Printed at the Atheneum

LO/N—1

BEAUX-ARTS
Ᵽ; 1972—
Montreal. 3625 St. Laurent Blvd.

BEE
A weekly journal devoted to news, politics,
literature, agriculture
w; vol.1,no.1— vol.3,no.52 1835—8
Pictou, N.S.
ed. James Dawson

BEEHIVE
Ᵽ; vol.1,no.1—3 1874—5
Toronto

BEHIND THE PALETTE
a; 1939—40
Vancouver. Vancouver School of Art

BELFORD'S MONTHLY MAGAZINE
A magazine of literature and art
m; vol.1,no.1— vol.3,no.6 1876—8
Toronto
Merged with CANADIAN MONTHLY AND

NATIONAL REVIEW (q.v.) to form ROSE
BELFORD'S CANADIAN MONTHLY AND
NATIONAL REVIEW (q.v.)

LO/N—1

BLACK IMAGES
A critical quarterly on Black culture
Ᵽ; vol.1,no.1 1972—
Toronto. Box 280, Sta F, Toronto, Ont. M4Y 2L7
ed. Lennox Brown
ISSN 0315—7784

LD/U—1: vol.1,no.2   LO/U—2   MA/U—1
OX/U—1: vol.1,no.2—4

BLACK MAGAZINE
Ᵽ; no.1 1962—
Montreal. 3504 Durocher

BLACK MOSS
Ᵽ; 1st series no.1 1969—73   2nd series no.1
1976—
Windsor, Ont. Black Moss/Bandit P.,
Box 22, 2450 Byng Rd.
ed. C. H. Gervais
ISSN 0067—9097

LO/U—2

BLACK WALNUT
Ᵽ; no.1 1970—
Waterloo, Ont. Wilfrid Laurier U.

BLACKFISH
t; no.1 1971—
Burnaby, B. C. Blackfish P., 1851 Moore St.
eds. B. T. Brett and Allan Safarik
ISSN 0045—2270

LO/U—2   OX/U—1

BLAND
Toronto

BLOORSTONE WHAT
no.1 197——
Toronto
ISSN 0319—5368

BLUE JEANS
no.1—3 1960s?
Sarnia, Ont.

BLUENOSE
A journal of progress
m; vol.1,no.1—13 1900
Halifax, N.S.

BLUENOSE
Nova Scotia's own magazine
*c.*1936
Halifax, N.S.

BLUENOSE RAMBLER
q; 1969–
Western Shore, N.S. P.O. Box 32 Western Shore,
N.S. B0J 3MU
ed. Blanche Fralic

BOGTROTTER POST
z(1 issue); no.205 i.e. no.1 1962
Vancouver, B.C. Box 2566

BOOSTER AND BLASTER
Montreal Free Post
þ; vol.1,no.1–2 1972
Montreal. 6580 MacDonald St., Montreal, Quebec

BOTTOM IRON
See IRON 1966–

BRANCHING OUT
Canadian magazine for women
f; no.1 1973–
Edmonton. Box 4098, Edmonton, Alberta
T6E 4T1
ISSN 0382–5264

BRICK
A journal of reviews
t
London, Ont. Applegarth Follies, P.O. Box 40,
Station B, London, Ont. N6A 4V3

BRITISH AMERICAN MAGAZINE
m; vol.1–2 1863–4
Toronto. Rollo & Adams

LO/S65

BRITISH-CANADIAN REVIEW
m; vol.1,no.1–3 1862–3
Quebec

BRITISH COLONIAL MAGAZINE
w; vol.1,no.1–26 1852–3
Toronto

BRITISH COLONIST
1827–?
ed. John Hooper

BRITISH COLUMBIA ARGONAUT
A magazine devoted to the literary genius of
British Columbia

m; vol.1,no.1–2 1931
Victoria, B.C.

BRITISH COLUMBIA MONTHLY
m; vol.1,no.1– vol.27,no.2 1911–27
Vancouver

BRITISH COLUMBIA MONTHLY
Canada's national magazine
þ; vol.1,no.1 1972–
Vancouver. P.O. Box 8884, Postal Station H,
Vancouver, B.C. V6B 4E2
ed. Gerry Gilbert
ISSN 0382–5272

LO/U–2: vol.1,no.1–4

BRITISH NORTH AMERICAN MAGAZINE AND
COLONIAL JOURNAL
vol.1,no.1 1831–?
Halifax, N.S.
ed. Edmund Ward

BROAD-AXE
1871
Charlottetown, P.E.I.

BRUISES
þ; no.1 1973–
Montreal. John Abbot College

BUST
þ; no.1–3 1968 published in 2 issues, the second
containing 2–3
Toronto. The Bust P.
ed. Doug Fetherling
ISSN 0045–3676

LO/U–2

BYSTANDER
A monthly review of current events, Canadian
and general
þ; vol.1–2 1880–1 new series no.1–12 (also
called vol.3) 1883–90
Toronto. Hunter Rose

LO/S65: n.s. no.1–12   QL/P–1: vol.1–3,
no.1

CALDERA
þ; no.1 1965–
Sudbury, Ont. Literary Society, Laurentian U.

CAMPUS CANADA
A national student magazine/un magazine
national étudiant
þ; vol.1,no.1–2 1963

Vancouver. National Federation of Canadian
University Students, Brock Hall, U. B.C., Vancouver 8

CANADA
A monthly journal of religion, patriotism, science
and literature
m; vol.1,no.1– vol.2,no.8 1891–2
Benton, N.B.

CANADA CHAPBOOKS
z(1 issue); vol.1,no.1 1919
Quebec. St. Anne de Bellevue

CANADA PUBLISHING COMPANY
q; no.1 1969–
Tweed, Ont. Madoc-Tweed Art and Writing
Centre
ed. Roy Cadwell
Supersedes ART AND LITERARY DIGEST (q.v.)

CANADA WEST MONTHLY
m; vol.1–24 1907–18
Winnipeg, Manitoba. Vanderhoof-Gunn, Silvester
Willson Bldg.
ed. Herbert Vanderhoof

LO/S65: vol.5,no.6– vol.23,no.1

CANADAPA
ϸ; 197––
Oakville. The Canadian Amateur Press Alliance,
P.O. Box 213, Oakville, Ont. L6J 3K7

OX/U–1: no.18–19

CANADIAN ACADEMY
Eastern Canada's magazine
q; vol.1,no.1 1912–?
Dominion, N.S.

CANADIAN AUTHORS
Creative writing by children of Northern Alberta
ϸ; 1973–
Edmonton. Children's services division, Edmonton
Public Library, 7 Winston Churchill Sq.,
Edmonton, Alberta T5J 2V4

CANADIAN AUTHORS' ASSOCIATION:
VANCOUVER BRANCH BULLETIN
z(9 p.a.); 1960?–
Burnaby, B.C. 3555 Keswick Ave., Burnaby, B.C.
V3J 1M5
ed. Pixie McGeachie

CANADIAN AUTHORS' ASSOCIATION:
WINNIPEG BRANCH NEWSLETTER
z(8 p.a.)

Winnipeg. 6 Oriole St., Winnipeg, Manitoba.
R3T OK3
ed. Joyce Collins

CANADIAN CASKET
e; vol.1,no.1–18 1831–2
Hamilton, Ont.

CANADIAN CHILDREN'S LITERATURE
q; vol.1,no.1 1975–
Guelph, Ont. Canadian Children's Literature
Association, CCL P., P.O. Box 335, Guelph, Ont.
N1H 6K5
ISSN 0319–0080

ED/N–1   OX/U–1

CANADIAN CHRISTIAN WRITER
m; vol.1,no.1 1956–
Kitchener, Ont. Canadian Christian Writers,
132 Spadina Rd. E.
ed. Lilian Churchill

CANADIAN COMMENT
ϸ; vol.1,no.1– vol.7,no.5 1932–8
Toronto. Current Publications

CANADIAN COMMENTATOR
q; vol.1,no.1– vol.6,no.9 1957–62
Toronto
ISSN 0010–2644
Superseded by COMMENTATOR (q.v.)

CANADIAN COURIER
A national weekly
w; vol.1,no.1– vol.26,no.1 1906–20
Toronto

LO/N–1: vol.1,no.1– vol.25,no.1

CANADIAN FORUM
An independent journal of opinion and the arts
m; vol.1,no.1 1920–
Toronto. Survival Foundation, 3 Church St.,
Suite 401, Toronto, Ont. M5E 1M2
ed. Denis Smith
ISSN 0008–3631

ED/N–1: 1976–   LD/U–1: vol.54,no.646–
LO/N–1: vol.1,no.1– vol.15,no.180
LO/S26: 1972–   LO/S65: vol.17–30,35–
LO/T22: vol.50,no.594–   LO/U–2: vol.42,
no.502–   LO/U–8: vol.42,no.504–
QL/P–2   QS/Q29

CANADIAN GARLAND
ϸ; vol.1,no.13–26 1833

Hamilton, Ont.
Supersedes GARLAND (q.v.)

CANADIAN GEM AND FAMILY VISITOR
A literary and religious magazine
m; vol.1,no.1 1848—
Toronto
ed. J. H. Leonard
ISSN 0382—5809

CANADIAN HOME
m; vol.1—2 1904—5
Toronto
Merged with NATIONAL MONTHLY OF
CANADA (q.v.) to form NATIONAL MONTHLY
AND CANADIAN HOME (q.v.)

LO/N—1

CANADIAN ILLUSTRATED MAGAZINE
m; vol.1,no.1— vol.7,no.3 1916—22
Montreal. Canadian Steamship Lines Ltd.

CANADIAN ILLUSTRATED NEWS
m; vol.1,no.1— vol.3,no.11 1862—4
Hamilton, Ont.

CANADIAN ILLUSTRATED NEWS
w; vol.1,no.1— vol.28,no.26 1869—83
Montreal

LO/N—1: vol.7—12,14—19,23,26—28
QM/P—2: vol.1—12

CANADIAN LIFE
þ; vol.1,no.1— vol.2,no.3 1949—52
Toronto. Advance Publishing Co.

CANADIAN LIGHTS
þ; c.1968
Warkworth, Ont.
ed. Ivy Painting

LO/U—2: 1968

CANADIAN LITERARY JOURNAL
Devoted to select, original literature and the
interest of Canadian literary societies
m; vol.1,no.1—11 1870—1
Toronto
Superseded by CANADIAN MAGAZINE (q.v.)

CANADIAN LITERARY MAGAZINE
m; vol.1,no.1—3 1833
Toronto. George Gurnett
ed. J. Kent

CANADIAN LITERATURE CLUB OF
TORONTO: MONTHLY CIRCULAR LETTER
m
Toronto. 'The Living Room', Maurice Dody Hall,
227 Bloor St. E.
ed. J. V. Horne

CANADIAN MAGAZINE
Religion, science, literature, morality, agriculture
and fiction
m; vol.1,no.1—4 1833
York, Toronto, Ont.
ed. W. Sibbald

CANADIAN MAGAZINE
m; vol.1,no.1— vol.2,no.1 1871—2
Toronto. Irving Flint
ed. A. Ridgeway
Supersedes CANADIAN LITERARY JOURNAL
(q.v.)

ED/N—1

CANADIAN MAGAZINE
of politics, science, art and literature
m; vol.1,no.1— vol.91,no.4 1893—9
Toronto
ed. J. Gordon Mowat
Merged with MASSEY'S MAGAZINE (q.v.) in
1897

LO/S65: vol.1—9,12—29,31—32,34—62

CANADIAN MAGAZINE AND LITERARY
REPOSITORY
m; vol.1,no.1— vol.4,no.24 1823—5
Montreal. Joseph Nickless

LO/N—1: vol.1—3   LO/S65: vol.1—2

CANADIAN MERCURY
m; vol.1,no.1—7 1928—9
Montreal
eds. F. R. Scott and Leo Kennedy

CANADIAN MISCELLANY
Or the religious, literary and statistical intelligence
m; vol.1,no.1—6 1828
Montreal

CANADIAN MONTHLY AND NATIONAL REVIEW
m; vol.1,no.1— vol.13,no.6 1872—8
Toronto. Adam Stevenson & Co.
Supersedes BELFORD'S MONTHLY MAGAZINE
(q.v.) Superseded by ROSE BELFORD'S
CANADIAN MONTHLY AND NATIONAL
REVIEW (q.v.)

LD/P–1: vol.1–9,11–12   LO/N–1
LO/S65: vol.1   OX/U–1: vol.1–3

CANADIAN MOSAIC
1970s
Ottawa

CANADIAN NOTES AND QUERIES
ɸ; no.1 1968–
Kingston, Ont. Queen's U.
ed. W. F. E. Morley

ED/N–1

**CANADIAN QUARTERLY REVIEW AND
FAMILY MAGAZINE**
Devoted to national politics and interesting family
literature
q; vol.1,no.1– vol.2,no.4 1863–6
Hamilton, Ont.

CANADIAN READER
m; vol.1,no.1 1959–
Toronto. Readers' Club of Canada, 35 Britain St.,
Toronto 229, Ont.
ISSN 0008–4891

CANADIAN REVIEW
ɸ; vol.1,no.1 1974–
Ottawa. P.O. Box 8316, Alta Vista Terminal
ed. Graham Pomeroy
ISSN 0315–1190

LD/U–1: vol.1,no.3–4   LO/U–2: vol.1,no.3–4

**CANADIAN REVIEW AND JOURNAL OF
LITERATURE**
m; vol.1,no.1– vol.2,no.11 1855–6
Montreal

CANADIAN REVIEW AND MAGAZINE
ɸ; vol.1,no.1– vol.3,no.5 1824–6
Montreal. *Montreal Gazette*
some issues called CANADIAN REVIEW AND
LITERARY AND HISTORICAL JOURNAL

**CANADIAN REVIEW OF MUSIC AND OTHER
ARTS**
ɸ; vol.1,no.1– vol.6,no.4 1942–8
Toronto

CANADIAN SUNRISE
ɸ; no.1 1968
Burlington, Ont. A. J. Evans, Flat 705,
2067 Prospect St.

CANADIAN WRITER AND EDITOR
m; 1945–

Montreal. Cooke Publishing Co.
ISSN 0383–1590

CANADIANA
ɸ; no.1–7 1944–56
Foleyet, Ont.

CAPE BRETON MAGAZINE
ɸ; vol.1,no.1– vol.2,no.1 1901–2
Sydney, N.S.
ed. Robert P. Bell

CAPE BRETON'S MAGAZINE
b; no.1 1973–
Cape Breton, N.S. Wreck Cove

ED/N–1

CAPILANO REVIEW
f; vol.1,no.1 1972–
Vancouver. Capilano College, 2055 Purcell Way,
North Vancouver V7J 3H5
ISSN 0315–3754
ed. Bill Schembrucker

LO/S26: vol.6,no.1–   LO/U–2

CAPTAIN GEORGE'S PENNY DREADFUL
w; 1968–
Toronto. The Vast Whizzbang Organization,
594 Markham St., Toronto, Ont. M6G 2L8

CATALYST
q; no.1 1975–
Brantford, Ont. Prison Arts Foundation, 143 5th
Ave., Brantford, Ont. N3S 1A3
ed. Etienne Boisjoli
ISSN 0381–5005

CATARAQUI REVIEW
ɸ; vol.1,no.1–2 1951
Kingston, Ont.
eds. George Whalley and Arnold Edinborough
ISSN 0411–2466

CATHERINE STREET GOOD
ɸ; no.1 1968–?
Vancouver

LO/U–2: no.2

CAUSEWAY
ɸ; vol.1,no.1 1966–
Toronto
ed. Myer Signer
ISSN 0576–9655

LO/U–2: vol.1,no.4

CENTURION
z(1 issue); no.1 1964
Victoria, B.C.

CHANGING IMAGE
a
Kitchener, Ont.
ISSN 0380–7118

CHEAP THRILLS
z(1 issue); n.d. *c*.1970
Burnaby, B.C. Simon Fraser U.

CHELSEA JOURNAL
Canadian periodical of social comment, literature
and religion
b; 1975–
Saskatoon, Sask. All Seasons Publishing Co.,
1437 College Drive, Saskatoon, Sask. S7N 0W6
ed. A. de Valk
ISSN 0317–2147

CHIAROSCURO
a; 1957–1975?
Waterloo, Ont. Student Board of Publications,
Wilfrid Laurier U.
ISSN 0069–3200
Originally printed as a supplement to CORD (q.v.)

LO/U–2: no.9

CHIEN D'OR/THE GOLDEN DOG
ϕ; no.1–4 1972–4
Montreal/Ottawa
ed. Michael Gnarowski
ISSN 0315–467X

LO/U–2

CHOICE PARTS
Ottawa

CHRISTIAN MIRROR
Devoted to the interests of religion and general
literature
w; vol.1,no.1– vol.3,no.52 1841–4
Montreal
ed. John E. L. Miller

CIRCULAR CAUSATION
ϕ; vol.1,no.1–4 1969–72
Vancouver. Intermedia P., P.O. Box 6254, Station
G. Vancouver 8, B.C.
eds. George Heyman and Scott Lawrence

LO/U–2

CIV/n
ϕ; no.1–7 1953–4

Montreal
ed. Aileen Collins
ISSN 0412–6602

CLOUD NINE
a; 1970–
Victoria, B.C. 1050 St. David St.
ed. Roger Sward

COLONIAL PEARL
A volume devoted to polite literature, science
and religion
w; vol.1,no.1– vol.4,no.20 1838–40
Halifax, N.S.

COMBUSTION
ϕ; no.1–15 1957–66
Toronto. Island P.
ed. Raymond Souster
ISSN 0588–5663

COMMENTATOR
m; no.6–14 1962–70
Toronto. 104, 150 King St. W., Toronto, Ont.
ISSN 0010–2644
Supersedes CANADIAN COMMENTATOR (q.v.)

COMMUNICATOR
ϕ; vol.1,no.1 1971–
Springhill, N.S. Nova Scotia Springhill Penitentiary,
Box 2140
ed. Bob Ely

COMMUNIQUÉ
z(1 issue); no.1 1974
Toronto. Secretariat, Canadian Conference of the
Arts, 49 Wellington St. E., Toronto 215, Ont.

LO/S65

COMPASS
w; no.1–7 1877
Quebec

CONNEXION
t; vol.1,no.1– vol.3 1968–70
Windsor, Ont. Mythical P., 3491 Mark Ave.

CONTACT MAGAZINE
c.1970s
Montreal

CONTEMPO
no.1– *c*.1970s
Scarborough, Ont.

COPPERFIELD
An independent Canadian literary magazine of

the land and the North
ƅ; no.1 1969–
Hamilton. 206 Maplewood St., Hamilton 22, Ont.
ed. Douglas Brown
ISSN 0069–9942

LO/U–2: no.2–   OX/U–1: no.2–

CORD
c. 1950s
Waterloo, Ont. Waterloo College
see also CHIAROSCURO

COSMOPOLITAN
w; no.1–7 1877
Quebec

COTOPAXI
ƅ; no.1 1968–
Toronto

CREATIVE CAMPUS
z(1 issue); no.1 1961
Winnipeg, Manitoba. U. Manitoba
ISSN 0590–062X

CREATIVE QUARTERLY
q; vol.1,no.1 1964?–
Winnipeg, Manitoba. U. Manitoba
see also CREATIVE CAMPUS

CRITICAL LIST
b; vol.1,no.1 1975–
Toronto. 32 Sullivan St., Toronto, Ont. M5T 1B9
eds. Ken Wyman and Jerry Green

CRUCIBLE
A quarterly publication dedicated to Canadian
literature in the making
q; vol.1,no.1 – vol.9,no.2 1932–43
Toronto

CYCLIC LITERARY MAGAZINE
ƅ; vol.1,no.1–3 1965–7
Montreal. 2820 Ekers Ave.
ed. Ronald Hollis
ISSN 0011–4308

LO/U–2: vol.1,no.1–2

CYGNET
z(1 issue); no.1 1961
Ottawa

DA VINCI
t; no.1 1973–
Montreal. Vehicule art (Montreal) Inc., P.O. Box
813, Station A, Montreal, Quebec, H3C 2V5

ed. Allan Bealy
ISSN 0315–9914

DANDELION
a; no.1–2 1975–6
Calgary, Alberta

DEM DAYS LABRADOR
q; 1970s?
Labrador, Newfoundland. P.O. Box 589, Goose
Bay

DESCANT
Literary supplement of the Graduate English
Association
t; no.1 1970–
Toronto. Descant, Station F, P.O. Box 314,
Toronto, Ont. M5S 2S8
ed. Karen Mulhallen

LO/U–2: no.2–   OX/U–1

DIAL-OG
q; no.1 1971–
Toronto. 6 Charles St. E., Toronto 285

DIME BAG
ƅ; no.1 1970–
Toronto. Rm C222 York Hall, Glendon Coll.,
2275 Bayview Ave., Toronto, Ont. M4N 3M6
Supersedes VENTILATOR (q.v.)

DIRECTION
A magazine containing poems and stories by
young Canadian writers
ƅ; vol.1–10 1943–
Outremont, Quebec
eds. William Goldberg, David Mullen, Raymond
Souster

DIRECTION
1975–
Toronto

DIVERSIONS
a; 1969–
Burnaby. Burnaby Creative Writers' Society,
6450 Gilpin St., Burnaby, B.C. V5J 2H7
ed. Orlee Lord

DOMINION ILLUSTRATED
w; vol.1,no.1 – vol.7,no.182 1888–91
Montreal
Superseded by DOMINION ILLUSTRATED
MONTHLY (q.v.)

LO/S65

DOMINION ILLUSTRATED MONTHLY
m; vol.1,no.1– vol.3,no.6 1892–5
Montreal
Supersedes DOMINION ILLUSTRATED (q.v.)

LO/S65

DREADNAUGHT
♭; no.1–3 1970–1
Toronto. Rainmaker Pubs.
eds. Jim Christy and Robert Macdonald

LO/U–2

DUEL
z(1 issue); no.1 1969
Montreal. Communications Board of Students'
Assn., Sir George Williams U., now Concordia U.
ed. Michael Rival

LO/U–2

DUO
no.1 1958–?
Vancouver
ISSN 0418–1654

EARTH AND YOU
A vehicle of current ideas for modern people
♭; no.1 1970– numbering irregular
Toronto. 1608 Eglinton Ave. W.
ed. Russell McHooley
ISSN 0085–011X

LO/S26: no.7   LO/U–2: no.8

ECHO
♭; no.1 1975–
Vancouver. P.O. Box 728, Station A, Vancouver,
B.C. V6C 2N7
ed. Hank Johnsen

EDGE
An independent periodical
♭; no.1–9 1963–9
Edmonton, Alberta
ed. Henry Beissel
ISSN 0424–3943

LO/U–2   OX/U–1

EDMONTON CULTURE VULTURE
m; no.1 1975–
Edmonton, Alberta. P.O. Box 1784, Edmonton,
Alberta T5J 2P2
ed. Vic Yanda

EITHER/OR
a; no.1 1965–
Wolfville, N.S. Students' Union, Acadia U.

ISSN 0424–7124
1975 issue entitled MUD CREEK MAGAZINE
1976 issue entitled FROM THE HORSE'S
MOUTH. Supersedes AMETHYST (q.v.)

ELBOW DRUMS
♭; no.1 1972–
Calgary, Alberta. Calgary Indian Friendship
Centre, 140 2nd Ave., S.W. Calgary
ed. Pat Burnett

ELLIPSE
t; no.1 1969–
Sherbrooke, Quebec. Faculté des arts, Université
de Sherbrooke
ed. Larry Shouldice
ISSN 0046–1830

EMERITUS
a; no.1–2 1965–6
London, Ontario
ISSN 0424–9127

ENDANGERED FAECES
♭; no.18 1975–
Vancouver. Strange Faeces P., P.O. Box 3622
349 W. Georgia St., Vancouver, B.C. V6B 3Y6
ed. Opal L. Nations
Supersedes STRANGE FAECES (q.v.)

LO/U–2

ENGLISH CANADIAN
w; vol.1,no.1 1891
Toronto. Yonge St.

LO/S65: vol.1,no.1

ENGLISH QUARTERLY
q; vol.1,no.1 1968–
Toronto. Canadian Council of Teachers of
English, LS Center, 155 College St., Toronto,
Ont.
ed. John North
ISSN 0013–8355

LD/U–1: vol.5,no.1

ENQUIRER
A Quebec publication
m; vol.1,no.1–12 1821–2
Quebec

ENTERPRISE
no.1 1948–
Toronto

ENTERTAINMENT
c.1970s
Toronto

EPHEMERA
ƀ; vol.1,no.1–2 1974
Montreal
ISSN 0316–6775

ERASMUS IN ENGLISH
no.1 1970–
Toronto

ERBIVORE
ƀ; 1965–
Montreal. 8198 Ave. de l'Epée, Montreal, Quebec
H3N 2G1
ed. Philip J. Currie
ISSN 0071–1071
Former title: FANTASTIC WORLDS OF
BURROUGHS AND KLINE

EVENT
t; vol.1,no.1 1971–
New Westminster, B.C. Dept. of English, Douglas
Coll., P.O. Box 2503, 426 Columbia St., New
Westminster, V3L 5B2
ed. John Levin
ISSN 0315–3770

LO/U–2   OX/U–1

EVERY MAN HIS OWN FOOTBALL
197–
Montreal

EVERY SATURDAY
z(1 issue); vol.1,no.1 1886
Ottawa

EVIDENCE
ƀ; no.1–10 1960–7
Toronto. Evidence Pubs.
eds. Kenneth Craig and Alan Bevan
ISSN 0531–4968

LD/U–1: no.9–10   LO/U–2: no.8–10

EXCHANGE
ƀ; vol.1,no.2– vol.2,no.3 1961–2
Montreal
ed. Stephen Vicinczcy
ISSN 0531–5166

EXILE
A literary quarterly
q; vol.1,no.1 1972–
Downsview, Ont. P.O. Box 546, Downsview
ed. Barry Callaghan

LO/U–2   OX/U–1: vol.1,no.2

EXPLORATIONS
Studies in culture and communication
t; vol.1–9 1953–9
Toronto. Toronto U.P.

BH/U–1: vol.7–9

FAMILY HERALD AND WEEKLY STAR
Practical, agriculturist and popular magazine
ƀ; 1870–1968
Montreal

LO/N–1: vol.34,no.46, vol.43,no.45– vol.46,
no.1

FANTASTIC WORLDS OF BURROUGHS AND
KLINE
Details not known superseded by ERBIVORE
(q.v.)

FAR POINT
f; no.1–8 1968–73
Winnipeg. Manitoba U.P., P.O. Box 35, Winnipeg
19, Manitoba
ed. Myron Turner and George Amabile
ISSN 0014–7621
Superseded by NORTHERN LIGHT (q.v.)

LD/U–1: no.1   LO/U–2   OX/U–1

FIFTH PAGE
a; 1963
Toronto. Ryerson Institute of Technology,
340 Victoria St., Toronto 200, Ont.

52 PICK UP
c.1970s
Toronto

FIG LEAF
1954–?
Montreal
ISSN 0426–0910

FIGMENT
no.1 1964–
Halifax, N.S.

FILE
For those to whom living is a fine art
ƀ; no.1 1972–
Toronto. Art Official

LO/U–2

FIREFLOWER
m; no.1 1967–
Whitehorse, Yukon. P.O. Box 2170
ed. Eugene Hoy

FIRST ENCOUNTER
a; 1969–
Sackville, N.B. Student Administrative Council,
Mount Allison U.
Supersedes TRIAL

FIRST STATEMENT
ɴ; vol.1,no.1– vol.3,no.1 1942–5
Montreal. First Statement P.
eds. John Sutherland, Irving Layton and Louis
Dudek.
Superseded by NORTHERN REVIEW (q.v.)

LO/U–2: vol.2

FIVE CENT REVIEW
A monthly review of the arts in Canada
ɴ; Forerunner issue, vol.1,no.1–3 1968–71
Montreal
ed. Barry Lord

LO/U–2

FLAT SINGLES
ɴ; c. 1970s
Windsor, Ont.

FLOORBOARDS
ɴ; no.1 1968–
St. John, N.B.
eds. Louis Cormier and Dan Dawson

FOLIO
ɴ; vol.1,no.1– vol.4,no.4 1966–9
Toronto. Metropolitan Society for the Encouragement and Development of Canadian Talent

FOLIO
A literary magazine
ɴ; vol.1 no.1– vol.24 1947–72
London, Ont. U. Western Ontario
eds. Larry Hutchman, Radi Spire and Peter Block-
Hansen

LD/U–1: vol.20,no.3, vol.24

FORGE
a; no.1 1956–
Montreal. Montreal Students' Society, McGill U.

FORM
ɴ; no.1–2 1967
Vancouver. Pons P., West 11th Ave.
ed. Greydon Moore

FOUNTAIN MAGAZINE
Devoted to short stories submitted to a competi-
tion sponsored by Founder's College

z(1 issue); n.d.
Downsview, Ont. York U.

FROM THE HORSE'S MOUTH
see EITHER/OR

FRONT
q; no.1 1974–
Kingston, Ont. P.O. Box 1355
eds. Jim Smith and others
also called IT NEEDS TO BE SAID

GALLARDIA
a; 1962–
Calgary, Alberta. Students' Union, U. Alberta

GAMBIT
ɴ; 1958–63
Toronto. Wayout P., Box 163
ed. John Richmond

GARLAND
ɴ; vol.1,no.1–12 1832
Hamilton, Ont.
Superseded by CANADIAN GARLAND (q.v.)

GASPÉ MAGAZINE AND INSTRUCTIVE
MISCELLANY
m; vol.1,no.1– vol.2,no.11 1849–50
New Carlisle, Quebec

GENERATION
Creative work by the students of University of
Windsor
f; no.1 1963–
Windsor, Ont. U. Windsor
ISSN 0533–7291

GERMINATION
ɴ; no.1 1976–
Scarborough, Ont.

GOLDEN TAFFY
a; 1971–2
Saskatoon, Sask. Saskatchewan English Teachers
Assn., 2317 Arlington Ave., Saskatoon, Sask.
27J 2H8
ISSN 0319–6690

GRAIN
f; vol.1,no.1 1973–
Saskatoon, Sask. Saskatchewan Writers' Guild,
P.O. Box 1885, S7K 3S2
ed. Caroline Heath
ISSN 0315–7423

LO/U–2

GROUND
A literary magazine
z(1 issue); no.1 1957
Halifax, N.S.
ISSN 0434–6963

GROUP THREE-O
↯; 1971
Burlington, Ont. United Amateur P., Flat 705,
2067 Prospect St.
ed. A. J. Evans

GUARDIAN
A monthly magazine of education and general
literature
m; vol.1,no.1–9 1860
St. John, N.B.
eds. Edward Manning and Robert Aiken

GUERILLA
↯; vol.1,no.1– vol.3,no.32 1970–5
Toronto

GYPSY
z(1 issue); vol.1,no.1 1970
Vancouver. Gypsy Pubs., 1350 East Georgia St.,
Vancouver 3, B.C.
ed. I. Todoruk

HALCYON
a; 1954–5
Ottawa. Student Assn. Literary Society, Carleton U.

HALIFAX MONTHLY MAGAZINE
m; vol.1–3 1830–3
Halifax, N.S. Cunabell
ed. John Sparrow Thompson
Supersedes ACADIAN MAGAZINE (q.v.)

HARBINGER
Southern Alberta Writing
z(1 issue); no.1 1973
Calgary, Alberta

HARP
A magazine of general literature
m; vol.1,no.1– vol.7,no.12 1874–82
Montreal

HERE AND NOW
A Canadian quarterly magazine of literature and
art
↯; vol.1,no.1– vol.2,no.4 1947–9
Toronto
eds. Catherine Harmon and Paul Arthur

LO/S65

HERETIC
z(1 issue); no.1 1963
Vancouver, B.C.

HESPERIAN
z(1 issue); vol.1no.1 1930
London, Ont.

Hh
↯; no.1 1976–
Montreal

HIGH IRON
see IRON 1966–

HILLTOP
z(1 issue); vol.1,no.1 1948

HYPERBOLE
f; no.1–12 1962–4
Morin Heights, Quebec. Upbank P.

ICONOMATRIX
Polemical and iconoclastic quarterly
q; no.1 1975–
Fredericton, N.B. Box 2, Postal Station A,
Fredericton, N.B. E3B 4Y2
eds. J. A. Brebner and J. C. Mahanti
ISSN 0382–876X

IMAGES AND INFORMATION
Sort of an art magazine
↯; vol.1,no.1–5 1975
Calgary, Alberta. Ap. 2319, 608 9th St.
ed. Don Mabie

IMAGO
↯; no.1–20 1964–74
Vancouver, B.C., 2499 West 37th Ave., Vancouver
B.C., V6M 1P4
ed. George Bowering
ISSN 0085–1744

LD/U–1: no.2,7   LO/N–1   LO/U–2
OX/U–1: no.2–20

IMPRESSION
Published quarterly for the encouragement and
development of the arts in Canada
↯; vol.1,no.1–4 1950–3
Vancouver,B.C., U. B.C.
ISSN 0442–3690

IN BETWEEN TIMES
c.1937?
Toronto. Upper Canada College

IN REVIEW
Canadian books for children
q; vol.1,no.1 1967–
Toronto. Provincial Library Service, 14th Floor,
Mowat Block, Queen's Park
ISSN 0019–3259

ED/N–1

IN STORE
z(1 issue); no.1 1969
Kitchener, Ont. Barry Lord's writing class at
Conestoga College

INGLUVIN
Anthology of new Canadian writing
þ; no.1–2 1970–1
Montreal
eds. P. Huse and K. Hertz

LO/U–2; no.2

INLAND SEA
f; vol.1,no.1 1971–
Winnipeg, Manitoba. Students' Union, U. Manitoba

INNIS HERALD
'let's go nummies'
m; vol.1,no.1 1965–
Toronto. Innis College Student Society, U.
Toronto
ed. J. McEvoy

INQUIRER
m; 1821–2
Quebec

INSCAPE
A journal of new Canadian writing
q; vol.1,no.1 1959–?
Ottawa. Dept. of English, U. Ottawa, K1N 6N5
ed. John Nause
ISSN 0020–1782

LO/U–2: vol.11,no.1– vol.14,no.3
OX/U–1: vol.11,no.3– vol.14,no.3

INSIDE
þ; no.1 1975–
Nelson. Ursa Major P., Ap. 302, 60 High St.,
Nelson, B.C. V1L 3Z4
ed. E. Kluge
ISSN 0380–2957

INSIDE
m; vol.1,no.1– vol.2,no.4 1964–5
Edmonton, Alberta. Undergraduate newspaper
of U. Alberta
Superseded by PULPINSIDE (q.v.)

INTERCOURSE
þ; no.1–16 1966–71
Quebec. Poverty P., P.O. Box 513, Station B
ed. Louis Cormier
ISSN 0020–5311

LO/U–2: 1967   OX/U–1: no.15–16

INTERNATIONAL FORUM
A West Coast monthly
m; vol.1,no.1–3 1926
Vancouver

INTERVALES
A literary magazine published by the Arts Society
of the University of New Brunswick
a; 1959–67
Sackville, N.B. Arts Soc., U. New Brunswick
ISSN 0539–2101

IRON
þ; no.1–9 1966–75
Last five issues unnumbered but given the following titles: SPRING IRON, no.10, BOTTOM IRON,
no.11, PUNK IRON, no.12, SERIOUS IRON,
no.13, HIGH IRON, no.14
Burnaby, B.C. Simon Fraser U.
ed. Brian Fawcett

LO/U–2: no.4

IRON
z(1 issue); no.1 1975
Burnaby, B.C.

ISLAND
Vancouver Island's quarterly review of poetry
and fiction
z(1 issue); no. 1 1972
Nanaimo, B.C.

ISLANDER
s; no.1 1973–
Toronto. York U.

IT NEEDS TO BE SAID
A new look at Canadian literature
q; no.1 1974–
Kingston, Ont. P.O. Box 1355
also called THE FRONT
eds. Jim Smith and others

JABBERWOCKY
t; no.1 1963–
Waterloo, Ont. Student Board of Publications,
Waterloo U.

JARGON
ƀ; no.1 1958–
Toronto. Students' Administrative Council,
U. Toronto
ISSN 0447–6042

JAW BREAKER
A little magazine of poetry, fiction and literary
opinion
ƀ; no.1–3 1971–2
Westmount, Montreal
ed. L. Russo

LO/U–2

JEWISH DIALOGUE
q; vol.1,no.1 1970–
Toronto. 1498 Yonge St., Suite 7, Toronto, Ont.
M4T 1Z6
eds. David Cohen and Joe Rosenblatt

JOYCEVILLE JOURNAL
Kingston, Ont. P.O. Box 880

JUBILEE
A magazine of Canadian writing
f; no.1 1974–
Gorrie, Ont. R.R.2, Gorrie, Ont. N0G 1X3
ISSN 0316–8417

JUNCTION 21–22
a; no.1–2 1967–8
Victoria, B.C. Alma Mater Society, U. Victoria

JUNK MAIL
A man's kind of art
z(1 issue); c.1971
Vancouver

KARAKI
f; 1971–
Victoria, B.C. English Dept., U. Victoria,
Victoria, B.C., V9A 1S3
ed. Ken Fernstrom

LO/U–2: no.2   OX/U–1: no.2

KENOMADIWIN NEWS
Thunder Bay, Ont.
ed. Val Chapman

LO/U–2: vol.11,no.9

KENSINGTON MAGAZINE
Toronto

KILLALY CHAPBOOKS
ƀ; 1972–
London, Ont. 764 Dalkeith Ave., London, Ont.

N5X 1R8
ed. Clarke E. Leverette

KIT BAG
m; vol.1,no.1–3 1903–4
Fredericton, N.B.
ed. Theodore Roberts

LAID BARE
ƀ; vol.1,no.1 1969–
Vancouver. Siwash Publishing Co.

LAKE MAGAZINE
m; vol.1,no.1–9 1892–3
Toronto

LAOMEDON REVIEW
f; vol.1,no.1 1975–
Mississauga. U. Toronto, 3359 Mississauga Rd.,
Mississauga, Ont. L5L 1C6

LATEST SCAVENGER
ƀ; vol.1,no.1 1968–
Toronto

LAURENTIAN UNIVERSITY REVIEW
no.1 1968–
Sudbury, Ont.
ISSN 0023–9011

LEACOCK FESTIVAL OF HUMOUR ANNUAL
a; 1975–
Orillia, Ont. Leacock Festival of Humour
Foundation, 992
Orillia, Ont. L3V 6K8
ISSN 0319–311X

LEFT COAST REVIEW
Vancouver. U. B.C.

LENNOXVILLE MAGAZINE
m; vol.1,no.1–9 1867–8
Montreal

BH/U–1

LIFELINE
b; 1974–
Cobalt. Highway Book Shop, Cobalt, Ont. P0J 1C
ed. Douglas C. Pollard
ISSN 0316–0602
also called PUBLISHERS', WRITERS', BROAD-
CASTERS', ILLUSTRATORS' LIFELINE

LIGHTNING BUG
c. 1970s
Toronto

LIMBO
Ⴘ; vol.1,no.1— vol.2,no.7—8 1964—7;   preceded
by a 'Manifesto Issue'
Vancouver. Neo-Surrealist Research Foundation,
4193 Postal Stn. D
ed. Murray Morton
ISSN 0024—3531

LO/U—2: lacks 'Manifesto issue'   OX/U—1:
vol.1,no2— vol.2,no.7—8

LINK
Ⴘ; 1974—
Scarborough, Ont. The Missing Link P., 78 Chelwood Rd., Scarborough, Ont. M1K 2K8
eds. Hans and Edwin Jewinski

LITERARY ECHO
m; vol.1,no.1—21 1874—5
Charlottetown, P.E.I.

LITERARY GARLAND AND BRITISH NORTH
AMERICAN MAGAZINE
A monthly repository of tales, sketches, poetry,
music, etc.
m; vol.1,no.1— vol.4,no.12 1838—42;   new
series vol.1,no.1— vol.9,no.12 1843—51
Montreal. James Lovell, St. Nicholas St.

CA/U—1: vol.1—3   QM/P—2: n.s. vol.3—5

LITERARY MISCELLANY
1832
Niagara Falls, Ont.

LITERARY MISCELLANY
q; vol.1—5 1908—12
Toronto. N.Y. Sherman

LITERARY TRANSCRIPT
c; 1838
Quebec

LODGISTIKS
Ⴘ; no.1 1972—
Kingston, Ont. Divine Order of the Lodge,
P.O. Box 764, Kingston, Ont. K7L 4X6
ISSN 0315—0623

LO/U—2

LOGOS
Ⴘ; vol.1,no.1 1967—
Montreal. Sagitarius Publishing Co.

LO/U—2: vol.2,no.1, vol.4,no.1

LOS
c.1970s
Montreal

LOUNGER
m; vol.1,no.1 1896—?
Ottawa

LOVE NOW
Ⴘ; no.1 1969—
Toronto

LOVING COUCH PRESS
Ⴘ; no.1 1969—
Winnipeg, Manitoba. 728—416 Main St.
ed. Steve Jones

MAGAZINE
Ⴘ; no.1 1968—
Winnipeg, Manitoba.
Loving Couch P., 728—416 Main St.

MAGENTA FROG MAGAZINE
Ⴘ; no.1 1970—
Vancouver. Talon P., 201—1019 Cordova St.,
Vancouver 6, B.C.
eds. Gordon Fidler and Arnold Saba
ISSN 0076—2350

LO/U—2   OX/U—1

MAKAR
Ⴘ; vol.1,no.1—3 1967—8
Burnaby, B.C. Simon Fraser U.
ISSN 0580—4965

MAKER
1976—
Montreal

MANDALA
a; 1967—73
Winnipeg, Manitoba. Students' Assn., U. Manitoba
230 Lockhart Hall, 515 Portage Ave., Winnipeg 2,
Man.
ed. K. K. Kossmann
ISSN 0076—373X

MAPLE LEAF
Or Canadian annual: a literary souvenir
a; 1847—9
Toronto

MAPLE LEAF
A juvenile monthly magazine
m; vol.1,no.1— vol.4,no.6 1852—4
Montreal

MARCH
The literary magazine of the University of Alberta
a; 1962—4
Calgary, Alberta. Students' Union of the U.

Alberta
Supersedes STET

MARIJUANA
z(1 issue); 1968
Vancouver. Multiple Magic Media

MARITIME MONTHLY
A magazine of literature science and art
m; vol.1,no.1– vol.5,no.6 1873–5
St. John, N.B.

LO/N–1: vol.1,no.1,6

MASSES
ɸ; vol.1,no.1– vol.2,no.12 1932–4
Toronto

MASSEY'S ILLUSTRATED
A journal of news and literature for rural homes
m; vol.1–7 1882–8; new series vol.1–7 1889–95
Toronto

MASSEY'S MAGAZINE
m; vol.1,no.1– vol.3,no.6 1896–7
Toronto. Massey P., 927 King St. W., Toronto,
Ont.
Merged into CANADIAN MAGAZINE of politics,
science, art and literature (q.v.)

LO/N–1

MATRIX
f; vol.1,no.1 1975–
Lennoxville, Quebec. P.O. Box 510
ed. Nigel Spencer
ISSN 0318–3610

MAY DAY MAGAZINE
no.1 1975–
Vancouver

MAYFLOWER
Or Ladies' Acadian newspaper
m; vol.1,no.1–9 1851–2
Halifax, N.S.
ed. Mary E. Herbert

MEDIA FREE TIMES
ɸ; vol.1,no.1 1974–
Vancouver. Ap.15, 1209 Thurlow St.
eds. Steve Dilkus, Lora Lippert and Ron Boychuck

MERRY DEVIL OF EDMONTON
ɸ; no.1 1969–
Edmonton, Alberta, Long Spoon P.
eds. Douglas Barbour and Stephen Scobie

METHODIST MAGAZINE AND REVIEW
m; vol.1–64 1875–1906
Toronto

MILL NEWS LETTER
f; no.1 1965–
Downsview. Toronto U.P., 5201 Dufferin St.
Downsview, Ont. M3H 5T8
eds. John M. Robson and Michael Laine
ISSN 0026–4253

MINDSIGHT UN LTD.
z(1 issue); 1971
Vancouver. Intermedia P.

MISSING LINK MAGAZINE
q; c.1970s
Scarborough, Ont. Missing Link P., 78 Chelwood
Rd., Scarborough, M1K 2K8
eds. Greg Gatenby and Hans Jewinski

MISTRAL
q; no.1 1975–; vols. lack designation
Halifax. 6023 Bliss St., Halifax, N.S. B3H 2A8
eds. C. Blackmore and B. Merlin
ISSN 0318–2088

MITRE
a; 1893–1970
Lennoxville, Quebec. Bishop's U.
Superseded by NEW MITRE (q.v.)

MODICUM
ɸ; vol.1,no.1 1969–; temporarily suspended
1973–4
Carlisle, Ont. Branstead P.
ed. Brender a Brandis
ISSN 0381–0739

MOMENT
ɸ; no.1–7 1960–2
Montreal
eds. Milton Acorn, A1 Purdy and Gwendolyn
MacEwan
ISSN 0540–6080

MONGOOSE
1972–?
Montreal

MONTHLY MAGAZINE
m; 1831–62
Montreal

MOONGOOSE
q; no.1 1971–
Montreal. 5252 Borden Ave., Montreal 265,
Quebec, H4V 2T1
ed. Ralph Alfonso

MOTION
b; no.1–6 1962
Vancouver, B.C.

MOUNT ALLISON ACADEMIC GAZETTE
z(1 issue); no.1 1853
Sackville, N.B.

MOUNT ALLISON GAZETTE
ϕ; no.1–2 1863
Sackville, N.B.

MOUNTAIN
ϕ; no.1–3 1962–3
Hamilton, Ont.
ed. David McFadden
ISSN 0541–1998

MOUSE EGGS
Montreal

MOUTH
ϕ; 1972–?
Scarborough, Ont. 6 Warfield Drive, Willowdale,
Scarborough, Ont. M2J 3S3

MUD CREEK MAGAZINE
see EITHER/OR

MUSEUM
Or Journal of Literature and the Arts
vol.1,no.1 1832?–4
Montreal

MUSKEG REVIEW
a; 1973–
Thunder Bay, Ont. Arts and Literary Society,
c/o Lakehead University Student Union, Oliver
Rd., Thunder Bay, Ont. P7B 5E1
ed. Diane Schoemperlen
ISSN 0316–9243

NATIONAL MONTHLY AND CANADIAN HOME
m; vol.1,no.1– vol.55,no.2 1905–58
Toronto. National Monthly Publishing Co.
Supersedes CANADIAN HOME (q.v.) and
NATIONAL MONTHLY OF CANADA (q.v.)

LO/S65: vol.10,no.1– vol.11,no.3

NATIONAL MONTHLY OF CANADA
m; vol.1,no.1– vol.4,no.12 1902–5
Toronto. Joseph Phillips, 241 Roncesvalles,
Toronto
Merged with CANADIAN HOME (q.v.) to form
NATIONAL MONTHLY AND CANADIAN
HOME (q.v.)

LO/N–1   LO/S65

NATURAL FAUNA
a; no.1 1974–
Victoria. 3440 Upper Terrace, Victoria, B.C.
V8R 6E7
ed. David MacWilliam
ISSN 0315–9051

NEITH
m; no.1–5 1903–4
St. John, N.B.
ed. A. B. Walker

NEW BRUNSWICK COURIER
1811–?
ed. Henry Chubb

NEW BRUNSWICK LITERARY JOURNAL
1840
ed. H. B. Sancton

NEW BRUNSWICK MAGAZINE
q; vol.1,no.1– vol.5,no.1 1898–1905
St. John, N.B.

LO/N–1: vol.1,no.1

NEW BRUNSWICK RELIGIOUS AND LITERARY
JOURNAL
b; no.1–6 1829–30
St. John, N.B.
ed. Revd. Alexander McLeod

NEW BRUNSWICK REPORTER AND
FREDERICTON ADVERTISER
1844–?
Fredericton, N.B.
ed. James Hogg

NEW CANADA
z(10 p.a.); vol.1,no.1 1970–
Toronto. New Canada P., Box 6088, Stn. A.

NEW CAPTAIN GEORGE'S WHIZZBANG
The Canadian magazine of popular culture
q; no.1–18 1968–74
Toronto. 594 Markham St., Toronto, Ont.
M6G 2LA
ISSN 0028–4408

NEW DOMINION MONTHLY
m; vol.1,no.1– vol.4,no.3 1867–79
Montreal. John Dougall & Son

LO/N–1

NEW FRONTIER
A monthly magazine of literature and social
criticism

m; vol.1,no.1– vol.2,no.5 1936–7
Toronto, Ont.

NEW FRONTIERS
b; vol.1,no.1– vol.5,no.2 1952–6
Toronto
ISSN 0545–1299

NEW LIBERTY
m; vol.24 1947–
Toronto/Montreal
Continues LIBERTY a Chicago magazine;
absorbed NEW WORLD ILLUSTRATED (q.v.)

CA/U–1   ED/N–1   LO/N–1
OX/U–1

NEW MITRE
Students' literary magazine
a; no.1 1971–
Lennoxville, Quebec. Bishop's U. Students'
Executive Council, Lennoxville, Quebec J1M 1Z7
ed. Paulina Grant
ISSN 0315–7458
Supersedes MITRE (q.v.)

LO/U–2: no.1–3

NEW STATEMENTS
t; 1971–
Ottawa. Suite 1000, 151 Slater St., Ottawa 4.

NEW THURSDAY
b; no.1–2 1974
Red Deer, Alberta. Red Deer College P., P.O.
Box 5005, Red Deer T4N 5H5
Supersedes THURSDAY (q.v.)

NEW WORLD ILLUSTRATED
m; vol.1,no.1– vol.9,no.1 1940–8
Toronto/Montreal
Merged with LIBERTY to form NEW LIBERTY
(q.v.)

LO/N–1: vol.1,no.2– vol.7,no.2

NEWEST REVIEW
q; vol.1,no.1 1975–
Edmonton, Alberta

NEWFOUNDLAND REVIEW
f; no.1 1972–
St. John's. Memorial U. of Newfoundland
ed. Gary Popp

NEWS FROM NOWHERE
b; 1971–
Edmonton, Alberta. Box 2827, Stn. A.

NEWSLETTER: SASKATCHEWAN WRITERS'
GUILD
b; 1966–73
Regina. Saskatchewan Writers' Guild and Sask-
atchewan Arts Board P.O. Box 1005, Regina,
Sask., S4P 0N0
Superseded by FREELANCE (q.v.)

NEWSPACKET
b; vol.1,no.1 1970–
Orillia, Ont. Stephen Leacock Associates,
P.O. Box 854

NEXT YEAR COUNTRY
Saskatchewan's news magazine
b; vol.1,no.1 1972–
Regina, Sask. Box 3446
ed. Sheila Kuziak
ISSN 0315–758X

NO MONEY FOR THE GOVERNMENT
c.1970s
Vancouver

NORTH COUNTRY
b; 1973–4
Waterloo, Ont.
Superseded by ONTARIO REPORT (q.v.)

NORTHERN JOURNEY
b; no.1–8/9 1971–6
Ottawa. NJ Press, P.O. Box 4073, Postal Stn E,
Ottawa, Ont. K1S 5B1
eds. Craig Campbell, Valerie Kent, David Mc-
Donald and Fraser Sutherland
ISSN 0315–3630

NORTHERN LIGHT
f; no.1 1974–
Winnipeg, Manitoba. 605 Fletcher Argue Blg.,
Manitoba U.P., Winnipeg R3T 2N2
ed. George Amabile
ISSN 0317–0586
Supersedes FAR POINT (q.v.)

NORTHERN NEIGHBOURS
The magazine of socialism in action
m; 1950–
Gravenhurst, Ont. N. N. Publishing Assn., Box
1000, Gravenhurst, Ont. P0C 1G0
ed. Herbert Dyson Carter
ISSN 0029–3199

NORTHERN REVIEW
b; no.1–7 1945–56
Montreal. First Statement P.

Supersedes FIRST STATEMENT (q.v.) and
PREVIEW (q.v.)

NOVA SCOTIA MAGAZINE
And comprehensive review of literature, politics
and news
m; vol.1—5 1789—92
Halifax, N.S. John Howe
ed. Revd. William Cochran

NOVA SCOTIA AND NEW BRUNSWICK
Or historical, literary, theological and miscellaneous repository
1806
Halifax, N.S.

NOVA SCOTIA NEW MONTHLY MAGAZINE
m; vol.1,no.1—3 1842
Halifax, N.S. Joseph Kirk

NUMBER 6
c.1970s
Toronto

O
A publication of the arts
q; no.1 1975—
Toronto. Ethnic P., 226 Roncesvalles Ave.,
Toronto, Ont. M6R 2L7
ed. Anna Wadon

OCCASIONAL MAGAZINE
b; vol.1,no.1—3 1895
Halifax, N S.

OLIFANT
q; no.1 1973—
Winnipeg, Manitoba. U. Manitoba, American
Canadian branch, Société Rencevals, Winnipeg,
Man. R3T 2N2
ed. John R. Allen
ISSN 0381—9132

ON THE BIAS
a; 1967—9
Toronto. Student Society, Innis College, U.
Toronto, M5S 1J5
Superseded by WRIT (q.v.)

ONTARIO REPORT
b; 1975—
Toronto. Editorial Board, P.O. Box 6851, Postal
Stn A, Toronto
ed. Paul Craven
ISSN 0371—1043
Supersedes NORTH COUNTRY (q.v.)

ONTARIO REVIEW
A North American journal of the arts
f; no.1 1974—
Windsor, Ont. 6000 Riverside Dr. E., Windsor,
Ont. N8S 1B6
ed. Raymond J. Smith
ISSN 0316—4055

ED/N—1   OX/U—1

OPEN LETTER
A Canadian quarterly of writing and sources
q; 1st series no.1—9 1965—9;   2nd series no.1—9
1971—4;   3rd series no.1 1974/5—
Toronto. Coach House P., 401 (rear) Huron St.,
Toronto, Ont. M5S 2G5
ed. Frank Davey
ISSN 0048—1939

LD/U—1   LO/U—1   LO/U—2
OX/U—1

OPINION
Poetry and prose by students of Toronto schools
t
Toronto. 40 St. Clair Ave. E., Toronto, Ont.
M4T 1M9
ISSN 0318—2207

ORANGE BEAR READER
m; no.1—9 1970
Windsor, Ont. 2655 Sierra Dr.

OSTARA
no.1 1970—
Ottawa

OUR CHEERFUL FRIEND
m; 1879—90
Ottawa

OUR JOURNAL
w; 1852—3
Quebec

OUR MONTHLY
A magazine of Canadian literature, science and
art
m; vol.1,no.1—2 1870
Toronto

OWL
m; vol.1—2 1888—9
Ottawa. U. Ottawa

OYSTER IN THE OOZE
z(1 issue); vol.1,no.1 1972
Ottawa. 7 Bullock Ave.

PM MAGAZINE
An independent literary magazine
þ; vol.1,no.1–3 1951
Vancouver

PACIFIC NATIONS
t; no.1 1967–
Vancouver, B.C. 4570 W. 1st Ave.
ed. Robin Blaser
ISSN 0030–8773

PACIFIC PROFILE
z(1 issue); vol.1,no.1 1961
Vancouver, B.C.
ISSN 0479–1037

PANIC BUTTON
c.1960s
Islington, Ont.

PARACHUTE
q; no.1 1974–
Peterborough, Ont. P.O. Box 1471
ed. Dennis Tourbin

PARALLEL
b; vol.1,no.1– vol.2,no.7 1966–7
Montreal. 1110 Sherbrooke St. W.
ed. Peter Désbarats
ISSN 0553–190X

PEARL
w; 1837–40
Halifax, N.S. Cunabell
ed. John Sparrow Thompson

PEAT MOSS
c.1970s
Windsor, Ont. Black Moss P.

PEDESTAL
þ; vol.1,no.1– vol.6,no.2 1969–74
Vancouver

PEGASUS
t; no.1 1963–
Vancouver
ed. Stewart Newton

PEGASUS
q; vol.1,no.1 1969–
Dartmouth, N.S. Scotian Pen Guild, Box 173
ed. Hazel Firth Goddard
ISSN 0031–4072
Supersedes INNOVATOR (q.v.) Superseded by
AMBER (q.v.)

PEOPLE'S MAGAZINE AND WEEKLY JOURNAL
w; vol.1,no.1–52 1846–7
Montreal

PHANTASM
c.1970s
Vancouver. Vancouver City College

PIQUE
q; 1956–7
Vancouver. Young Bourgeois Artists' and
Authors' Assn., U. B.C.

PLUCK
þ; no.1–3 1968
Edmonton. Dept. of English, U. Alberta

POPPIN
vol.1,no.1– vol.2,no.1 1968–9
Vancouver

LO/U–2: vol.2,no.1

PORCEPIC
þ; no.1 1971–
Toronto. 70 Main St.

PREVIEW
þ; no.1–23 1942–5
Montreal, Quebec
ed. Patrick Anderson
Superseded by NORTHERN REVIEW (q.v.)

PRINCE EDWARD ISLAND MAGAZINE
m; vol.1,no.1– vol.7,no.1 1899–1905
Charlottetown, P.E.I.

PRINCE EDWARD ISLAND REGISTER
1823–?
Charlottetown, P.E.I.
ed. James Douglas Hazard

PRISM
þ; vol.1,no.1–2 1955–6
Montreal. Sir George Williams College (now
Concordia University) Literary Society

LO/U–2: vol.1,no.1

PROCESS
Montreal

PROGRESS MAGAZINE
m; vol.1,no.1–2 1867
Summerside, P.E.I.
ed. Thomas Kirwin

PROVINCIAL
Or Halifax monthly
m; vol.1,no.1– vol.2,no.12 1852–3
Halifax, N.S.*
ed. Mary Jane Katzmann

PUGN
c.1970s
Nanaimo, B.C.

PULP
e; vol.1,no.1 1972–
Vancouver. Pulp P., P.O. Box 8806, Stn. H

LO/U–2

PULPINSIDE
m; no.3 1966
Edmonton, Alberta. Undergraduate newspaper
of U. Alberta
Supersedes INSIDE (q.v.) Superseded by
ANTENNAE (q.v.)

PUNK IRON
see IRON 1966–

QOLUS
q; no.1 1967–?
Vancouver. 7707 Yukon St.

QUARRY
q; vol.1,no.1 1965–
Kingston, Ont. Oberon P., P.O. Box 1061,
Kingston, Ont. K7L 4Y5
ed. Gail Fox
ISSN 0033–5266

BH/U–1: vol.15,no.1–   LD/U–1: vol.16,no.4–
LO/T22: vol.15,no.2, vol.17,no.1,3, vol.18,no.1
LO/U–2: vol.13,no.1–   OX/U–1: vol.13,
no.1–

QUARTERBACKS
ƀ; no.1 1970–
Lasalle, Que. 351 Gerald St., Lasalle, Que.
H8P 2A4
ed. Glen Siebrasse

OX/U–1

QUEBEC MAGAZINE
m; vol.1–4 1792–4

QUEEN STREET MAGAZINE
A multi-media journal
ƀ; vol.1,no.1 1973–
Toronto. P.O. Box 25, Station B, Toronto, Ont.
M5T 2WI
ed. Angelo Sgabellone

QUERY
q; no.1 1970–
Saskatoon, Sask. Saskatchewan Teachers' Federation, P.O. Box 1108, Saskatoon, Sask. S7K 3N3

QUILL
The Canadian short story magazine
m; vol.1,no.1–9 1923
Toronto

RADIO FREE RAIN FOREST
z(1 issue); 1968
Vancouver. Intermedia P.
ed. Gerry Gilbert
ISSN 0319–373X

LO/U–2

RAINCOAST CHRONICLES
ƀ; vol.1,no.1 1972–
Madeira Park, B.C. Raincoast Historical Society,
Harbour Publishing, P.O. Box 119 VON 2HO
ed. Howard White

RAPIER
ƀ; 1970?
Toronto

RAVEN
Literary magazine
ƀ; vol.1,no.1–10 1955–62
Vancouver. U. B.C.
ed. Ted Nicholson
ISSN 0484–0062
Supersedes THUNDERBIRD (q.v.)

LD/U–1: vol.1,no.1–3, 5–7

READING
m; vol.1,no.1–3 1946
Toronto
eds. Ronald Hambleton, Allan Aderson and Lister
Sinclair

REBEL
ƀ; no.1–4 1917–20
Toronto

RECOGNITIONS
c.1970s
Dundas, Ont.
ISSN 0318–0689

REGION
ƀ; no.1–9 1961–8
London, Ont.

RENAISSANCE
b; 1974–
Scarborough, Ont.
ISSN 0319–6402

REPOSITORY
q; no.11 1975–
Prince George. Repository P., R.R. 7 Buckhorn
Rd., Prince George, B.C. V2N 2J5
eds. Bob Atkinson and John Harris
ISSN 0317–0845
Supersedes SEVEN PERSONS REPOSITORY (q.v.)

RETURNING
b; Returning Press no.1   Returning two no.2
Return three no.3 1972–3
Vancouver
ed. Judith Copithorne
ISSN 0318–5230

REVUE II
no.1 1976–
Vancouver

RIKKA
q; 1974–
Toronto. Rikka Publishing House, P.O. Box 6031,
Stn. A, Toronto, Ont. M5W 1P4
ed. George Yamada

RINTRAH
1972–
London, Ont.

RIVERS BEND REVIEW
b; no.1–9 1973–4
Rexdale, Ont.

RIVERSIDE QUARTERLY
q; vol.1,no.1 1964–
Regina, Sask. Box 40, U. Stn.
ISSN 0035–5704
eds. Lee Shapiro and others

LO/U–1: vol.4,no.4   OX/U–1: vol.5,no.3

ROOM OF ONE'S OWN
A feminist journal of literature and criticism
q; vol.1,no.1 1975–
Vancouver. Growing Room Collective, 1918
Waterloo St., Vancouver, B.C. V6R 3G6
eds. Gayla Reid and Gail van Varseveld
ISSN 0316–1609

ROSE BELFORD'S CANADIAN MONTHLY
AND NATIONAL REVIEW
m: vol.1,no.1– vol.8,no.12 1878–1882

Toronto
Supersedes BELFORD'S MONTHLY MAGAZINE
(q.v.) and CANADIAN MONTHLY AND
NATIONAL REVIEW (q.v.)

LO/N–1

ROSEHARP
For beauty, loyalty and song
z(1 issue); no.1 1835
Toronto. York U.C.

ROSS'S WEEKLY
w; 1859–63
ed. John Ross

RUFANTHOLOGY
a; no.1 1975–
Montreal

RUNE
b; vol.1,no.1–3 1974–6
Toronto. The Student Council, St. Michael's Coll.,
P.O. Box 299, U. Toronto, Toronto, Ont. M5S 1J4
eds. E. J. Carson, Brian Henderson, S. Solecki

SAELALA
a; vol.1,no.1 1960–
Toronto. York U.

SAINT JOHN MONTHLY MAGAZINE
m; vol.1,no.1–6 1836
St. John, N.B. J. T. Younghusband
ed. Patrick Bennett

SAND
c.1970s
Williams Lake, B.C. Cariboo College

SAND PATTERNS
q; no.1 1972–
Charlottetown, P.E.I. P.O. Box 321, Charlottetown, P.E.1., C1A 7K7
ed. Betty Campbell
ISSN 0316–5167

SATURDAY ECHO
w; no.1–5 1893
Ottawa

SATYRDAY
c.1970s
Toronto

SCARAB
z(1 issue); 1972
Peterborough, Ont.

SCARBOROUGH FAIR
An anthology of literature
a; 1973–
West Hill, Ont. Scarborough Coll., U. Toronto
ed. Jars Balan
ISSN 0318–1499

SCHOOL
m; vol.1,no.1– vol.6,no.2 1913–7
Toronto. Toronto U.P. Faculty of Education

LO/S65: vol.2,no.8– vol.6,no.2

SCRIBBLER
w; vol.1,no.1– vol.10,no.184 1821–7
Montreal

SCRUNCHEONS
A review of creative literature published in Newfoundland
b; 1972–
St. John's, Newfoundland. Memorial U. of Newfoundland
ed. G. T. Popp

SERIOUS IRON
see IRON 1966–

SESAME
Annual publication of the women graduates and
undergraduates of U. Coll. Toronto
a; no.1–3 1897–1900
Toronto. U. Coll. Toronto

SEVEN PERSONS REPOSITORY
b; no.1–10 1972–4
Prince George, B.C.
eds. Bob Atkinson and John Harris
ISSN 0317–0845
Superseded by REPOSITORY (q.v.)

SHEET
b; vol.1,no.1– vol.5 1960–2
Toronto

SIFT
b; no.1 1974–
Halifax, N.S. St. Mary's U.
ISSN 0380–6693

SINCLAIR'S MONTHLY CIRCULAR AND
LITERARY GAZETTE
m; vol.1–3 1855–7
Quebec

SNOWDROP
m; vol.1–3 1847–50;   new series vol.1–5

1851–3
Montreal

SOMETHING ELSE
z(1 issue); no.1 1963
Ottawa

SPARE CHANGE
b; no.1–2 1971
Vancouver

SPEAK UP
m; vol.1,no.1 1975–
Toronto. Speak Up Publishing Group, Box 272,
Stn. B, Toronto, Ont., M5T 2W2

SPHINX
A magazine of literature and society
f; no.1 1974–
Regina, Sask. Dept. of English, Regina U. Regina,
Sask. S4S 0A2
ed. Aydon Charlton
ISSN 0319–0188

SPIRITUAL TOPOGRAPHIES
b; no.1 1974–
Forest Grove, B.C.
ed. William Scharf

OX/U–1: no.1

SPLIT LEVEL
f; 1974–
Winnipeg. Split Level Publishing House, Box 791,
Winnipeg, Manitoba, R3C 1P7
eds. Barry Chamish and Harry Peters
ISSN 0317–0039

SPRING IRON
see IRON 1966–

SQUARE DEAL MAGAZINE
1970
Charlottetown, P.E.I.

SQUATCHBERRY JOURNAL
f; no.1 1975–
Geraldton, Ont. P.O. Box 205, Geraldton, Ont.
P0T 1MO
ed. Edgar Lavoie

STEWART'S LITERARY QUARTERLY
q; vol.1–5 1867–72
St. John, N.B.
ed. George Stewart, Jnr.

STORY SO FAR
b; no.1–3 1971–4

Toronto Coach House P., Huron St., Toronto
181, Ont.
ISSN 0316–0645

STRANGE FAECES
q; no.1–17 1969–75
Vancouver. Strange Faeces P., P.O. Box 3622
ed. Opal L. Nations
Superseded by ENDANGERED FAECES (q.v.)

LO/U–2: no.5–17

STROBE
b; vol.1,no.1 1967–
Montreal. Que. McGill Hillel Students Society
and Zionist Organization, 3460 Stanley St.,
Montreal 112, Que
ISSN 0049–2345

STUFFED CROCODILE
b; no.1 1972–
London, Ont. Killaly P., 764 Dalkeith Ave,
London, Ont. N5X 1R8
ed. Clarke E. Leverette
ISSN 0315–0496

LO/U–2

STYLE
z(1 issue); no.1 1967
Toronto

SUNYATA MAGAZINE
b; no.1 1967–
Montreal. P.O. Box 1012, Montreal, Que, 3
ed. Tyndale Martin
ISSN 0039–5463

LO/U–2; no.1

TALON
b; vol.1,no.1– vol.5,no.1 1963–8
Vancouver. Talonbooks
ISSN 0082–1543

LO/U–2

TARGYA
b; vol.1,no.1–2 1973
Saskatoon, Sask. 25th Street House Theatre,
1023 8th St. E. Saskatoon, Sask. S7H 052
ISSN 0318–6008

TAWOW
Canadian Indian cultural magazine
q; vol.1,no.1 1970–
Ottawa. Cultural Development Division, 400
Laurier Ave. W., Ottawa 4, Ont.

ed. Mary E. Jamieson
ISSN 0039–9930

LO/T22   MA/U–1   OX/U–9

TEANGADOIR
b; no.1–5 1953–63
Toronto. 52 Derwyn Rd.
eds. P. O'Broin and Hazel Yake
ISSN 0497–0101

ED/N–1

TEMPO
b; vol.1–2,no.2 1968–70
Windsor, Ont.

TERMINAL CITY EXPRESS
e; no.1–12 1972–3
Vancouver

THIS MAGAZINE
Education, culture, politics
b; vol.1,no.1 1966–
Toronto, Ont. Red Maple Publishing Co., 3
Church St., Suite 401, Toronto, Ont. M5E 1MZ
ed. Rick Salutin

3 CENT PULP
Famous magazine
b; vol.1,no.1 1972–
Vancouver. Pulp P., P.O. Box 48806, Stn. H

THUNDERBIRD
t; vol.1,no.1– vol.5,no.1 1946–9
Vancouver. U. B.C.
Superseded by RAVEN (q.v.)

THURSDAY
a; 1969–73
Red Deer, Alberta. Red Deer College P., P.O. Box
5005, Red Deer, Alberta. T4N 5H5
Superseded by NEW THURSDAY (q.v.)

THURSDAY'S CHILD
z(1 issue); n.d.
Vancouver. U. B.C.

TIDE
b; no.1 1968–
Montreal. Wandering Albatross P.
ed. Philip Des Jardins

TITMOUSE REVIEW
b; no.1–5 1972–4
Vancouver. Titmouse International, 720 W. 19th
Ave.

eds. Arron and Linda Hoffman

LO/U–2: no.2–5   OX/U–1: no.2

TORCH
w; vol.1,no.1–34 1877–8
St. John, N.B.

TOUCHSTONE
b; no.1–2 1965
Toronto. P.O. Box 631, Stn. F.
ed. Peter Cameron

TOWTRUCK
þ; no.1–4 1969
Toronto

TRIDENTINE
Peterborough, Ont. Trent U.

TRINITY UNIVERSITY REVIEW
f; vol.1,no.1 1888–
Toronto. Coach House P., 401 Huron St. (rear)
ed. Richard G. R. Lawrence

LO/N–1: vol.15,no.6, vol.26,no.8–
LO/S65: vol.28,no.5–   vol.51,no.1

TRUTH
1867–85
Toronto

TUATARA
f; no.1–12 1969–74
Toronto. Coach House P., 401 Huron Street
(rear), Toronto, Ont.
ed. Mike Doyle
ISSN 0041–3852

LO/U–2   OX/U–1

TWELVE-MILE CREEK
þ; no.1 1971–
St. Catherine's, Ont.

TWENTY CENTS MAGAZINE
z(10 p.a.); vol.1,no.1 1966–
London, Ont. P.O. Box 151, Stn. B
ed. Robert C. McKenzie
ISSN 0049–4895

2 O'CLOCK RAP
a; no.1 1972–
Toronto. 40 St. Clair Ave., Toronto, Ont. M4T 1M9
ed. F. Murray
ISSN 0318–1189

TWO PENNY MAGAZINE
A weekly museum of literary amusement and

instruction
w; 1834
St. John, N.B.

UNDERGRAD
þ; no.1 1959–
Toronto. Literary and Athletic Society, U. Coll.,
Toronto

UNDIPLOMATIC COURIER
a; no.1–2 1964–5
Toronto, Ont.

UNITY PRESS
m; vol.1,no.1–2 1970
Windsor, Ont.

UNIVERSITY COLLEGE GARGOYLE
Toronto. U.Coll., Toronto

UNMUZZLED OX
q; vol.1,no.1 1971–
Kingston, Ont. P.O. Box 1581
ed. Michael André
ISSN 0049–5557

LO/U–2

URCHIN
Fredericton, N.B.

VANE
Hamilton, Ont. McMaster U.

VENTILATOR
f; no.1–3 1965–8
Toronto. Rm C 222 York Hall, Glendon Coll.,
2275 Bayview Ave., Toronto, Ont. M4N 3M6
Superseded by DIME BAG (q.v.)

VERSUS
þ; no.1 1976–
Montreal

VICTORIA HOME JOURNAL
vol.1,no.1 – vol.4,no.16 1891–5
Victoria, B.C.

VICTORIA MAGAZINE
A cheap periodical for Canadian people
m; vol.1,no.1–12 1847–8
Belleville, Ont.
eds. Susanna and J. W. D. Moodie

LD/U–1

VIEW FROM THE SILVER BRIDGE
t; no.1 1975–

Campbell River, B.C. 201 Alder St., Campbell
River, B.C. V9W 2N5
ed. Bill Standeven

VIGILANTE
ɸ; no.1–3 1970–1
Calgary, Alberta
ed. P. Piffer

LO/U–2   OX/U–1

VOYAGER
s; 1895–6
Toronto

WAGTAIL
q; no.1 1969–
Sarnia, Ont. 111 North Victoria St.
ed. J. Highfield
ISSN 0042–9988

LO/U–2   OX/U–1: no.1

WALSH'S MAGAZINE
m; vol.1,no.1–5 1895–6
Toronto

WATERLOO REVIEW
f; no.1–6 1958–61
London, Ont.
ISSN 0511–3792
Superseded by ALPHABET (q.v.)

WAVES
York University magazine
t; vol.1,no.1 1972–
Downsview, Ont. York U., Rm S-713, Ross Bldg,
Downsview, Ont. M3J 1P3
ed. Bernice Lever
ISSN 0315–3932

LD/U–1: vol.2,no.3   LO/U–2
OX/U–1: vol.3,no.1

WEEK
A Canadian journal of politics, society and
literature
w; vol.1,no.1– vol.13,no.52 1883–96
Toronto

LO/N–1: vol.8,no.1– vol.13,no.52

WEST COAST REVIEW
A tri-annual magazine of the arts
t; vol.1,no.1 1966–
Burnaby, B.C. English Dept., Simon Fraser U.,
Burnaby, B.C. V5A 1S6
ed. Frederick Candelaria
ISSN 0043–311X

LD/U–1: vol.2,no.3   LO/S26: 1969–
LO/U–2

WESTMINSTER
A paper for the home
m; no.1–23;   new series no.1–13;   3rd series
no.1–29   1895–1916
Toronto. The Westminster Co.

LO/N–1: 1st series no.2–3   LO/S65: 3rd
series, no.2–7,10–15,18–25,28–29

WHAT IS
c.1970s
Montreal

WHETSTONE
a; 1971–
Lethbridge, Alberta U. Lethbridge
ed. M. A. Oordt

WHITE PELICAN
A quarterly review of the arts
q; vol.1,no.1 1971–
Edmonton, Alberta. 8918 Windsor Rd.
eds. Shiela Watson and Stephen Scobie

LO/U–2   OX/U–1: vol.1,no.1

WHITE WALL REVIEW
no.1 1976–
Toronto

WHY NOT?
ɸ; vol.1,no.1 1975–
Halifax, N.S. AYF Enterprises Ltd.
ed. Antoine Francis

WILLISON'S MONTHLY
Canadian literature and politics
m; vol.1,no.1– vol.5,no.3 1925–9
Toronto. 34 King St. E.

WINDOWS
z(1 issue); no.1 1969
St. John, N.B. U. New Brunswick
ed. Eddie Chinton

WOMB
A literary magazine
ɸ; 1976–
Port Arthur, Ont.
ed. George Spentzos

WORDS FROM INSIDE
a; no.1 1971–
Brantford, Ont. Prison Arts Foundation, 143 5th
Ave., Brantford, Ont. N3S 1A3

ed. George McWhirter
ISSN 0316—8670

WORKSHEET
c.1970s
Vancouver. U. B.C.

WREATH
z(1 issue); no.1 1845
Fredericton, N.B.

WRIT
♭; no.1—6 1970—
Toronto. Innis College, U. Toronto, Toronto
M5S 1J5
ed. Roger Greenwald
ISSN 0316—3768
Supersedes ON THE BIAS (q.v.)

LO/S26: no.2   LO/U—2
OX/U—1: no.4—6

YELLOW JOURNAL
♭; no.1—9 1970
Vancouver

YES
♭; vol.1—19 1956—70
Pierrefonds, Quebec
eds. Michael Gnarowski and Glen Siebrasse
ISSN 0044—0353

LO/U—2: vol.1,no.2— vol.16   OX/U—1:
vol.16—19

YORK LITERARY SCENE
♭; 1969—
Toronto. York U.

YOUNGBLOOD
Revolutionary Youth paper
Vancouver

YOUTH'S MONITOR AND MONTHLY
MAGAZINE
m; vol.1,no.1—7 1836
Toronto

Academic and Critical

ACTA VICTORIANA
♭; vol.1,no.1 1875—
Toronto. Victoria College Union, 73 Queen's
Park Cres. E., Toronto 5, Ont.

LO/N—1: vol.3   LO/S65: vol.23,no.3
LO/U—2: vol.97,no.2   OX/U—1: vol.97,no.2

ALIVE
Independent Canadian literature
m; no.1—40 1969—75
Guelph, Ont. Alive P. Ltd., Box 1331
ed. Edward Pickersgill
ISSN 0044—7285
Superseded by ALIVE MAGAZINE (q.v.)

LO/U—2: no.20—40

ALIVE MAGAZINE
Literature and ideology
m; no.41—50 1975—6
Guelph, Ont. Alive P. Ltd., Box 1331
Supersedes ALIVE (q.v.) Superseded by NEW
LITERATURE AND IDEOLOGY (q.v.)

LO/U—2: no.41—50   OX/U—1: no.46—50

ANTIGONISH REVIEW
q; vol.1,no.1 1970—
(numbering changes: vol.2,no.3 = no.7)
Antigonish, N.S. Dept. of English, St. Francis
Xavier U.
ed. R. J. MacSween
ISSN 0003—5661

CA/U—1   ED/N—1   EX/U—2
LO/U—2

ARIEL
A review of international English literature
q; vol.1,no.1 1960—
Calgary, Alberta. U. Calgary, Alberta T2N 1N4
ed. James Black
ISSN 0004—1327

BH/U—1   CA/U—1   CB/U—1
EX/U—1   HL/U—1   LD/U—1
LO/S26   LO/T22   LO/U—1
NR/U—1   ST/U—1

BOOKS IN CANADA
m; vol.1,no.1 preceded by an introductory issue;
vol.1,no.1 1971—
Toronto. Canadian Review of Books Ltd., 501
Yonge St.
ed. Douglas Marshall
ISSN 0045—2564

ED/N—1   LO/T22

BRITISH COLUMBIA LIBRARY QUARTERLY
q; vol.1,no.1 1938—
Vancouver. British Columbia Library Assn.,
3127 Thunderbird Cres.
ed. B. L. Bacon

CANADIAN AUTHOR AND BOOKMAN
q; vol.1,no.1 1921—

Niagara, Ont. Canadian Authors' Assn., Box 120,
Niagara-on-the-Lake, Ont. LOS 1JO
ed. Duncan S. Pollack
ISSN 0008—2937
Absorbs CANADIAN POETRY (q.v.)

LO/N—1: vol.9,no.1— vol.10,no.3,5
LO/S65: vol.12,no.1— vol.17,no.4, vol.24,no.1—4
LO/T22: vol.42,no.2—   OX/U—1: vol.13—

CANADIAN BOOKMAN
q; vol.1,no.1— vol.31,no.4 1919—39
Montreal. Toronto Industrial and Educational P.
Ltd.
ed. B. K. Sandwell

LO/S65: no.1—4

CANADIAN LITERATURE
A quarterly of criticism and review
q; no.1 1959—
Vancouver. U. B. C. P., 2075 Westbrook Place,
Vancouver, B.C., V6T 1N5
ed. George Woodcock
ISSN 0008—4360
LITTÉRATURE CANADIENNE

CA/U—1   ED/N—1   HL/U—1: no.3—
LD/U—1: no.13—   LO/N—1   LO/S26:
no.34—   LO/S65   LO/T22
LO/U—1: no.5—   MA/U—1: no.29—
OX/U—1   QL/P—2

CANADIAN REVIEW OF COMPARATIVE LITERATURE
t; no.1 1974—
Toronto. Canadian Comparative Literature Assn.,
U. Toronto P., 5201 Dufferin St., Downsview,
Ont. M3H 5T8
ed. Milan V. Dimic
ISSN 0319—051X
REVUE CANADIENNE DE LITTÉRATURE
COMPARÉE

ED/N—1: 1976—   OX/U—1

CHESTERTON REVIEW
f; no.1 1974—
Saskatoon. G. K. Chesterton Society, 1437
College Drive, Saskatoon, Saskatchewan S7N OW6
ed. J. Ian Boyd
ISSN 0317—0500

ED/N—1

COMPARATIVE LITERATURE IN CANADA
f; vol.1,no.1 1969—
Edmonton, Alberta. U. Alberta
ed. M. V. Dimic

CONTEMPORARY LITERATURE IN TRANSLATION
t; no.1 1968—
Vancouver. Dept. of Creative Writing, U. B.C.,
P.O. Box 3127, Mission City, B.C. VCV 4J3
ed. Andreas Schroeder
ISSN 0010—7492

LO/U—2: no.18—   MA/U—1

DALHOUSIE REVIEW
q; vol.1,no.1 1921—
Halifax, N.S. Dalhousie U.P., Rm 4413,
Killam Library
ed. A. R. Bevan
ISSN 0011—5827

CA/U—1: vol.43,no.1—   DR/U—1: vol.22,
no.1—   ED/N—1: vol.46,no.1—   ED/U—1
GL/U—1: vol.12,no.1—   LD/U—1: vol.38,
no.2—   LO/N—1: vol.17,no.1,4—
LO/S65   LO/T22: vol.38,no.1—
LO/U—1: vol.30,no.1—   MA/U—1: vol.37,
no.1—   OX/U—1   OX/U—9

ENGLISH STUDIES IN CANADA
q; vol.1,no.1 1975—
Toronto. Toronto U.P.

ED/N—1

ESSAYS ON CANADIAN WRITING
f; no.1 1975—
Downsview, Ont. S765 Ross Bldg., York U.,
4700 Keele St., Downsview, Ont. M3J 1P3
ed. Jack David
ISSN 0316—0300

OX/U—1

FIDDLEHEAD
q; no.1 1945—
Fredericton, N.B. Dept. of English,U. New Brunswick, Fredericton, N.B. E3B 5A3
ed. Roger Ploude
ISSN 0015—0630

ED/N—1: 1976—   LD/U—1: no.73—
LO/S26: no.79—   LO/T22: no.29,88—90,
94,96—   LO/U—2: no.63—

HORIZON
Canadian literary studies for Canadian Common-
wealth students
Saskatoon, Sask.

HUMANITIES ASSOCIATION BULLETIN
q; vol.1,no.1— vol.23,no.4 1951—72
Fredericton, N.B. Humanities Assn. of Canada,
769 George St.

ed. Fred Cogswell
Superseded by HUMANITIES ASSOCIATION
REVIEW (q.v.)

HUMANITIES ASSOCIATION REVIEW
q; vol.24,no.1 1973–
Kingston, Ont. Humanities Assn. of Canada,
John Watson Hall, Queen's U.
ed. P. W. Rogers
Supersedes HUMANITIES ASSOCIATION
BULLETIN (q.v.)

JOURNAL OF CANADIAN STUDIES
q; vol.1,no.1 1966–
Peterborough, Ont. Trent U.
ed. D. Smith
ISSN 0021–9495
REVUE D'ÉTUDES CANADIENNES

ED/N–1: 1976–   LO/S65   LO/T22:
vol.7,no.3–   LO/U–8: vol.1,no.2–

LAKEHEAD UNIVERSITY REVIEW
no.1 1968–
Thunder Bay, Ont.
ISSN 0023–7337

LITERATURE AND IDEOLOGY
ƥ; no.1–18 1969–74
Toronto/Montreal. Norman Bethune Institute
Superseded by ALIVE MAGAZINE (q.v.) See
also NEW LITERATURE AND IDEOLOGY

OX/U–1

McGILL DAILY LITERATURE SUPPLEMENT
w; 1924–5
Montreal. McGill U.
eds. A. J. M. Smith and Allan B. Latham

McGILL FORTNIGHTLY REVIEW
e; vol.1–2 1925–7
Montreal. McGill U.
eds. A. J. M. Smith and F. R. Scott

McGILL UNIVERSITY MAGAZINE
q; vol.1,no.1– vol.19,no.2 1901–20
Montreal. McGill U.

LO/N–1: vol.6,no.1– vol.19,no.2
OX/U–1: vol.6,no.1– vol.18,no.1

McMASTER UNIVERSITY MONTHLY
m; vol.1,no.1– vol.39,no.8 1891–1930
Hamilton, Ont.

McMASTER UNIVERSITY QUARTERLY
q; no.1–60 1921–51
Hamilton, Ont.

MALAHAT REVIEW
q; no.1 1967–
Victoria, B.C. U. Victoria, Box 1700, Victoria,
B.C. V8W 2Y2
ed. Robin Skelton
ISSN 0025–1216

BT/U–1   CB/U–1   ED/N–1
EX/U–1   LO/N–1   LO/T22: no.27–
LO/U–2   MA/U–1   NR/U–1
OX/U–1

MANITOBA ARTS REVIEW
f; 1938–58
Winnipeg. U. Manitoba

DR/U–1   GL/U–1: no.1–6

MODERNIST STUDIES
Literature and culture, 1920–1940
t; vol.1,no.1 1974–
Edmonton, Alberta. Dept. of English, U. Alberta,
Edmonton, Alberta T6G 2E1
eds. Shirley Rose and Ernest Griffin

MOKO NEWSLETTER
f; vol.1,no.1 1973–
Saskatoon, Sask. Canadian Assn. for Commonwealth Literature and Language Studies
(CACLALS) Dept. of English, U. Saskatchewan
S7N 0WO
ed. R. T. Robertson

LO/S26: vol.1,no.4–   LO/S65

MOSAIC
A journal for the comparative study of literature
and ideas
q; vol.1,no.1 1967–
Winnipeg, Manitoba. Manitoba U.P., Room 208,
Tier Bldg., Winnipeg, Man. R3T 2N2
eds. R. G. Collins and John Wortley
ISSN 0027–1276

BH/U–1: vol.5–   CA/U–1   CB/U–1:
vol.2–   ED/N–1   ED/U–1
HL/U–1: vol.1,no.3, vol.2,no.2–   LO/N–1
LO/T22   LO/U–1: vol.1,4   NR/U–1:
vol.5–   OX/U–1

NEW LITERATURE AND IDEOLOGY
q; no.19 1976–
Toronto. Norman Bethune Institute, Box 727,
Adelaide Station, Toronto, Ont. M5C 2J8
Supersedes ALIVE MAGAZINE (q.v.) See also
LITERATURE AND IDEOLOGY

OX/U–1

PATTERNS OF LITERARY CRITICISM
þ
Toronto. Toronto U.P.
eds. E. Sirluck, R. J. Shoeck and M. McLuhan

PROCEEDINGS AND TRANSACTIONS OF
THE ROYAL SOCIETY OF CANADA
a; 1st series vol.1−11,   2nd series vol.1−12,
3rd series vol.1−55,   4th series vol.1− 1882−
Toronto. Royal Society of Canada

BH/U−1   LD/U−1   LO/S65: (lacks 3
ser. vol.18,no.29)   LO/U−1: 1882−1925

QUARTERLY OF CANADIAN STUDIES
q; vol.1,no.1 1971−
Toronto. P.O. Box 816, Station F, Toronto 5,
Ont.
ed. Andrew Z. Kerekes

QUEEN'S QUARTERLY
q; vol.1,no.1 1893−
Kingston, Ont. McGill-Queen's U.P.
ed. Kerry McSweeney
ISSN 0033−6041

BH/U−1: vol.18,no.3−   CA/U−1: vol.3,no.3−
CB/U−1: vol.77,no.1−   ED/N−1: 1976−
GL/U−1: (lacks vol.1,no.2)   LD/U−1:
vol.14,no.2, vol.18,no.4− vol.40,no.4, vol.64,no.1−
LO/N−1: vol.11,no.3−   LO/S65
LO/T22: vol.63,no.4−   LO/U−1: vol.15,
no.1−   LO/U−8: vol.76,no.4−   MA/U−1
OX/U−1: vol.18,no.4−

QUILL AND QUIRE
b; vol.1,no.1 1935−
Toronto. Greey de Pencier Pubs., 56 The
Esplanade

SATURDAY NIGHT
m; vol.1,no.1 1887−
Toronto. Second Century Canada Pubs., 69 Front
St. E, Ont. M5E 1R3
ed. Robert Fulford
ISSN 0036−4975

ED/N−1: 1975−   LO/S26: vol.81,no.11−
LO/T22: vol.83,no.7−

SATURDAY READER
w; vol.1,no.1− vol.4,no.104 1865−7
Montreal

LO/N−1: vol.1,no.1−26

SCAN LITERARY SUPPLEMENT
z(1 issue): 1966
Toronto, Box 7, Station B

Being the literary supplement to SCAN:
JOURNAL OF THE COMMUNIST PARTY
YOUTH, vol.2,no.6 1966

STUDIES IN CANADIAN LITERATURE
f; vol.1,no.1 1976−
Fredericton, N.B. Dept. of English, U. New
Brunswick
eds. Barrie Davies and others
ISSN 0380−6995

HL/U−1

T. S. ELIOT NEWSLETTER
þ; vol.1,no.1−2 1974
Downsview, Ont. Dept. of English, York U.,
Ross Bldg. 7655, Downsview, Ont. M3J 1P3
ed. Shyamal Bagchee
Superseded by T. S. ELIOT REVIEW (q.v.)

ED/N−1

T. S. ELIOT REVIEW
þ; vol.2,no.1 1975−
Downsview, Ont. Dept. of English, York U., Ross
Bldg. 7655, Downsview, Ont. M3J 1P3
ed. Shyamal Bagchee
Supersedes T. S. ELIOT NEWSLETTER (q.v.)

TAMARACK REVIEW
q; no.1 1956−
Toronto. Toronto U.P., P.O. Box 15a, Station K.,
Toronto, Ont. M4P 2G5
ed. I. M. Owen
ISSN 0039−9256

ED/N−1: 1976−   HL/U−1: no.49−52,56−
LD/U−1: no.40−   LO/S26: no.41−
LO/T22   LO/U−2: no.49−   OX/U−1
ST/U−1: no.14−

TRANSACTIONS OF THE LITERARY AND
HISTORICAL SOCIETY OF QUEBEC (Old
Series)
þ; 1829−56
Quebec. Thomas Cary & Co., Freemasons' Hall

CA/U−1: vol.2,no.1−16   GL/U−1: vol.3,
no.1−2   LO/N−1: (lacks vol.2,no.30)
LO/S65: vol.1−2,5

TRANSACTIONS OF THE LITERARY AND
HISTORICAL SOCIETY OF QUEBEC (New
Series)
þ; vol.1−28 1863−1909
Quebec. Printed at the *Morning Chronicle* Office

LO/S65

TRANSACTIONS OF THE OTTAWA LITERARY
AND SCIENTIFIC SOCIETY
∅; vol.1–4 1897–1907
Ottawa. E. J. Renolds, 127 Sparks St.

LO/N–1 LO/S65

UNIVERSITY OF MANITOBA QUARTERLY
q; vol.1,no.1– vol.7,no.3 1926–33
Winnipeg, Manitoba

UNIVERSITY OF OTTAWA REVIEW
vol.1–17 1898–1915
Ottawa
Supersedes OWL (q.v.)

UNIVERSITY OF TORONTO QUARTERLY
q; vol.1,no.1– vol.3,no.2 1895–6
Toronto

UNIVERSITY OF TORONTO QUARTERLY
q; vol.1,no.1 1931–
Toronto. Toronto U.P.
ed. F. W. Blissett

BH/U–1: vol.17– BT/U–1: vol.39–
CA/U–1 CB/U–1: vol.29– ED/U–1
EX/U–1: vol.42,no.4– HL/U–1: vol.22–
LO/S26: 1971 LO/S65 LO/T22:
vol.26,no.2– LO/U–1: vol.19–
MA/U–1 NR/U–1: vol.30– SH/U–1:
vol.19– ST/U–1: vol.39–

UNIVERSITY OF TORONTO REVIEW
An undergraduate publication
q; 1968–
Toronto

UNIVERSITY OF WINDSOR REVIEW
f; vol.1,no.1 1965–
Windsor, Ont. English Dept., U. Windsor
ed. Eugene McNamara
ISSN 0042–0352

CA/U–1 CB/U–1 LO/U–1
OX/U–1: vol.3,no.1–

WASCANA REVIEW
f; vol.1,no.1 1966–
Regina, Sask. U. Regina, Regina Campus
ed. William Howard
ISSN 0043–0412

CB/U–1: vol.2,no.1– ED/N–1
HL/U–1 LD/U–1: vol.1,no.2, vol.2,no.1–2,
vol.3– LO/N–1: vol.2,no.1– LO/S26:
vol.3,no.1– LO/U–1 OX/U–1: vol.2,
no.1–

WESTERN CANADIAN STUDIES IN MODERN
LANGUAGES AND LITERATURE
q; no.1 1970–
Regina, Sask. Dept. of Modern Languages, U.
Saskatchewan
eds. Oliver Abrioux and others

CA/U–1 CB/U–1 HL/U–1
LO/U–1

Drama

CANADIAN DRAMA
f; vol.1,no.1 1975–
Waterloo, Ont. Dept. of English, U. Waterloo,
Waterloo, Ont., N2L 3G1
ed. Rota Lister
ISSN 0317–9044
L'ART DRAMATIQUE CANADIEN

CANADIAN THEATRE REVIEW
q; no.1 1974–
Downsview, Ont. York U.
ed. Don Rubin
ISSN 0315–0836

ED/N–1: 1976– LO/T22 OX/U–1:
no.3–

DRAMA AT CALGARY
∅; no.1 1966–
Calgary, Alberta. Drama Division, U. Calgary

ENCORE
∅; no.1 1963–
Hawkesbury, Ont.
ISSN 0424–964X

MODERN DRAMA
q; vol.1,no.1 1958–
Toronto. Graduate Center for the Study of
Drama, Massey College, 554 Spadina Crescent,
Toronto, Ont. M5S 2J9
ed. Jill Levenson
ISSN 0026–7694

NR/U–1

PERFORMING ARTS
t; vol.1,no.1 1962–
Toronto. Canadian Stage and Arts Pubs., 49
Wellington St. E.
eds. Stephen Mezei and Arnold Edinborough
ISSN 0031–5230

ED/N–1 LO/T22: vol.7,no.1–

Fiction

BENT
ƀ; 196?–
Victoria, B.C. 1111 Bewdley Ave.
ed. Byrd Lukinuk
ISSN 0067–5733

BLUE JAY
A monthly magazine of short stories
ƀ; vol.1,no.1 – vol.2,no.8 1904–5
Niagara Falls, Ont.

CANADIAN FICTION MAGAZINE
q; no.1 1971–
Vancouver. P.O. Box 36422, Postal Station G,
Vancouver, B.C. V6R 4G7
ed. Geoffrey Hancock
ISSN 0045–477X

LO/S26: no.10–   LO/U–2: no.12–
OX/U–1

CANADIAN SHORT STORY MAGAZINE
q; vol.1,no.1 1975–
Lethbridge, Alberta. 518 26th St. S., Lethbridge,
Alberta T1J 3Y5
ed. Louis Burke
ISSN 0317–1949

CANADIAN STORIES
Canada's first popular all-fiction magazine ·
m; vol.1,no.1–6 1928
Deseronto, Ont.

CANADIAN WRITING
ƀ; vol.1,no.1–2 1950–1
Montreal. Montreal Writers' Workshop

EXAMPLES
z(1 issue); 1968
Toronto. New Writers' Workshop, 602A
Markham St.

LO/U–2

54′ 40″
Writing from Barry McKinnon's creative writing
classes at the College of New Caledonia
a; no.1–3 1970–3
Prince George, B.C.

FREELANCE
b; 1974–
Regina, Sask. Saskatchewan Writer's Guild and
Saskatchewan Arts' Board, P.O. Box 1005,
Regina, Sask., S4P 0N0
ed. Pat Krause

Supersedes NEWSLETTER: SASKATCHEWAN
WRITERS' GUILD (q.v.)

GEORGIA STRAIGHT WRITING SUPPLEMENT
ƀ; no.1–8 1971–2
Vancouver. York Street Commune

OX/U–1

GROUNDWORK
a; 1971–
Prince George, B.C. Barry McKinnon's creative
writing workshop

INNOVATOR
ƀ; vol.1,no.1–4 1967–72
Dartmouth, N.S. New Writing Club of Nova
Scotia
ed. Hazel Firth Goddard
ISSN 0537–7218
Superseded by PEGASUS (q.v.)

INTERNATIONAL FICTION REVIEW
f; vol.1,no.1 1974–
Fredericton, N.B. International Fiction Assn.,
U. New Brunswick
ed. Saad Elkhadem
ISSN 0315–4149

ED/N–1: 1976–   SH/U–1

INTRODUCTIONS FROM AN ISLAND
New writing by the students in the creative
writing programme of the University of Victoria
a; no.1 1969–
Victoria, B.C. U. Victoria, P.O. Box 1700,
Victoria, B.C. V8W 2Y2
ed. R. Skelton
ISSN 0318–3270

JOURNAL OF CANADIAN FICTION
q; vol.1,no.1 1972–
Montreal. Bellrock P. Assn., 2050 Mackay St.,
Montreal, H3G 2J1
ed. John R. Sorfleet
ISSN 0047–2255

ED/N–1   LD/U–1   LO/T22: vol.3,no.4–
LO/U–1: vol.1,no.2   OX/U–1

MARSH AND MAPLE
q; 1975?–
Dartmouth, N.S. Scotian Pen Guild, P.O. Box 173

NARRATOR MAGAZINE
no.1 1934–?
Toronto

NEBULA
f; no.1 1975–
North Bay, Ont. Nebula P., 509 Lakeshore Dr.,
North Bay, Ont. P1A 2E3
ed. Ken Stange
ISSN 0137–2104

NEW CANADIAN STORIES
ɸ; no.1 1972–
Ottawa, Ont. Oberon Press, 555 Maple Lane,
Ottawa, Ont. K1M ON7
eds. David Helwig and Joan Harcourt
ISSN 0316–7518

ORIGINS
A magazine based on creative writing
q; vol.1,no.1 1967–
Hamilton, Ont. Box 72, Station E, Hamilton,
Ont. L8S 4K9
ed. H. Barrett
ISSN 0048–2234

LO/U–2

PERIODICS
A magazine devoted to prose
ɸ; no.1 1977–
Vancouver, B.C. P.O. Box 69375 Postal Station K,
Vancouver, B.C. V5K 4W6
eds. Paul de Barros and Daphne Marlatt
ISSN 0701–2748

LO/S26

POTLACH
ɸ; no1–8 1964–7
Vancouver. Dept. of Creative Writing U. B.C.,
Vancouver 8
ISSN 0551–7001

PRISM
A magazine of contemporary writing
ɸ; no.1–3 1959–63
Vancouver. Dept. of Creative Writing, U. B.C.,
Vancouver 8
ISSN 0032–8790
Superseded by PRISM INTERNATIONAL (q.v.)

LO/U–1: no.2

PRISM INTERNATIONAL
A journal of contemporary writing
f; no.4 1964–
Vancouver. Dept. of Creative Writing, U. B.C.,
Vancouver 8.
ed. Michael Bullock
ISSN 0032–8790
Supersedes PRISM (q.v.)

ED/N–1   LO/S26: vol.12,no.3–
LO/T22: vol.14,no.2–   LO/U–2: vol.2,no.2,
vol.4,no.1–2,4

SALT
A little magazine of contemporary writing
ɸ; 1969–
Moosejaw, Sask. Tegwar P., 1119–13th Ave.,
N.W. Moosejaw, Sask.
ed. Robert Currie
ISSN 0085–5863

LO/U–2

SLESSE NEWS
m; vol.1,no.1 1964–
Chilliwack, B.C.
ISSN 0049–0717

**VANCOUVER WRITERS' GUILD MEMBERS'
JOURNAL**
Vancouver

Poetry

AIR
b; no.1 1971–
Vancouver. Box 688, Station H
ed. B. Lachance
ISSN 0044–6947

ALBERTA POETRY YEARBOOK
a; 1930–
Edmonton, Alberta. Edmonton Branch, Canadian
Authors' Assn., 13104 136th Ave. Edmonton,
Alberta T5L 403
ed. June L. Fritch
ISSN 0065–5996

ANOTHER POETRY MAGAZINE
ɸ; no.1–3 1970–1
Toronto. 32 Marchmount Rd.
eds. Dale and Margery Zieroth

LO/S26: no.3   LO/U–2

ANTHOL
a; 1972–
Pointe Claire, Quebec, P.O. Box 208,
71 Pardo Ave.
ed. Robert Morrison
ISSN 0316–2583

BLACK FLY
ɸ; no.1 1973–

Thunder Bay, Ont. P.O. Box 302, Postal Station P
ISSN 0319–1176

BLEWOINTMENTPRESS
♭; Issues given designations such as the Poverty
issue, Oil Slick issue, the Occupashun issue; 1963–
Vancouver, B.C. Blewointmentpress, 1611 Yew
St.
ISSN 0520–2728

LO/U–2: 1965–

BLOOD
z(1 issue); 1969
Vancouver. Intermedia P.

BLOODY HORSE
A magazine of poetry
z(1 issue); vol.1,no.1 1963
Montreal. Editions d'Orphée, 370 Marie Anne
St. E., Montreal 24

CV/II (CONTEMPORARY VERSE TWO)
q; vol.1,no.1 1975–
Winnipeg. P.O. Box 32, University Centre, U.
Manitoba, R3T 1EO
ed. Dorothy Livesay
ISSN 0319–6879

CANADA GOOSE
A Canadian poetry quarterly
♭; no.1–3 1973–4
Lethbridge, Alberta
eds. Dale Zieroth and Charles Noble

CANADIAN POETRY
q; vol.27,no.1– vol.31,no.4 1963/4–1967/8
Toronto. Canadian Authors' Assn.
Supersedes CANADIAN POETRY MAGAZINE
(q.v.) Absorbed by CANADIAN AUTHOR AND
BOOKMAN (q.v.)

LD/U–1: vol.30,no.4   LO/N–1   LO/T22
LO/U–2: vol.28,no.4, vol.31,no.4

CANADIAN POETRY MAGAZINE
q; vol.1–26 1936–62/3
Toronto. Canadian Authors' Assn.
ed. E. J. Pratt
Superseded by CANADIAN POETRY (q.v.)

LO/N–1: vol.16,no.4– vol.26,no.4
LO/T22: vol.10,no.4– vol.26,no.4

CATALYST
♭; no.1–2 1967–8
Toronto. U. Toronto
ISSN 0576–9140

CATAPULT
f; vol.1,no.1–2 1964
Montreal. 5684 Clark St., Montreal 14, Quebec
ISSN 0576–9221
Supersedes CATARACT (q.v.)

CATARACT
♭; vol.1–3 1961–2
Montreal. 5684 Clark St., Montreal 14, Quebec
ISSN 0576–923X
Superseded by CATAPULT (q.v.)

CONTACT
An international poetry magazine
♭; no.1–10 1952–4
Toronto. 28 Mayfield Ave.
ed. Raymond Souster
ISSN 0573–7818

OX/U–1: no.4

**CONTEMPORARY POETRY OF BRITISH
COLUMBIA**
z(1 issue); no.1 1970
Vancouver. Sono Nis P.
ed. J. Michael Yates
ISSN 0384–0433

LO/U–2   OX/U–1

CONTEMPORARY VERSE
A Canadian quarterly
q; no.1–39 1941–52
Victoria, B.C.
ed. Alan Crawley

LO/U–2: no.30,32,34–35

CRITICAL STUDIES IN CANADIAN POETRY
♭; 1976–
Ottawa. P.O. Box 5147, Postal Station E
eds. W. Glenn Clever and Frank M. Tierney

CROSS COUNTRY
A magazine of Canadian–U.S. poetry
t; no.1–4 1975 in 3 issues
Montreal. Apt. 14, 1935 Tupper St., Montreal,
Quebec
eds. Ken Norris, Robert Galvin and Jim Mele (U.S.)
ISSN 0318–6075

CYCLOPS
z(1 issue); no.1 1969
Scarborough, Ont. Huron P.
ed. Ian Young
Superseded by CATALYST (q.v.)

DELTA
A magazine of poetry and criticism

ɸ; no.1−26 1957−66
Montreal
ed. Louis Dudek
ISSN 0418−5951

LO/U−2: no.24,25   OX/U−1: no.26

EARTHWORDS
ɸ; no.1−6 1967−70
Ganges, B.C. Orphan Universe P., Box 14 Ganges,
B.C., V0S 1E0
ed. T. Balzac
ISSN 0070−7937
Supersedes WORDJOCK (q.v.) Superseded by
EMPTY BELLY (q.v.)

LO/U−2: no.6

ELPHIN PLOT
ɸ; 1969−72
Lake Louise, Alberta. Deodar Shadow P.
ed. Andrew Suknaski

EMPTY BELLY
A magazine of poetry and communication
ɸ; no.1−4 1972−5
Ganges, B.C. P.O. Box 14, Ganges, B.C. V0S 1E0
ed. Charles Tidler
ISSN 0316−9529
Supersedes EARTHWORDS (q.v.) and WORD−
JOCK (q.v.)

LO/U−2: no.2−4

FAZO
A magazine of poetry
z(1 issue); vol.1,no.1 1965
Burlington, Ont.
ed. T. Campbell

FOUR DECADES OF POETRY 1890−1930
f; no.1 1976−
Toronto. 231 Lonsmount Drive, Toronto, Ont.
M5P 2Y9
ed. Esther Fisher
ISSN 0308−0889

FULL TIDE
q; vol.1,no.1− vol.39,no.1 1936−74
Vancouver. Vancouver Poetry Society, 4602
Prospect Rd.
ed. Borghild Valeria
ISSN 0046−5267

GANGLIA
ɸ; series 1,no.1−7 1965−7;   series 2,no.1−2
Publication suspended 1967−9   1969 issue
called series 2,no.1   in series 1,no.6 not publ.
Orangeville, Ont. Ganglia P.

ed. B. P. Nichol (1st series?)
ISSN 0435−1142
No.6 of series 1 absorbed with GRONK (q.v.)

LO/U−2

GARGOYLE POETRY ANNUAL
a
Toronto. U. College Literary and Athletic
Society

GREASE BALL
ɸ; no.1 1969−
Toronto. Ganglia P., c/o Village Bookstore, 239
Queen St. West, Toronto, Ont. M5V 1Z4
Linked with GRONK (q.v.)

GRIPPER
ɸ
Toronto. Coach House P. 401 Huron St. (rear),
Toronto 181, Ont.
ed. Victor Coleman
ISSN 0072−7687

GRONK
ɸ; no.1 1967−
Toronto. Ganglia P. c/o Village Bookstore, 239
Queen St. West, Toronto, Ont. M5V 1Z4
eds. D. W. Harris, B. P. Nichol and Reah Smith
Connected with GANGLIA (q.v.) and GREASE
BALL (q.v.)
ISSN 0017−453X

LO/U−2: no.1−7

GUT
A magazine of prose, reviews and poetry
b; no.1 1973−
Toronto. 10 Wascana Ave., Toronto, Ont.
ed. Alfred Rushton

HAIKU
q; vol.1,no.1 1967−
Toronto. Haiku P., P.O. Box 866, Station F
ed. Eric W. Amann
ISSN 0017−6656

HYPHID
q; vol.1,no.1 1967−
Toronto. Weed/Flower P.
ed. Nelson Ball
Supersedes WEED (q.v.)

LO/U−2   OX/U−1

IMAGE NATION
ɸ; no.1−6? 1969?
Toronto. Rochdale College

eds. Victor Coleman and others
LO/U−2: no.5−6

IMPULSE
t; vol.1,no.1 1971−
Toronto. P.O. Box 238, Station M
ed. Peter Such
vol.2,no.3/4 is a double issue of PORCEPIC (q.v.)
no.2

IS
t; no.1 1966−
Toronto. Coach House P., 101 Kendal Ave.,
Toronto, Ont. M5R 1L8
ed. Victor Coleman
ISSN 0047−1526
Supersedes ISLAND (q.v.)

LO/U−2: no.3−15   OX/U−1: no.15

ISLAND
þ; no.1−8 1964−7
Toronto. Coach House P.
ed. Victor Coleman
ISSN 0578−8099
Superseded by IS (q.v.)

LO/U−2: no.2−3,6

LINDA
þ; introductory issue in 1968   vol.1,no.1 1971
Bloomfield, Ont. P.O. Box 69
ed. K. Rogers

LO/U−2: 1971

LIONTAYLES
a; vol.1,no.1−2 1967−8
Waterloo, Ont. Federation of Students, Waterloo U.
Supersedes VOLUME (q.v.)

LO/U−2: vol.1,no.2

LUV
för poëmz
þ; no.1−6 1967
Toronto. Fleye P.
ed. David W. Harris
ISSN 0460−0363

LO/U−2: no.1−5

MAINLINE
A magazine of poetry
t; no.1−13 1968−73
Windsor, Ont. P.O. Box 61, Sandwich Stn.
eds. Dorothy Farmiloe and others
ISSN 0025−0821

LO/N−1   LO/U−2   OX/U−1: no.7.

MANNA
A review of contemporary poetry
f; no.1−5 1972−4
Toronto. 21 Don Valley Dr.
ed. Lorne Shivinian

LO/N−1

MEASURE
c.1970s
Toronto

MONTREAL POEMS
þ; no.1 1974−
Dewittville, Quebec

MUSE
a; 1891−1967
Hamilton, Ont. Board of Publications, McMaster U.
ISSN 0380−1993

NEW BRUNSWICK CHAPBOOKS
þ; 1968−
Fredericton, N.B. 252 Stanley St. E3B 3A3
ed. Nancy Bauer

OLD NUN MAGAZINE
b; no.1 1976−
Toronto, Ont. 129 Seaton St., Toronto, Ont.
M5A 2T2
Supersedes OLD NUN NEWSLETTER (q.v.)
See also POETRY TORONTO NEWSLETTER

OLD NUN NEWSLETTER
þ; no.1−6 1975
Toronto, Ont. 129 Seaton St., Toronto, Ont.
M5A 2T2
Superseded by OLD NUN MAGAZINE (q.v.)
and POETRY TORONTO NEWSLETTER (q.v.)

OTHER VOICES
þ; no.1−10 1965−75
London, Ont. Alice in Wonderland P., 100
Duchess Ave., London, Ont. N6C 1N6
Supersedes POETS' WORKSHOP

LD/U−1: no.3−4   LO/U−2: no.7−10

PARNASSUS
A magazine of new poetry
þ; vol.1,no.1−6 1945
Toronto
ed. J. P. Rae

POEM COMPANY
b; Phase 1,no.1 1970−
Vancouver. Intermedia P., P.O. Box 3294,

Vancouver, B.C. V6J 3X9
eds. Henry Rappaport and others

POETRY CANADA
ɮ; no.1 1969–
Vancouver. League of Canadian Poets, 3323 W.
3rd Ave., Vancouver, B.C. V6R 1L3
ed. Leona M. Gom
ISSN 0316–036X

POETRY 70
z(1 issue); 1970
Toronto. Board of Education

POETRY TORONTO NEWSLETTER
m; no.1–2 1975–6
Toronto. Old Nun Publications, 224 St. George
Station, Apt. 709, Toronto, Ont. M5R 2N9
ed. Pier Giorgio Di Cicco
Supersedes OLD NUN NEWSLETTER (q.v.)
See also OLD NUN MAGAZINE

POETRY-WINDSOR-POÉSIE
t; vol.1,no.1 1974–
Windsor, Ont. Box 6, Sandwich P.O., Windsor,
Ont. N9C 3Y6
eds. A. Amprimoz, W. Schiller and A. van den
Hoven
ISSN 0317–0764

POM SEED
no.1, 1973–
London, Ont.

POSTER-POEM
1969
Vancouver

RE VISIONS
Street poetry
ɮ; vol.1,no.1 1970–
Toronto

REFUGEE JOURNAL OF POETRY
ɮ; vol.1,no.1 1968–
Melita, Manitoba. Black Dog Pubs., P.O. Box 28
ed. Joe McLellan

OX/U–1: vol.1,no.1

RYERSON POETRY CHAPBOOKS
ɮ
Scarborough, Ont. McGraw-Hill Ryerson Ltd.,
330 Progress Ave.

SASKATCHEWAN POETRY BOOK
a; 1934–
Regina, Sask. Saskatchewan Poetry Society,

3104 College Ave., Regina, Sask. S4T 1V7
ISSN 0080–6560

LO/N–1

SCRATCH
An anthology of Canadian student poetry
ɮ; 1973–
Victoria, B.C.

SNAPDRAGON POETRY
ɮ; vol.1,no.1–2 1963
Kitchener, Ont.

SPANISH FLEYE
A pepetual anthology for living peepl
z(1 issue); 1966
Toronto. Fleye P.
ed. David W. Harris
ISSN 0584–8032

LO/U–2   OX/U–1

STRUCTURIST
ɮ; no.1 1960–
Saskatoon, Sask. U. Saskatchewan
ed. Eli Bornstein

LO/U–2   OX/U–1

SUMMER POEMS
z(1 issue); no.1 1963

SUNDOG
ɮ; no.1 1973–
Wood Mountain, Sask.
ed. Andrew Suknaski

THIRTY-FIVE
An anthology
z(1 issue); no.1 1971
Vancouver. Journalism Dept. of City Coll.
eds. Shirley Culpin and Dennis Senger

LO/U–2

TISH
m; no.1–42 1961–8
Vancouver. W. 19th Ave. Vancouver 13, B.C. 720
eds. Frank Davey, George Bowering and Dan
Macleod
ISSN 0040–8158

LO/U–2: no.23–37

TOWER
a; 1952–
Hamilton. Tower Poetry Society, McMaster U.
ed. John Ferns

ISSN 0495–9701

LO/U–2: 1965–73

TWELFTH KEY
A poetry journal
t
London, Ont. Applegarth Follies, P.O. Box 40,
Station B, London, Ont. N6A 4V3

UP THE TUBE WITH ONE I (OPEN) – POMES
ƀ; no.1 1966–
North Burnaby, B.C. 4875 Albert St.
eds. C. W. Carlson, N. P. Lane and M. Kemp
ISSN 0083–4602

LO/U–2

V.P.S. CHAPBOOK
z(1 issue); vol.1,no.1 1925
Vancouver. Vancouver Poetry Society

VANCOUVER ISLAND POEMS
Cloud nine
a; 1973–
Victoria, B.C. Soft P. 1050 St. David St., Victoria,
B.C. V8S 4Y8

VILLAGE SQUIRE
m; 1975–
Blyth, Ont. Blyth Standard, P.O. Box 10

ed. Keith M. Rochston
ISSN 0382–0203

VOLUME
A bi-annual of Poetry
ƀ; no.1–6 1963–7   Title includes the last two
digits of the year, e.g. Volume 63
Waterloo, Ont. Students' Board of Publications,
U. Waterloo
eds. Nelson Ball and S. G. Buri
ISSN 0507–2816
Superseded by LIONTAYLES (q.v.)

LO/U–2

WEED
b; no.1–12 1966–7
Toronto. Weed/Flower P.
ed. Nelson Ball
ISSN 0511–4101
Superseded by HYPHID (q.v.)

LO/U–2

WEST COAST POETS
ƀ; no.1 1968–
Vancouver. Very Stone House

OX/U–1

WORDJOCK
ƀ; no.1–4 1967
Ganges, B.C.
ISSN 0512–2090
Superseded by EARTHWORDS (q.v.)

CARIBBEAN

Short-Title List by Country

Periodicals for the Caribbean are arranged alphabetically by title. A list of short titles under individual countries is given for ease of reference.

BARBADOS
(*cont.*)
Forum
Harrisonian
Lodge School Record
Queen's College Magazine
Weymouth Magazine

GUYANA

Artana
Chronicle Christmas Annual
Csakazertis
Expressionova
Georgetown College Journal
Kaie
Kyk Over Al
New World Fortnightly
Nu-crop
Plexus

JAMAICA

Buckatoro Journal
Bulletin of the African Studies'
  Association
Caribbean Quarterly
Focus
Jamaica Journal
Jamaica Journal and Kingston
  Chronicle
Jamaica Magazine
Jamaica Quarterly Journal and
  Literary Gazette
Jamaica Quarterly Journal of
  Literature
Jamaica Review
Jamaica and West Indian Review
Journal of the Institute of Jamaica
Kalaloo
New Jamaica Magazine
New World Quarterly
Now
Outlook
Pelican Annual
Pepperpot
Pimento
Planters' Punch
Plummer's Magazine
Public Opinion Christmas Annual
Savacou
Trifler
Victoria Quarterly
Watchman and Jamaica Free Press
West Indian Review
York Castle Quarterly

ST. KITTS

La Laps

ST. LUCIA
Link
Toutwelle
West Indian Enterprise

ST. VINCENT
Flambeau
Islands

TRINIDAD

Art and Man
Beacon
Caribbean Contact
Caribbean Watchman
Corlit
Corlit Newsletter
Kairi
New Voices
Opus
S.A.G.
Tapia
Themes
Trinidad
Trinidad Miscellany
Trinidad Monthly Magazine
Trinidad Review
Voices

ART AND MAN
þ; no.1–3 1968–9
Port of Spain, Trinidad. 36 Frederick St.
ed. Roy Mitchell

ARTANA
q; vol.1,no.1 1963–
Georgetown, Guyana. Guyana Centre of the Arts,
294 Murray St., Guyana.

LO/U–8: vol.1,no.1–3

BAJAN AND SOUTH CARIBBEAN
m; vol.1,no.1 1953–
Bridgetown, Barbados. Carib Publicity Co. Ltd.,
P.O. Box 718C
ed. T. A. D. Gale
ISSN 0005–4011

LO/S26   LO/S65   LO/U–8: vol.12,no.5–
                      OX/U–9: vol.4,no.11–

BEACON
þ; vol.1,no.1– vol.3,no.4 1931–3;   vol.4,no.1
1939
Port of Spain, Trinidad

ed. Albert Gomes

LO/U–8

BEE
w; vol.1,no.1– vol.2,no.14 1887–8
Bridgetown, Barbados
ed. E. G. Sinkler

BIM
f; vol.1,no.1 1942–
Christ Church, Barbados. 'Ferney', Atlantic
Shores
eds. Frank Colleymore and John Wickham
ISSN 0006–2766

CB/U–1: no.11–   CC/U–1: vol.8,no.32–
vol.9,no.33, vol.13,no.51   HL/U–1: vol.3,
no.12, vol.5,no.18–19, vol.6,no.23, vol.10,no.41,
vol.13,no.52   LD/U–1: vol.13,no.51–
LO/S26: vol.12,no.48–   LO/U–1: no.40–58
OX/U–1: no.56–   OX/U14: vol.1,no.4,
vol.2,no.5–6, vol.2,no.8, vol.3,no.9–14,
no.18–20,22–32,34–

BUCKATORO JOURNAL
m; no.1–6 1823
Kingston, Jamaica

LO/N–1

**BULLETIN OF THE AFRICAN STUDIES'
ASSOCIATION OF THE WEST INDIES**
þ; no.1 1967–
Kingston, Jamaica. African Studies' Assn. of the
West Indies, P.O. Box 222, Kingston 7

LD/U–1: no.4   LO/U–8: no.1–8

CARIB
m; vol.1,no.1–6 1895
St. Johns, Antigua
ed. Miss F. Cassin

LO/T83: vol.1,no.2–6

CARIBBEAN CONTACT
m; 1973–
Port of Spain, Trinidad. P.O. Box 876

CARIBBEAN QUARTERLY
q; vol.1,no.1 1949–
Kingston, Jamaica. Dept. of Extra-Mural Studies,
U. West Indies, P.O. Box 42
ed. Rex Nettleford
ISSN 0008–6495

BH/U–1   CA/U–1   CB/U–1: vol.12,
no.2–   DR/U–1: vol.11–   EX/U–1:
vol.3–   LO/N–1   LO/S26: 1953–

LO/S65   LO/U–1   LO/U–8
MA/U–1   NR/U–1: vol.14–   OX/U–1
OX/U–9   OX/U14   QL/P–2
LO/T83

CARIBBEAN WATCHMAN
m; vol.1,no.1– vol.6,no.6 1903–8
Port-of-Spain, Trinidad

LO/N–1: lacks vol.2,no.1,3–7, vol.6,no.2–3

CHRONICLE CHRISTMAS ANNUAL
a; no.1–8 1915–22
Georgetown, Guyana. *Daily Chronicle*

CORLIT
t; no.1 1973–
California, Trinidad. Corinth Teachers' Literary
Group, 41 Esperanza
ed. Vishnu Gosine

CORLIT NEWSLETTER
þ; no.1 1975–
California, Trinidad. Corinth Teachers' Literary
Group

CSAKAZERTIS
Just for all that
þ; no.1 1971–?
Georgetown, Guyana
ed. Thomas Kabdebo

LO/U–2: no.1

EXPRESSIONOVA
A magazine of creative writing from the Caribbean
þ; no.1 1966–   None issued in 1968
Turkeyen, Guyana
ISSN 0014–5335
early numbers called EXPRESSION

FLAMBEAU
q; no.1–9 1965–8
Kingstown, St. Vincent. Kingstown Study Group

LO/U–8

FOCUS
þ; no.1–4 1943–60
Kingston, Jamaica
ed. Edna Manley

FORUM
A quarterly review
q/þ; vol.1,no.1– vol.4,no.1;   new series vol.1–4
1943–5   A few scattered issues may have been
published between 1934 and 1943
Bridgetown, Barbados. The Forum Club

GEORGETOWN COLLEGE JOURNAL
Georgetown, Guyana

CA/U–1: vol.36–42 1908–14

HARRISONIAN
ƀ; 1917–
Bridgetown, Barbados. Harrison College

LO/S65: vol.13,no.2– vol.35

ISLANDS
z(1 issue); c.1973
St. Vincent

JAMAICA JOURNAL
no.1 1818–?
Kingston, Jamaica
ed. Mr. Rippingham

LO/N–1: no.1

JAMAICA JOURNAL
q; vol.1,no.1 1967–
Kingston, Jamaica. Institute of Jamaica, 12–6
East St.
ed. Shirley Maynier Burke
ISSN 0021–4124

CB/U–1   CC/U–1: vol.9,no.1–
LO/S26: vol.2,no.3–   LO/S65   LO/U–8
OX/U–9

JAMAICA JOURNAL AND KINGSTON
CHRONICLE
w; vol.1–4 1823–1826
Kingston, Jamaica

LO/N–1   LO/T83: vol.1,no.38– vol.2,no.36

JAMAICA MAGAZINE
Containing original essays, moral, philosophical
and literary
m; vol.1,no.1– vol.4,no.1 1812–3
Kingston, Jamaica. *Kingston Chronicle* Office,
Harbour St.

LO/N–1: vol.1,no.1– vol.2,no.2   LO/T83:
vol.1,no.1– vol.2,no.2

JAMAICA QUARTERLY JOURNAL AND
LITERARY GAZETTE
q; 181–? –?
Kingston, Jamaica. Conducted by a Society of
Gentlemen

LO/N–1: 1818,1819

JAMAICA QUARTERLY JOURNAL OF
LITERATURE, SCIENCE AND ART
q; vol.1,no.1 1860–?

Kingston, Jamaica, James Gall

LO/S65: 1861

JAMAICA REVIEW
m; vol1.no.1– vol.3,no.5 1925–8
Kingston, Jamaica. Coronation Buildings

LO/S65: vol.1,no.1– vol.3,no.2

JAMAICA AND WEST INDIAN REVIEW
q; 1963–70
Kingston, Jamaica
being the title of WEST INDIAN REVIEW (q.v.)
from 1963–70

JOURNAL OF THE INSTITUTE OF JAMAICA
ƀ; 1893–9
Kingston, Jamaica. Institute of Jamaica, Date
Tree Hall, East St.

LO/S65

KAIE
Official organ of the National History and Arts
Council of Guyana
ƀ; no.1 1965–
Georgetown, Guyana. National History and Arts
Council of Guyana

LO/S26: no.2–   LO/U–2: no.2–11
LO/U–8   OX/U14

KAIRI
ƀ; numbered by year and part 1974/1–
Port-of-Spain, Trinidad. 22 Fitt St., Woodbrook
ed. Christopher Laird

LO/S26

KALALOO
z(1 issue); no.1 1973
Kingston, Jamaica. Literary Society

KYK OVER AL
f; vol.1,no.1– vol.9,no.28 1945–61
Georgetown, Guyana. Argosy Publishing Co.

BT/U–1: no.11–25   LO/S65: no.1–4,7–13,
15–28   OX/U14: no.13,15–24

LA LAPS
ƀ; vol.1,no.1 1976–
Basseterre, St. Kitts. National Publishing House

LINK
ƀ; vol.1,no.1– vol.2,no.3 1968–70
Castries, St. Lucia. Link Publications

LODGE SCHOOL RECORD
a; 1911–
St. John, Barbados. Lodge School

NEW JAMAICA MAGAZINE
f; vol.1–3 1798–9
Kingston, Jamaica. Lunan & Lewis

OX/U–1

NEW VOICES
f; vol.1, 1973–   no.5=vol.3,no.5
Diego Martin, Trinidad. 1 Sapphire Drive
ed. Anson Gonzales

LO/S26

NEW WORLD FORTNIGHTLY
e/m; no.1–50 1964–7
Georgetown, Guyana
no.49–50 entitled NEW WORLD MONTHLY
ed. David de Caires

LO/U–8

NEW WORLD QUARTERLY
q; vol.1,no.1– vol.5,no.4 1963–72
Kingston, Jamaica. New World Group Ltd., Box
221, Kingston 7
ed. Vaughan Lewis

CB/U–1: 1967–9   LO/U–2: vol.2,no.3–
vol.5,no.1   LO/U–8   OX/U14: vol.3,
no.1– vol.5,no.4

NOW
þ; no.1n.d. no.2–4/5 1973–4
St. Ann, Jamaica. P.O. Box 14, Brown's Town
ed. Stewart Brown

LO/S26: no.2–3   LO/U–2: no.2–3

NU-CROP
Organ of the students of the Guyana School of
Agriculture
f; no.1 1968–
Georgetown, Guyana. Guyana School of Agriculture
ed. Clement Map

OPUS
A review
t; no.1–3 1960
Port-of-Spain, Trinidad. P.N.M. Publishing Co.,
P.O. Box 461
eds. John Wickham and Ronald Benge

OUTLOOK
A monthly review of life and literature reflecting

progressive thought
m; c.1930s
Kingston, Jamaica

LO/N–1: 1933

PELICAN ANNUAL
a; 1955–
Mona, Jamaica. Guild of Undergraduates, U. West
Indies

PEPPERPOT
Annual Jamaican pot-pourri
þ; no.1–9 1951–69
Kingston, Jamaica. P.O. Box 75, Kingston 6
ed. Elsie Barsoe

LD/U–1   LO/S26

PIMENTO
With a dram of common sense
e; vol.1,no.1–4 1927
Kingston, Jamaica
ed. Pat à Beckett

LO/S65   LO/T83

PLANTERS' PUNCH
þ; vol.1,no.1– vol.5,no.6 1920–45
Kingston, Jamaica
ed. Herbert G. de Lisser

PLEXUS
A magazine of young writing
Georgetown, Guyana

PLUMMER'S MAGAZINE
A Jamaica literary magazine
m; vol.1,no.1–2 1913
Kingston, Jamaica

LO/S65: vol.1,no.1

PUBLIC OPINION CHRISTMAS ANNUAL
a; 1966–
Kingston, Jamaica. City Printery Ltd.

QUEEN'S COLLEGE MAGAZINE
þ; no.1 1918–
Bridgetown, Barbados. Queen's College

S.A.G.
Arts and the world
þ; vol.1,no.1– vol.2,no.2 1970–2
San Fernando, Trinidad. Studio Arts Group,
9 Irving St. North
eds. Irma Thomas, Wilfrid Shepherd and Patricia
Allum

LO/S26: vol.1,no.2–3, vol.2,no.2   LO/S65

SAVACOU
A journal of the Caribbean artists' movement
q; vol.1,no.1 1970–
Kingston, Jamaica. The Herald Ltd.
eds. Edward Brathwaite, Kenneth Ramchand and
Gorden Rohlehr
ISSN 0036–5068

CB/U–1   LD/U–1: vol.1–2   LO/S26
LO/U–2: vol.3,7–8   LO/U–8: vol.1,no.2–
OX/U–9   OX/U14: vol.3–8

STROMBUS
The premier Bahamian magazine
m; vol.1,no.1– vol.3,no.1 1913–5
Nassau, Bahamas. Tribune Office

LO/S65

TAPIA
ƥ; vol.1,no.1 1969–
Tunapuna, Trinidad. Tapia Publishing Co., Tuna
Puna Rd.
ed. Allan Harris

LO/S26 [3-year file]   LO/U–2   LO/U–8

THEMES
Verse and prose from the Campus
ƥ; no.1–3 1970–2
St. Augustine, Trinidad. Literary and Debating
Society, U. West Indies

TOUTWELLE
ƥ; vol.1,no.1 1976–
Castries, St. Lucia

TRIFLER
m; vol.1–2 1822–3
Kingston, Jamaica

LO/N–1

TRINIDAD
ƥ; c.1930s
Port-of-Spain, Trinidad
eds. C. L. R. James and Alfred Mendes

TRINIDAD MISCELLANY
A monthly magazine of politics, literature,
religion and sociology
m; vol.1,no.1 1903–?
Port-of-Spain, Trinidad

LO/N–1: vol.1,no.1

TRINIDAD MONTHLY MAGAZINE
m; no.1 1871–?
Port-of-Spain, Trinidad

LO/N–1: no.1

TRINIDAD REVIEW
A monthly magazine for everybody
m; vol.1,no.1 1911–?
Port-of-Spain, Trinidad

LO/N–1: vol.1,no.1

VICTORIA QUARTERLY
q; vol.1,no.1– vol.4,no.4 1889–92
Kingston, Jamaica. De Souza, 7 Church St.
ed. J. C. Ford

LO/N–1: vol.4,no.2–3   LO/S65

VOICES
ƥ; vol.1,no.1– vol.2,no.2 1964–70;   new
series no.4 1977–
Port-of-Spain, Trinidad
ed. Clifford Sealy

CB/U–1: vol.1,no.1–6   ED/N–1
LO/S26: 1970–   OX/U–1   OX/U14

WATCHMAN AND JAMAICA FREE PRESS
c; no.1 1832–?
Kingston, Jamaica

LO/S65: no.56–104

WEST INDIAN ENTERPRISE
m; no.1–67 1931–7
Castries, St. Lucia. The Voice
ed. Miss Lockhart

LO/S65: no.1,47,49,56,59–61,63–7

WEST INDIAN REVIEW
q; vol.1,no.1– vol.6,no.10 1934–40;   2nd series
vol.1–6,no.4 1944–9;   3rd series 1949–55;
4th series 1956–60;   5th series 1961–70;
6th series 1971–
Kingston, Jamaica. Arawak P., 46 East St.
ed. Esther Chapman Hepher
ISSN 0021–4086
Incorporated JAMAICA from 1949 Renamed
JAMAICA AND WEST INDIAN REVIEW
1963–70

CA/U–1: 6th series vol.1,no.1–   LO/N–1:
3rd series vol.2,no.19–   LO/S65
LO/U–1: vol.1,no.1– vol.3,no.2, vol.5,no.7

WEYMOUTH MAGAZINE
ƥ; vol.1,no.1–4 1939–49
Bridgetown, Barbados. Weymouth Club

YORK CASTLE QUARTERLY
q; no.1 1889–?
Kingston, Jamaica

LO/N–1: no.1–2

HONG KONG

CHIMES
a; 1961–
Hong Kong. English Society
0069–3642

ENGLISH SOCIETY MAGAZINE
♭; no.1 1974–
Hong Kong. New Asia College

LD/U–1: no.1

JOURNAL OF THE HONG KONG BRANCH OF
THE ROYAL ASIATIC SOCIETY
q; vol.1,no.1 1961–
Hong Kong. P.O. Box 13864

LO/U14

LION
a; 1931–4
Hong Kong. Central British School

LO/S65

OCEAN LITERATURE
m
Hong Kong. Ocean Literary P., 3 on Ning Lane,
Sai Ying Pun.

ODDS AND ENDS
b; vol.1,no.1–5 1896–7
Hong Kong. J. P. Braga, 9 Zetland St.

LO/N–1   LO/S65

MALAYSIA AND SINGAPORE

BERITA PELAJAR
b; no.1 1969–
Kuala Lumpur. National Union of Malaysian
Students

BERITA PELAJAR SPECIAL
♭; vol.1,no.1 1969–
Kuala Lumpur. U. Malaya

CAULDRON
♭; vol.1–3 1947–9
Singapore. Medical College Union Literary and
Debating Society
Superseded by NEW CAULDRON (q.v.)

COMMENTARY
♭; vol.1,no.1 1968–
Singapore. U. Singapore Society, Guild House,
5 Dalvey Estate, Singapore 10

ed. Kwa Chong Guan
ISSN 0084–8956

EVENING OF POETRY AND MUSIC
q; no.1–4 1969–70
Singapore. Literary Society, U. Singapore

FOCUS
a; vol.1,no.1– vol.5,no.1 1961–5   New series
no.1–3 1967–70
Singapore. Literary Society, U. Singapore

LD/U–1: vol.2,no.1–3, vol.3,no.3, vol.4,no.1,
vol.5,no.1, n.s. no.1–3   LO/S26: n.s. no.2–3
LO/U–2: vol.2,no.1, vol.3,no.3, vol.4,no.1,
vol.5,no.1, n.s. no.1–3

FORWARD
a; no.1 1955–

Singapore. Pulaw Bukom English School

LO/N−1

GULA MALAKA
Magazine
a; no.1−2 1913−4
Singapore. Kelly and Walsh
eds. W. S. Ebden and O. T. Dussek

IMPRESSION
Quarterly magazine of the University of Singapore
Society
z(1 issue); vol.1,no.1 1965
Singapore. U. Singapore Society, L. M. Creative
Publicity Ltd.

INTISARI
♭; vol.1,no.1 1964−
Singapore. Malaysian Sociological Research
Institute Ltd.

JOURNAL OF THE INDIAN ARCHIPELAGO
AND EASTERN ASIA
q; vol.1−9 1847−55   New series vol.1−4 1856−9
Penang, Singapore
ed. J. R. Logan

LO/N12: lacks n.s. vol.3   LO/S65: vol.1−8
LO/U−1

JOURNAL OF THE MALAYSIAN BRANCH OF
THE ROYAL ASIATIC SOCIETY
♮; vol.1,no.1 1923−
Singapore. National Meseum
From vol.1−36 (1923−63) known as JOURNAL
OF THE MALAYAN . . . SOCIETY

JOURNAL OF NANYANG UNIVERSITY
♭; vol.1,no.1 1967−
Singapore. Nanyang U.

CB/U−1: vol.2,no.1−

KESUSA STERAAN NANYANG
♭; no.1−3 1959−60
Singapore. Lian Yock Fang

LIDRA
♭; no.1 1960−
Kuala Lumpur. Literary and Dramatic Society,
U. Malaya

LO/U−2: no.5

LITERARY MISCELLANY
z(1 issue); no.1 1968
Singapore. Dept. of Modern Language and
Literature, Nanyang U.

MAGAZINE
♭/a; vol.1−10 1931−40   New series no.1−3
1946/7−8/9   3rd series 1949/50−57/60
Singapore Students' Union, U. Malaya

MAJALLAH/QUEENSWAY/MAGAZINE
a
Singapore. Queensway Secondary School

LO/N−1: 1965

MALAYAN UNDERGRAD
♭; no.1−15 1948−66
Singapore. Raffles College Students' Union

MONSOON
a; vol.1,no.1−2 1961−2
Singapore. G. H. Kiat & Co.

NEW CAULDRON
a; 1950−6
Singapore. Raffles Society, U. Malaya.
Supersedes CAULDRON (q.v.)

NEW DIRECTIONS
vol.1,no.1 1973−
Singapore. Times Publishing

PAPER BOATS
An anthology of Malaysian creative writing
z(1 issue); no.1 1967
Kuala Lumpur. Literary and Dramatic Society,
U. Malaya

PAS PAN
♭; no.1−8 1938
Penang, Singapore
Official organ of the Writers' Assn. of Malaya

LO/N−1

PHOENIX
a; 1960−74
Singapore, U. Singapore

POETRY SINGAPORE
t; no.1 1968−
Singapore. U. Singapore, Dept. of English, Buhit
Timah Rd., Singapore 10
ed. Edwin Thumboo
ISSN 0032−2164

LO/U−2: no.1−2

PRIMA
z(1 issue); 1969
Kuala Lumpur
eds. Kolej Tuanku and Abdul Rahman

PROSPECT
m; vol. 1,no. 1 1969—
Singapore. Educational Publications Bureau

PSYCHE
a; 1963—
Singapore. U. Singapore

RAFFLES GIRLS' SCHOOL MAGAZINE
a; no. 1 1949—
Singapore

LO/N—1

REPOSITORY
ƥ
Singapore. Life P.

SAYA
ƥ; no. 1—12 1969—75
Singapore. 323 Upper East Coast Rd., Singapore 16

LO/S26

SINGAPORE UNDERGRAD
q; vol. 1,no. 1— vol. 10,no. 2 1967—76
Singapore. Singapore Students' Union

SPOKESMAN
a; no. 1 1968—
Kuala Lumpur. U. Malaya

STAMFORD JOURNAL
m; vol. 1,no. 1 1969—

Singapore. Stamford College

SULOH NANTAH
ƥ; no. 1—24 1960—4
Singapore. English Society, Nanyang U.

TENGGARA
f; vol. 1,no. 1 1967—   Supplements 1968, 1969
Kuala Lumpur. Dept. of English, U. Malaya
eds. Lloyd Fernando and others

HL/U—1   LD/U—1: vol. 1,no. 1   LO/S26:
vol. 1,no. 2—6   LO/U—2: vol. 1,no. 4—6
LO/U14

TRAVELLERS' PALM
z(1 issue); vol. 1,no. 1 1967
Singapore
ed. P. M. Williams

TUMASEK
ƥ; no. 1—3 1964
Singapore

VARSITY
Kuala Lumpur. Students' Union, U. Malaya

WRITE
An independent student publication of the
University of Malaya
ƥ; no. 1—5 1957—8
Singapore

MEDITERRANEAN

Cyprus

Malta

ATHENAEUM MELITENSE
q; vol. 1,no. 1—4 1926—7
Malta

CYPRUS REVIEW
m; vol. 1,no. 1 1944—
Nicosia, Cyprus

LO/S65: vol. 6,no. 7— vol. 12,no. 2

CYPRUS TODAY
b; vol.1,no.1 1963—
Nicosia, Cyprus. Public Information Office

LO/S26: vol.1,no.5—   LO/U14

FERMENT
ϕ; no.1—7 1966—9
Malta

JOURNAL OF THE FACULTY OF ARTS:
ROYAL UNIVERSITY OF MALTA
ϕ; vol.1,no.1 1957—
Msida, Malta. Malta U.P.
ed. Prof. J. Aquilina

CB/U—1: vol.1,no.4—   LO/U—8: vol.2,no.1—
LO/U14

JOURNAL OF MALTESE STUDIES
ϕ; no.1 1961—
Malta

JOURNAL OF THE MALTA UNIVERSITY
LITERARY SOCIETY
ϕ; vol.1—5 1932—53
Msida, Malta

LINK
t; no.1—12 1948—54
Malta

MALTA PENNY MAGAZINE
w; vol.1—2 1839—41
Valletta, Malta

LO/S65

MEDITERRANEAN LITERARY REGISTER
ϕ; no.1—24 1827—8
Malta

MELITA
An English and Italian monthly periodical
m; vol.1—5 1921—5
Valletta, Malta

LO/S65

POEZIJA
ϕ; no.1 1971—
Malta. Malta Poetry Society, 8 Naxxar Rd., San
Gwann
ed. Victor Fenech and others

LO/S26

VALLETTA
Journal of literary and miscellaneous information
m; no.1—4 1838
Valletta, Malta

VITA NOVA
Review of literature, art and science in English
and Italian
ϕ; no.1—4 1901
Malta

NEW ZEALAND

A1 MAGAZINE
Gems of thought from noble thinkers, the bright-
est reading beneath the Southern Cross, the most
up to date prose imaginable
w; 1894
Wanganui

ACT
Incorporating New Zealand Theatre Federation
Magazine

q; vol.1,no.1 1967—
Wellington, P.O. Box 9441
ed. Laurie Atkinson

LO/T20

ANVIL
ϕ; no.1—2 1945—6
Auckland. Anvil Club

AOTEAN
New Zealand's national monthly fiction magazine
m; no.1 1927—?
Christchurch. Aotean Publishing Co.

ARACHNE
A literary journal
b; no.1—3 1950—1
Wellington. Literary Society, Victoria U. of
Wellington
Supersedes HILLTOP (q.v.)

LO/T20

ARENA
A literary magazine
b; 1943—75
Te Aro, Wellington. Box 6188
ed. Noel Farr Hoggard
ISSN 0004—0959

LD/U—1: no.44—   LO/U—2: no.2,5,7—8,61—
OX/U—1: no.70—

ARGOT
b; no.1—29 1969—72
Wellington. Students' Assn., Victoria U. of
Wellington
ISSN 0004—1130

LD/U—1: no.20   LO/U—2: no.16—29

ART IN NEW ZEALAND
q; vol.1,no.1— vol.17,no.6 1928—45
Wellington. Harry H. Tombs Ltd.
ed. C. A. Morris
Superseded by YEARBOOK OF THE ARTS IN
NEW ZEALAND (q.v.)

LO/N—1   LO/S65: vol.1,no.1, vol.2,no.6,
vol.3, vol.4,no.15—16, vol.5, vol.7—11, vol.13—15,
vol.16,no.1—2, vol.17,no.4—5   LO/T20:
vol.8,no.4, vol.10,no.2—3, vol.11,no.1—
vol.13,no.4, vol.14,no.4   OX/U—1

ARTS AND COMMUNITY
m; ?—1973
Taupo. Huka Falls Arts Centre, Wairakei Tourist
Park, Box 95

LO/T20: vol.5,no.5,7,10— vol.6,no.1,7,8,11,
vol.7,no.4,8, vol.8,no.2,7—9, vol.9,no.11,
vol.10,no.1,3—4

ATEA
b; no.1—3 1899
Wellington. Wesleyan Literary and Debating
Society
ed. J. W. Black

ATOM QUARTERLY
A magazine written and illustrated by the girls
of New Zealand
q; vol.1,no.1— vo..4,no.4 1899—1903
Auckland. Cannings, Queen St.
ed. Dora E. Moor

BOOK
b; no.1—9 1941—7
Christchurch. Caxton P.

LO/T20: no.9

BRIGHT
no.1 1941—?
Masterton

BROADSHEET
A miscellany of literary and general comments
b; no.1 1957—
Wellington
ed. Brian Bell

BROADSHEET
b; no.1 1973—
Auckland. Women's Liberation, P.O. Box 47—261

LO/U—2: no.6—

CANTERBURY UNIVERSITY COLLEGE
REVIEW
b; no.1—91 1897—1948
Christchurch. Students' Assn.

CAVE
Magazine of the arts
t; no.1—8 1972—4
Dunedin. P.O. Box 1458
ed. Trevor Reeves
Included a supplement, OUTRIGGER (q.v.)
Superseded by NEW QUARTERLY CAVE (q.v.)

LD/U—1: no.6—8   LO/U—2: no.1—4

CHAPBOOK
b; no.1—28 1944—50
Wellington. Chapbook Society
ed. Ronald B. Castle

LO/N—1: no.20—21

CHAPMAN'S NEW ZEALAND MONTHLY
MAGAZINE
Literary, scientific and miscellaneous
m; no.1—5 1862
Auckland. G. T. Chapman

COLONIST'S FAMILY HERALD
A journal for the instruction and amusement of

the people
w; vol.1,no.1– vol.3,no.69 1864–5
Wellington. Daily Southern Cross

COLOPHON
Miscellany from the Library School, Wellington
ƥ; no.1–3 1946
Wellington. National Library Service

COMMENT
A New Zealand quarterly review
q; no.1 1959–
Wellington. Comment Publishing Co., P.O. Box
1746
eds. Spiro Zavos and P. J. Downey
ISSN 0010–2555

LD/U–1: no.2,4,6–8,12–15,17–20,22–23,
25–42

CONSPECTUS
Annual publication of the Literary Club, Auckland
University College
ƥ; Issues unnumbered 1949, 1950, 1952, 1964
Auckland. Auckland U. Literary Club

CRITIC
A New Zealand journal of public opinion
e; vol.1–3 1923–4
Auckland. Critic Publishing Co.

CRUCIBLE
ƥ; no.1–4 1966–9
Auckland. P.O. Box 5574
ed. William Wilcox

LO/U–2

DRUM
Essays, criticism, comment
ƥ; no.1 1961–
Wellington
eds. K. Lawson and P. Craddock

DUNEDIN REVIEW
ƥ; vol.1–6 1882–6
Dunedin.
ed. J. G. S. Grant
Superseded by LITERARY MAGAZINE (q.v.)

EARWIG
The magazine with chomp
f; no.1 1969–   no.8 called 8½
Auckland. Earwig Graphics, 10 Norfolk St.
Auckland 2
ed. John Milne

LO/U–2

EDGE
t; vol.1,no.1–6 1971–3
Christchurch. P.O. Box 25042 Victoria St.
ed. D. S. Long
ISSN 0046–1253
Includes supplements EDGE NEWSLETTERS
and HOBSON'S BAY BROADSHEETS Superseded by HOBSON'S BAY BROADSHEET (q.v.)

LD/U–1   LO/U–2

EGRESS
z(1 issue); no.1 1946
Wellington
eds. Patrick Hayman and Hubert Witheford

ENTERPRISE
m; no.1–5 1935
Auckland

EST I ROM
z(1 issue); no.1 1955
Wellington. 42 Tiber St.
ed. D. G. Harris

EXPERIMENT
ƥ; no.1 1956–
Wellington. Literary Society, Victoria U. of
Wellington
ed. Renato Amato

LO/U–2: no.10–11,13

FERNFIRE
ƥ; no.1–14 1957–66
Auckland. Unity Writers
ed. Murray Gitos

LO/U–2: no.5–14

FRAGMENTS
ƥ; no.1 1970–
Christchurch. 18 Maxwell St.
ed. David Young

LO/U–2: 3 issues, no dates or numbering

FREED
ƥ; no.1–4 1969–71
Auckland. Students' Assn. Literary Society
eds. Alan Brunton, Jim Stevenson and M. D.
Edmond

LO/U–2

FRONTIERS
A magazine of the arts
ƥ; vol.1,no.1– vol.2,no.2 1968–70
Christchurch. P.O. Box 1659

ed. David Prescott

LO/U−2

GAUDEAMUS
An independent student journal
m; no.1−5 1951
Christchurch. Caxton P.

HERE AND NOW
An independent monthly review
m; vol.1,no.1− vol.4,no.4 1949−54
new series no.39−62 1954−7
Auckland. Pelorus P.

LO/N−1

HILLTOP
A literary magazine
b; no.1−3 1949
Wellington. Literary Society, Victoria U. of
Wellington
Superseded by ARACHNE (q.v.)

LO/N−1   LO/T20: no.3

HOBSON'S BAY BROADSHEET
Ɋ; no.1 1974−
Christchurch. Edge P., 161 Taylor's Mistake Rd.,
Christchurch 8
ISSN 0090−9300
Superseds EDGE (q.v.)

HUIA
A New Zealand annual
a; no.1 1903−?
Auckland
ed. Howard Kampe

HUTCHISON'S
New Zealand pioneer of general literature and
colonial progress
w; no.1−12 1866
Wanganui
ed. William Hutchison

IMAGE
Ɋ; no.1 1958−
Auckland. 5 Taumata Rd., Castor Bay
ed. Robert Thompson

LD/U−1: no.5−6   LO/T20: no.4−8

ISLANDS
A New Zealand quarterly of arts and letters
q; vol.1,no.1 1972−
Auckland. 4 Sealy Rd., Torbay, Auckland 10
ed. Robin Dudding

CA/U−1: vol.2,no.1−   ED/N−1

LD/U−1   LO/S26: vol.2,no.1−   LO/S65
LO/T20   LO/U−2   OX/U−1
SH/U−1: vol.2,no.1−

ISSUE
Ɋ; no.1−2 1952
Christchurch

KIWI
The magazine of the Auckland University College
a; 1905−11
Auckland
eds. C. K. Stead and R. R. Dyer

LANDFALL
A New Zealand quarterly
q; no.1 1947−
Christchurch. Caxton P., 119 Victoria St.
ed. Leo Bensemann
ISSN 0023−7930

BH/U−1   BT/U−1   CA/U−1
DR/U−1: no.11−   ED/U−1   EX/U−1:
no.18−   HL/U−1: no.1−17,23−
LD/U−1   LO/S26   LOS65   LO/T20
LO/U−1   LO/U−2: no.32−   LO/U−8:
no.18−   NR/U−1: no.28−   OX/U−1
SH/U−1: no.18−

LIPSYNC
Ɋ; no.1 1972−
Wellington. 40 Orangi-Kaupapa Rd.

LITERARY MAGAZINE
Ɋ; no.1−8 1885
Dunedin
ed. J. G. S. Grant
Supersedes DUNEDIN REVIEW (q.v.)

MAGAZINE
Ɋ; no.1−39 1945
Christchurch
ed. Dennis McEldowney

MAORILANDER
A weekly magazine
w; no.1−7 1901
Auckland

MATE
f; no.1 1957−
Wellington. Box 10153, The Terrace
ed. Alistair Paterson
ISSN 0025−5130

BH/U−1: no.12−   CA/U−1: no.12−
LD/U−1: no.4,6,12−14,16−   LO/S26: no.13−

LO/T20   LO/U−1: no.2−   LO/U−2
OX/U−1: no.12−

MIRROR MAGAZINE
z(1 issue); no.1 1910
Christchurch

MONOCLE
The New Zealand monthly magazine
m; vol.1,no.1− vol.3,no.4 1937−9
Wellington

NEW ARGOT
m; vol.1,no.1 1973−
Wellington. New Zealand U. Students' Assn.,
1 Marion St.

LO/U−2: vol.1,no.1

NEW NATION
A monthly journal of public affairs, art and
literature
m; vol.1,no.1− vol.2,no.6 1924−5
Wellington. New Nation Publishing Co.

NEW QUARTERLY CAVE
An international review of arts and ideas
q; no.1 1975−
Hamilton. Outrigger Publishers Ltd., 1 von
Tempsky St.
ed. Norman Simms
ISSN 0110−0076
Supersedes CAVE (q.v.) See also OUTRIGGER

NEW TRIAD
m; vol.1no.1− vol.3,no.4 1937−42
Wellington
ed. N. F. Hoggard
Supersedes SPILT INK (q.v.)

NEW ZEALAND BEST POEMS
a; 1932−43
Wellington. Harry H. Tombs Ltd.

LO/T20: 1939, 1943

NEW ZEALAND BOOKWORLD
b; no.1 1973−
Wellington, P.O. Box 9405
ed. William Riley

LO/T20

NEW ZEALAND FORTNIGHTLY REVIEW
e; no.1−6 1933
Auckland

NEW ZEALAND ILLUSTRATED ANNUAL
a; 1880−1

Christchurch
ed. M. Mosley

NEW ZEALAND ILLUSTRATED MAGAZINE
m; vol.1,no.1− vol.12,no.6 1899−1905
Auckland
ed. Thomas Cottle

LO/S65: vol.1−9

NEW ZEALAND MAGAZINE
q; vol.1,no.1−2 1850
Wellington. W. E. Vincent & Co.
ed. W. E. Grimstone

LO/N−1

NEW ZEALAND MERCURY
m; vol.1,no.1− vol.3,no.12 1933−6
Wellington
ed. Helen Longford

NEW ZEALAND MONTHLY REVIEW
m
Christchurch. Monthly Review Society, P.O. Box
345

NEW ZEALAND NEW WRITING
a; no.1−4 1942−5
Wellington. Progressive Publishing Society,
P.O. Box 956
ed. Ian A. Gordon

LO/T20

NEW ZEALAND POETRY YEARBOOK
b; no.1−11 1951−64
Wellington. Pegasus P., P.O. Box 2836
ed. Louis Johnson

LO/N−1   LO/T20   OX/U−1

NEW ZEALAND QUARTERLY REVIEW
And magazine of general and local literature
q; no.1−3 1857
Wellington. New Zealand Spectator

LO/N−1: no.1−2

**NEW ZEALAND UNIVERSITIES ARTS
FESTIVAL YEARBOOK**
z(1 issue); 1969
Dunedin. New Zealand Universities Arts Festival
Committee
eds. Bill Manhire and John Dickson

LD/U−1

NEW ZEALAND UNIVERSITIES' LITERARY
YEARBOOK
ƅ; 1960–
Christchurch. New Zealand Arts Festival Committee
ed. Florence Jones

LD/U–1: 1960   LO/U–2: 1972

NEW ZEALAND VERSE
z(1 issue); no.1 1934
Oamaru. Handcraft P.

NEW ZEALAND WOMEN WRITERS' SOCIETY
BULLETIN
ƅ
Wellington. 2 Carlton Flats, 243 The Terrace

NEW ZEALAND WRITER AND DRAMATIST
z(1 issue); no.1 1934
Wellington. Bryant Duplicating Bureau

NUCLEUS
ƅ; no.1 1957–
Auckland. Dobbic P.
eds. W. Curnow and P. Crookes

LO/U–2

NUMBERS
A quarterly review
ƅ; vol.1,no.1– vol.3,no.2 1954–9
Wellington
eds. J. K. Baxter, Charles Doyle and Louis Johnson

LD/U–1   LO/N–1   LO/T20: vol.1,no.1–
vol.2,no.2

ORIFLAMME
z(1 issue); no.1 1933
Christchurch. Caxton P.
Superseded by SIROCCO (q.v.)

ORIFLAMME
A literary journal of youth and the fine arts
q; vol.1,no.1– vol.2,no.4 1939–42
Wellington

ORPHEUS
ƅ
Mount Roskill
ed. Stephen Chan

LO/U–2: no.4

OTAGO UNIVERSITY REVIEW
ƅ; 1888–1954

Dunedin. Students' Assn., Otago U.
Superseded by REVIEW 1954– (q.v.)

OUTLINE
ƅ; no.1 1959–
Auckland. Pilgrim P.
eds. Denis Taylor and R. M. S. Tudehope

OUTRIGGER
b; no.1–9 1974–6
Hamilton. Outrigger Publishers, 1 von Tempsky St.
Published as a supplementary series to CAVE (q.v.)
and NEW QUARTERLY CAVE (q.v.)

LD/U–1: no.1–5,8–9

PENNY JOURNAL
w; vol.1,no.1– vol.2,no.61 1866–7
Auckland. Mitchell and Seffern

PHOENIX
A quarterly magazine published by the Literary
Club of Auckland University College
q; vol.1,no.1– vol.2,no.2 1932–3
Auckland

PILGRIM OF THE ARTS
t; vol.1,no.1 1976–
Christchurch. Pilgrim South P.

PLASTIC
z(1 issue); no.1 1970
Christchurch. Literary Society, Canterbury U.
Supersedes TROUBADOUR (q.v.)

LO/U–2

POETRY NEW ZEALAND
ƅ; no.1 1970–
Christchurch. Pegasus P.
ed. Frank McKay

LD/U–1   LO/T20   LO/U–2

QUILL
The magazine of the New Zealand Women Writers'
and Artists' Society
ƅ; no.1–4 1934–48
Auckland

RED FUNNEL
m; vol.1,no.1– vol.9,no.3 1905–9
Dunedin. Union Steam Ship Co.

LO/S65: vol.1–5

REVIEW
z(1 issue); no.1 1939

Wellington. John O'London Literary Club
ed. M. S. Butterton

REVIEW
a; 1954—
Dunedin. Students' Assn., Otago U.
Supersedes OTAGO UNIVERSITY REVIEW (q.v.)

LD/U—1: 1975   LO/U—2: 1971

SALIENT
An organ of student opinion at Victoria University
b; no.1—3 1952—5
Wellington

SATURDAY REVIEW
b; no.1—119 1864—71
Dunedin
ed. J. G. S. Grant

SIROCCO
z(1 issue); no.1 1933
Christchurch. Caxton P.
Supersedes ORIFLAMME (q.v.)

SOUTHERN
Monthly magazine
m; vol.1,no.1— vol.5,no.6 1863—6
Auckland. Creighton and Scales
eds. D. Giles and H. H. Lusk

SPILT INK
A journal issued in the interests of New Zealand
writers
b; vol.1,no.1— vol.4,no.8 1932—7
Auckland
ed. N. F. Hoggard
Superseded by NEW TRIAD (q.v.)

TOM BRACKEN'S ANNUAL
a; 1896—7
Wellington

TRIAD
A monthly magazine of music, science and art
m; no.1—34 1893—1937
Dunedin

TROUBADOUR
z(1 issue); 1969
Christchurch. Literary Society, Canterbury U.
Superseded by PLASTIC (q.v.)

LO/U—2

VERBATIM
z(1 issue); no.1 1955
Christchurch. Caxton P. Literary Club,
Canterbury U.

VERSE
A quarterly
q; no.1—12 1935—8
Otaki

VERSE
f; 1950—?
Wellington

VERSE ALIVE
a; no.1—2 1936—7
Christchurch. Caxton P.
ed. H. Winston Rhodes and Denis Glover

LO/T20

VIEW
An independent journal for free men
m; vol.1,no.1— vol.2,no.10 1940—2
Christchurch

WEEKLY BUDGET
A journal devoted to literature and the discussion
of social and political questions
z(1 issue); no.1 1886
Auckland

WOODEN HORSE
A literary magazine of New Zealand interest
q; vol.1,no.1— vol.2,no.4 1950—4
Christchurch
ed. C. R. Allen

YEARBOOK OF THE ARTS IN NEW ZEALAND
a; no.1—7 1945—51
Wellington
Supersedes ART IN NEW ZEALAND (q.v.)

LO/N—1: no.2—7   LO/T20   OX/U—9:
no.2—7

YOUNG WRITER
m; no.1—3 1953—4
Auckland. 47 Canal Road, Avondale

YOUTH WRITES
b; 1973—
Wellington. 182 Wakefield St.
ed. Marcia Kirsten

ZEALANDIA
A monthly magazine of general New Zealand
literature by New Zealand authors
m; vol.1,no.1—12 1889—90
Dunedin
ed. William Freeman

LO/S65

PACIFIC ISLANDS

Fiji

Papua New Guinea

FOCUS
ƀ
Boroko, Papua New Guinea. New Guinea News
Service, P.O. Box 5050

GIGIBORI
f; vol.1,no.1 1974—
Boroko, Papua New Guinea. Institute of Papua
New Guinea Studies, Ningini P., P.O. Box 1432
ed. Ulli Beier

KIVUNG
t; vol.1,no.1 1968—
Boroko, Papua New Guinea. Linguistic Society
of the U. Papua New Guinea, P.O. Box 1140
ed. John Lynch
ISSN 0023—1959

KOVAVE
A journal of New Guinea literature
f; vol.1,no.1— vol.5,no.1 1969—75   Preceded
by a 'pilot issue'
Queensland, Australia. Cultural Centre of the
U. Papua New Guinea, Jacaranda P., 65 Park Road,
Milton, Qld. 4064
eds. Apisai Enos and Kama Kerpie
ISSN 0023—4303

LO/S26: vol.3,no.1— vol.5,no.1   LO/U—2

MANA ANNUAL OF CREATIVE WRITING
a; 1930—75
Sydney, Australia. South Pacific Creative Arts
Society, Pacific Publications
Produced as a supplement to PACIFIC ISLANDS
MONTHLY (q.v.)
Superseded by MANA REVIEW (q.v.)
For holdings see PACIFIC ISLANDS MONTHLY

MANA REVIEW
ƀ; vol.1,no.1 1976—
Suva, Fiji. South Pacific Creative Arts Society,
P.O. Box 5083
Supersedes MANA ANNUAL OF CREATIVE
WRITING (q.v.)

LO/N—1   LO/S26

NEW GUINEA WRITING
See PAPUA NEW GUINEA WRITING

PACIFIC ISLANDS MONTHLY
m; vol.1,no.1 1930—
Sydney, Australia. Pacific Publications, P.O.
Box 3408
Contains writing supplement, MANA (q.v.)

LO/N—1: vol.21,no.6—   LO/S26: vol.28,no.2—
LO/S65: vol.7,no.1—   LO/U—8: vol.35,no.1—
OX/U—9

PAPUA NEW GUINEA WRITING
q; no.1 1970—
Konedobu, Papua New Guinea. Literature
Bureau, P.O. Box 2312
ed. Jack Lahui
Previously NEW GUINEA WRITING

LD/U—1

SPAN
Newsletter of the South Pacific Association for
Commonwealth Literature and Language Studies
f; no.1 1975—
Brisbane. South Pacific Assn. for Commonwealth
Literature and Language Studies, U. Queensland
ed. Chris Tiffen
ISSN 0313—1459

LO/S26

SOUTH ASIA

General

AFRO-ASIAN WRITINGS
ƿ; vol.1,no.1−4 1967−70
Cairo, Egypt. Permanent Bureau of Afro-Asian
Writers, 104 Kasr el Aini St.
Superseded by LOTUS (q.v.)

LO/S26   LO/U14

JOURNAL OF SOUTH ASIAN LITERATURE
q; vol.9,no.1 1973−
East Lansing, Michigan, U.S.A. Asian Studies
Center, Michigan State U., 101 International
Center, East Lansing, Michigan 48824
ISSN 0025−0503
Supersedes MAHFIL (q.v.)

HL/U−1   LO/S26   LO/U14

LOTUS
Afro-Asian writings
q; no.1 1971−
Cairo, Egypt. Permanent Bureau of Afro-Asian
Writers, 104 Kasr el Aini St.
ed. Youssef El Sebai
ISSN 0002−0664
Supersedes AFRO-ASIAN WRITINGS (q.v.)

LO/S26: no.1−16   LO/U14

MAHFIL
A quarterly of South Asian Literature
q; vol.1,no.1 − vol.8,no.4 1964−72
East Lansing, Michigan, U.S.A. Asian Studies
Center, Michigan State U., 101 International
Center, East Lansing, Michigan 48824
ISSN 0025−0503
Superseded by JOURNAL OF SOUTH ASIAN
LITERATURE (q.v.)

HL/U−1   LO/S26: vol.5,no.1−2
LO/U14

Bangladesh
(formerly East Pakistan)

BANGLA ACADEMY JOURNAL

f; vol.4,no.1 1973−
Dacca. Bangla Academy, Burdwan House, Dacca, 2.
ed. Mazharul Islam
Supersedes BENGALI ACADEMY JOURNAL
(q.v.)

LO/S26

BENGALI ACADEMY JOURNAL
f; vol.1,no.1 − vol.3,no.2 1970−2
Dacca. Bengali Academy, Burdwan House, Dacca, 2
ed. Dr. Neelima Ibrahim
Superseded by BANGLA ACADEMY JOURNAL
(q.v.)

LO/S26

DACCA UNIVERSITY STUDIES PART A
ƿ; 1935−
Dacca. Library, Dacca U.

BH/U−1   LD/U−1: vol.1,no.1, vol.7,no.2
LO/N12   LO/U−1   LO/U14

LIFE AND LIGHT
A rational quarterly in English
q; vol.1,no.1 1964−
Dacca. Turun Bangladesh Publishers, 5 Purana
Paltan
ed. M. Rahman

NEW VALUES
ƿ; c.1960s
Dacca. Dacca U.

SCHOLAR
q; vol.1,no.1 1970−
Chittagong. 1 Nizam Rd.
ed. Anwar Nasreen
ISSN 0036−6323

India

General

AAVESH
A rejoinder of writings by Indian youth biased

to liberated thinking
f; no.1 1968—
New Delhi. 62–3 Rajendra Nague, New Delhi 5
ed. Ramesh Bakshi
ISSN 0001–3064

ADVENT
q; no.1 1944—
Pondicherry. Sri Aurobindo Ashram

DR/U–4: no.4 1947—

ARTIST
a; no.1–2 1971–2
Calcutta. 26 Doctor Lane, Calcutta 14
ed. A. Paul Ahibhusan Malik

ARYAN PATH
m; vol.1,no.1 1930—
Bombay. Theosophy Hall, 40 New Marine Lines,
Bombay 400020
ed. Sophia Wadia

CA/U–1   ED/N–1   LO/N12: vol.1,no.2–
LO/U–1: vol.1–12   LO/U–2: vol.26,no.8,10,
vol.27,no.1,3–4   LO/U14: vol.1,no.3–6,12
OX/U–1

ASIATIC OBSERVER
Or religious, literary and philosophical miscellany
q; vol.1,no.1 – vol.2,no.4 1823–4
Calcutta. Baptist Mission P.

LO/N–1   LO/S65: vol.1

ASIATICK MISCELLANY
q; vol.1–2 1785–6
Calcutta
ed. Daniel Stuart
Superseded by NEW ASIATIC MISCELLANY (q.v.)

CA/U–1   LO/N–1   LO/S65: vol.1
LO/U14   OX/U–1

ASSAM ACADEMY REVIEW
q; vol.1,no.1 1961—
Gauhati, Assam. Assam Academy for Cultural
Relations

AVENUES
A monthly of trends and ideas
m; vol.1,no.1 1968—
New Delhi. Gondals P.

BANASTHALI PATRIKA
q; no.1 1957?—
Banasthali, Rajasthan. Banasthali Vidyapith
ed. Rameshwar Gupta

LD/U–1: no.12–17/18

BENARES MAGAZINE
ƥ; vol.1,no.1– vol.8,no.2 1848–53
Calcutta. Thacker & Co., Orphan School P.

LO/N12   OX/U–1: vol.1,no.5– vol.8,no.2
(lacks vol.1,no.6– vol.2,no.1, vol.7)

BENGAL ANNUAL
A literary keepsake
a; 1830–6
Calcutta. Samuel Smith & Co.
ed. David Lester Richardson

ED/U–1: 1830   LO/N–1: (lacks 1832–3)
OX/U–1: 1834

BENGAL MAGAZINE
w; vol.1,no.1–126 1872–3
Calcutta. Esplanade Row
ed. Revd. Lal Behari Day

LO/N–1   LO/N12

BENGAL REVIEW
m; vol.1,no.1–12 1905
Calcutta
ed. Shumbhoo Chunder Dey

LO/N–1: vol.1,no.1–3   LO/N12: vol.1,
no.2–12

BENGALI LITERATURE
q; no.1 1966—
Calcutta. 53 Bidhan Polli, Jadavpur, Calcutta – 32.
ed. Ashis Sanyal
ISSN 0005–8815

BHAVAN'S JOURNAL
e; vol.1,no.1 1954—
Bombay. Bharatiya Vidya Bhavan, Kulapati
K. M. Munshi Marg, Bombay 400007.
ed. S. Ramakrishnan
ISSN 0006–0518

LO/S26 (keeps 1 year temporary file)

BHUBANESWAR REVIEW
f; no.1 1968—
Bhubaneswar, Orissa. Type Va, 10–4 Asoka
Nagar, Bhubaneswar–1.
ed. Sitakanta Mohapatra
ISSN 0006–0534

LD/U–1: no.1

BLITZ
w; no.1 1941—
Bombay. 17–17 H. Cowasji Patel St., Fort
Bombay, 1

ed. R. K. Karanjia
ISSN 0006—4882

BOMBAY MISCELLANY
m; vol.1,no.1— vol.5,no.30 1860—3
Bombay. Chesson & Woodhall
also called CHESSON AND WOODHALL'S
MISCELLANY

LO/N—1   OX/U—1

BOMBAY QUARTERLY REVIEW
q; vol.1,no.1— vol.7,no.14 1855—8
Bombay. Smith, Taylor & Co.

LO/N—1   LO/N12: vol.1,no.1— vol.3,no.12
OX/U—1   QL/P—1

BOMBAY MONTHLY TIMES
m; 1842—5
Bombay
Superseded by BOMBAY TIMES (q.v.)

LO/N—1

BOMBAY TIMES
Bi-monthly summary of intelligence
b; 1845—57
Bombay

LO/N—1

CALCUTTA CHRISTIAN ADVOCATE
1839—51
Calcutta

CALCUTTA JOURNAL
Or political, commercial and literary gazette
1818—24
Calcutta

ED/P—1: no.1—2

CALCUTTA LITERARY GAZETTE
A journal of belles-lettres, etc.
vol.1—10 1824—34
Calcutta

LO/N—1: vol.9—10

CALCUTTA LITERARY GLEANER
m; vol.1—2 1842—4
Calcutta

AD/U—1

CALCUTTA MAGAZINE
A journal of literature, politics, science and the
arts
m; vol.1,no.1— vol.6,no.2 1873—8

Calcutta
ed. Owen Aratoon

LO/N12

CALCUTTA MAGAZINE AND MISCELLANY
1814—5
Calcutta

CALCUTTA MAGAZINE AND MONTHLY
REGISTER
m; vol.1—4 1830—2
Calcutta. Samuel Smith & Co., Hare St.

LO/N—1   LO/N12: vol.1—3

CALCUTTA MONTHLY
A monthly review devoted to literary, scientific,
social, moral and sporting subjects
m; vol.1—4 1896—9
Calcutta. Mohammedan Sporting Club

LO/N—1: vol.1,no.1—6, vol.2,no.1—7, vol.3,
no.10—12, vol.4,no.4—9   LO/N12: vol.1,
no.3,6, vol.2,no.1—2,no.4—7, vol.3,no.10—
vol.4,no.2

CALCUTTA MONTHLY JOURNAL
m; vol.1—?   new series vol.1—4   3rd series
vol.1—7 1795—1841
Calcutta
LO/N—1: no.41—51,64—75,242,248,250—253,
268—428;   new series vol.3—4;   3rd series
(lacks 1837)

CARAVAN
The fortnightly of national resurgence
e; 1940—
New Delhi. Delhi P., E—3 Jhandewala Estate,
New Delhi 110055
ed. Vishwa Nath
ISSN 0008—6150

CENTURY REVIEW
q/m; vol.1,no.1— vol.8,no.30 1915—22
Calcutta
eds. N. C. Lebarry and J. J. Campos

LO/N—1: vol.1,no.1— vol.6,no.2   LO/N12

CHAMELEON
þ; no.1—4 1872—3
Mirzapor. Orphan School P.

LO/N12

CHARIOT
q; no.1 1972—
Cuttack, Orissa
ed. Shushil K. Patnaik

CHESSON AND WOODHALL'S MISCELLANY
See BOMBAY MISCELLANY

COMMONWEALTH QUARTERLY
A journal devoted mainly to Commonwealth
literature and Indian regional literatures
q; vol.1,no.1 1976—
Mysore. 2823 VIII Cross, V. V. Mohalla, Mysore 2
eds. S. N. Vikramraj Urs and Madhav Kulkarni

LO/S26

CONCORD
A monthly review
m; vol.1,no.1 1887—?
Calcutta. Concord Club, 8 Krishna Singhee's Lane
ed. Kali Chari Banurji

LO/N12: vol.1,no.1—6

CONFLUX
m; 1969—
New Delhi

CONSPECTUS
z(1 issue): vol.1,no.1 1965
New Delhi. India International Centre

BH/U—1

CONTEMPORARY INDIAN LITERATURE
m; vol.1,no.1 1961—75
New Delhi. H328 Narayana, New Delhi 28
ed. E. Lakshman Shastry
ISSN 0045—8333

CULTURAL FORUM
q; vol.1,no.1— vol.15,no.4 1958—75
New Delhi. Ministry of Cultural Affairs, Government of India
ISSN 0011—2852

CB/U—1: vol.10,no.3— vol.15,no.4
LO/U14: vol.4,no.1— vol.15,no.4

CULTURAL MEET
q; 1958—
Delhi

CULTURAL NEWS FROM INDIA
q; vol.1,no.1 1960—
New Delhi. Indian Council for Cultural Relations,
Azad Bhavan, Indraprastha Estate
ed. A. Srinivasan
ISSN 0011—2887
DR/U—4: vol.3,no.1— vol.4,no.6   ED/N—1:
vol.3,no.7— vol.4,no.6   LO/N12
LO/S65: vol.1,no.1— vol.4,no.5   LO/U14:

vol.1,no.4, vol.2,no.1,3,5, vol.3,no.1— vol.4,no.6
OX/U—1: vol.3,no.7— vol.4,no.6

DAMN YOU
A magazine of the arts
m; no.1 1965—
Allahabad, U. P. 37 Balrampur House, Allahabad—2
ISSN 0011—5940

LO/U—2: no.4,6

DEBONAIR
Diwana parody
m; 1974—
Bombay
A parody of DIWANA TEJ MONTHLY (q.v.)

DHARA
ɓ; vol.1,no.1 1966—
Delhi. Dhara Pubs., 88 Gupta Colony
ed. R. S. Yadav
ISSN 0012—1738

LD/U—1: vol.1,no.3   LO/S26: vol.1,no.2,
vol.2,no.3

DIONYSUS
ɓ; vol.1,no.1 1965—
Bombay. 96 Penso Villa, Dr. M. Raut Rd.,
Bombay 28
eds. S. V. Pradhan and A. S. Benjamin

DIWANA TEJ MONTHLY
m; 1970—5
New Delhi. Daily Tej Pvt. Ltd., 8—B Bahadurshah
Zafar Marg, New Delhi, 1
ed. V. B. Gupta

DRIFT
w; 1967—
Calcutta. Drift Publications, P—1 Hide Lane,
Calcutta 12
ed. N. K. Mitra
ISSN 0012—6217

EAST AND WEST
A monthly review
m; vol.1,no.1— vol.21,no.18 1901—21
Bombay
ed. Sardar Jogendra Singh

LO/N—1   LO/N12   OX/U—1: vol.1,no.1—
vol.13,no.1

EAST AND WEST
A quarterly of literature
q; vol.1,no.1 1956—
Secunderabad, A. P.

ed. Rayapral

LO/U—2: vol.1,no.2—3   OX/U—1

EQUALS ONE
z(1 issue); no.1 1969
Pondicherry. Aurobindo Society, Pondicherry
605002
eds. Medhananda and Maude Pickett Smith
ISSN 0013—9815

LO/U—2

FREEDOM FIRST
m; 1954
Bombay

GANDHI MARG (ENGLISH EDITION)
q; no.1 1957—
New Delhi. Gandhi Peace Foundation, 221/223
Deen Dayal Upadhyaya Marg, New Delhi 110002.
ed. T. K. Mahadevan
ISSN 0016—4437

HARMONY
s; no.1 1968—
Bhubaneswar, Orissa

HELICON
m; 1971—
Calcutta. 10—3c Nepal Bhattacharya St., Calcutta
26
eds. Jyotirmoy Chatterjee and Suddha Sattwa Bovt

HINDOOSTANEE INTELLIGENCER AND
ORIENTAL ANTHOLOGY
m; no.1—14 1801—2
Calcutta

LO/N—1: no.1—4   LO/U14

HINDU COMMENTATOR
1867—73
Calcutta

HINDU PIONEER
m; no.1—7 1835—6
eds. Kylas Chandra Dutta and Bhuvan Mohan Mitra

HINDUSTAN REVIEW
þ; vol.1,no.1 1900—
Patna, Bihar
ed. Sachchidananda Sinha

LO/N12: vol.3—87   LO/S65: vol.21,no.1—
vol.89,no.568 (incomplete)   LO/U14: vol.67—

ILLUSTRATED WEEKLY OF INDIA
w; vol.1,no.1 1880—

New Delhi. 7 Bahadurshah Zafar Marg
ed. Khushwant Singh
ISSN 0019—2430

LO/N—1: vol.57,no.30;   LO/S26: Literary
articles retained from vol.97,no.1—

IMPRINT
The best of reading every month
m; vol.1,no.1 1961—
Bombay. Business P., Surya Mahal, 5 Burjorji
Bharucha Marg, Bombay 400023
ed. R. V. Pandit
ISSN 0019—3046

INDIA
m; 1944—
Calcutta

INDIA
q; vol.1,no.1 1952—
New Delhi

INDIAN HORIZONS
q; vol.21,no.1 1972—
New Delhi. Indian Council for Cultural Relations,
Azad Bhavan, Indraprastha Estate, New Delhi
110001
ed. A. Srinivasan
Supersedes INDO-ASIAN CULTURE (q.v.)

LO/N12   LO/S26   LO/U14
OX/U—1

INDIAN INK
being splashes from various pens in aid of the
Imperial Indian War Fund
a; 1914—18
Calcutta
ed. Everard Digby

LO/S65: 1915—18   LO/U14: 1915—16

INDIAN LITERARY REVIEW
m; vol.1,no.1 1930—
Bombay. D. B. Taraporevala Sons & Co.
also called TARAPOREVALA'S INDIAN
LITERARY REVIEW

LO/N—1: vol.11,no.8— vol.12,no.3,8, vol.13,
no.2,4— vol.14,no.3,6—7, vol.15,no.4—9,11—13,
vol.16,no.2—   OX/U—1: vol.1,no.1—2

INDIAN LITERATURE
q; vol.1,no.1 1957—
New Delhi. Sahitya Akademi (National Academy
of Letters), Rabindra Bhavan, New Delhi 11001
ISSN 0019—5804

CA/U—1: vol.1,no.2—   CB/U—1: vol.13,no.1—

ED/U−1   LO/N12   LO/S26: vol.11,no.4
LO/U14   OX/U−1: vol.10,no.1−

INDIAN P.E.N.
b; vol.1,no.1 1934−
Bombay. P.E.N. All-India Centre, Theosophy Hall,
40 New Marine Lines, Bombay 400020
ed. Madame Sophia Wadia
ISSN 0019−6053

LD/U−1: vol.25,no.1− vol.40,no.1
LO/N12: vol.16−   ST/U−1: vol.40−

INDIAN REVIEW
Devoted to the discussion of all topics of interest
m; vol.1,no.1 1900−
Madras. Manian Natesan, 2−A Cathedral Rd.,
Madras 86
ed. M. C. Subhramanyam
ISSN 0019−6304

LO/N−1   LO/N12: vol.6,no.1− vol.43,no.6,
vol.51,no.1−   LO/S65: vol.6,no.12− vol.43
(incomplete)   LO/U14: vol.37,no.12−
vol.46,no.12   OX/U−1: vol.1−8 (incomplete)

INDIAN REVIEW
Containing the cream of current literature
q; vol.1,no.1− vol.7,no.39 1883−6
Calcutta. W. H. Targett
eds. F. J. Rowe and W. T. Webb

LO/N12

INDIAN WRITING
A quarterly
b; vol.1,no.1−4 1940−1   2nd series no.5 1942
London, U.K.
eds. I. Singh and others

CA/U−1   ED/N−1   LO/N−1
OX/U−1

INDIAN WRITING TODAY
A quarterly devoted to significant writing in
India
q; no.1−18 1967−71
Bombay. Nirmala-Sadanand Publishers, 35c
Tardeo Rd., Bombay 400034
eds. Sadanand G. Bhatkal and Prabhakar Padhye
ISSN 0019−6584

CA/U−1   DR/U−4: no.4,9−11,16,18
LD/U−1: no.2−6   LO/S26: no.3−18
LO/U14: no.2−18   OX/U−1

INDO-ASIAN CULTURE
a; no.1−20 1952−71
New Delhi. Indian Council for Cultural Relations

Superseded by INDIAN HORIZONS (q.v.)

LD/U−1: no.10,12,16−20   LO/N12: no.4−20
LO/S26: no.20   LO/S65: no.8−11
LO/U14   OX/U−1

INTELLECTUALS' RENDEZVOUS
m; no.1 1976−
New Delhi. Heritage Publishers, M−116 Connaught Circus, New Delhi 11001

JOURNAL OF INDIAN WRITING IN ENGLISH
A bi-annual devoted to creative and critical writing
in English
f; vol.1,no.1 1973−
Gulbarga, Mysore. Dept. of English, Post-Graduate
Centre, Gulbarga 585105
ed. G. S. Balarama Gupta

LD/U−1: vol.1,no.2   LO/N12   SH/U−1
LO/S26: vol.4,no.2−

KURINJI QUARTERLY
q; no.1 1973−
Calcutta. 536 Raja Basantha Roy Road
ed. M. Srinivasan

LITERARY PERSPECTIVES
b; no.1 1962−
Bombay. Asia Publishing House

LITERARY REVIEW
q; vol.1,no.1−4 1974
Niralanagar, Lucknow

LITERARY STUDIES
A quarterly review of literature and criticism
from the Punjab
q; vol.1,no.1 1970−
Patiala, Punjab. Razdan House, Sirhindi Darwaza
ed. Brij M. Razdan
ISSN 0024−4600

LORE
Magazine of new writing
m; no.1 1974−
New Delhi. Rami P., 48 Mandirwali Gali, Yusof Sarai
ed. M. C. Bose

MADRAS MISCELLANY
m; no.1−9 1839−40
Madras. Athenaeum P.
ed. J. B. Pharoah

LO/N12

MAHASHTRA PARICHAYA
q; no.1 1968−

New Delhi. Maharashtra Information Centre,
A—8 State Emporia Bldg.
ISSN 0025—0473

MAHRATTA
w; 1881—?
Poona, Maharashtra

MALABAR QUARTERLY REVIEW
q; vol. 1—10 1902—11
Ernakulam, Kerala
Superseded by MONTHLY REVIEW (q.v.)

LO/N—1: vol.4—5, vol.7,no.2— vol.10

MARCH OF INDIA
ƥ; vol.1,no.1— vol.15,no.9 1947—63
Delhi. United Publications

LO/N—1   LO/N12: vol.2,no.2— vol.15,no.9
LO/S65: vol.1,no.1

MINIMAX
Quarterly of creative and critical writing in English
q
Delhi. K—5/8 Model Town, Delhi 110009
ed. Durgadas Mukhopadhyay

MIRA
A monthly journal of Indian culture
m; 1933—?
Poona, Maharashtra. 10 Sadha Vaswani Rd.,
Poona 1
ed. Gangaram Sajandas
ISSN 0026—5780

MODERN REVIEW
A monthly review and miscellany
ƥ; vol.1,no.1 1907—
Calcutta. Prabasi P. Private Ltd., 77—2—1
Dharamtala St.
ed. Ashoke Chatterjee
ISSN 0026—8380

DR/U—4: vol.35,no.6—   LD/U—1: vol.62,
no.3—4, vol.65,no.2—5, vol.66,no.1,3
LO/N—1: vol.3,no.5—   LO/N12: vol.5,no.1—
vol.80,no.6 (incomplete), vol.81,no.1—
LO/S65: vol.1,no.1— vol.4,no.12, vol.7,no.1—
vol.8,no.12, vol.10,no.1— vol.15,no.12
LO/U14: 1922—   OX/U—1: vol.21,no.2—

MODERN WORLD
A monthly devoted to politics, science, literature,
art and philosophy
m; vol.1,no.1— vol.7,no.1 1911—4
Madras
ed. V. Mangalvedkar

LO/N—1   LO/N12: vol.1,no.1—4
LO/S65: vol.4,no.4—5

MONTHLY REVIEW
m; vol.11,no.1— vol.14,no.3 1911—5
Trivandram, Kerala
ed. Ramananda Chatterjee
Supersedes MALABAR QUARTERLY REVIEW
(q.v.)

LO/N—1   LO/N12

MOOKERJEE'S MAGAZINE
Of politics, sociology, literature, art and science
ƥ; vol.1—5 1861   new series vol.1,no.1— vol.5,
no.40 1872—6
Calcutta

CA/U—1: n.s. vol.1,no.1— vol.5,no.40
LO/N—1: vol.1,3—5, n.s. vol.1,no.1— vol.5,no.40
LO/N12: n.s. vol.1,no.1— vol.4,no.30

MOTHER INDIA
Review of culture
m; vol.1,no.1 1948—
Pondicherry. Sri Aurobindo Ashram Trust,
Pondicherry 605002
ed. K. D. Sethna
ISSN 0027—1543

NATIONAL MAGAZINE
A monthly magazine
m; vol.1,no.1— vol.2,no.12 1875—6
Calcutta

LO/N12

NEW ASIATIC MISCELLANY
a; vol.1 1789
Calcutta
ed. Daniel Stuart
Supersedes ASIATIC MISCELLANY (q.v.)

CA/U—1   LO/N—1

NEW ERA
m; vol.1,no.1— vol.2,no.2 1928—9
Madras

LO/N12

NEW LITERATURE
ƥ; 1962—
Delhi

NEW REVIEW
A Catholic journal
m; vol.1,no.1— vol.32 1935—50
Calcutta
ed. M. Ledrus

CA/U–1: vol.1,no.1– vol.5,no.2, vol.16,no.5–6, vol.17,no.1– vol.32   ED/N–1: vol.1,no.1– vol.5,no.2   LO/N–1   LO/N12: vol.1, no.1– vol.24,no.144   OX/U–1

OPINION LITERARY QUARTERLY
q; no.1–4 1973–4
Bombay. 'Purnima', 40C Ridge Rd., Bombay 400006

ORIENT
An Anglo-Indian monthly magazine of politics, literature, science and art
m; vol.1,no.1– vol.4,no.4 1881–6
Bombay

LO/N–1   LO/N12

ORIENT PEARL
a; 1835
Calcutta. T. Ostell
ed. W. Kirkpatrick

LO/N–1   LO/N12

ORIENTAL MISCELLANY
A monthly journal of politics, literature, science and arts
m; vol.1,no.1– vol.5,no.6 1879–83
Calcutta

LO/N–1: vol.1,no.3–4,6   LO/N12

ORIENTAL THOUGHT
q; vol.1,no.1 1954–
Nasik, Maharashtra

OX/U–1

PALM LEAVES
A monthly magazine
m; vol.1,no.1– vol.2,no.15 1873–4
Calcutta. Baptist Mission P.
ed. G. H. Rouse

LO/N12

PHAROS
b
New Delhi. J5–79 Rajouri Gardens
eds. Pradip Madan and Karuwarjit Singh

PPHOO
Intercontinental
þ; 1969–
Calcutta
ed. Pradip Chowdhuri

LO/U–2

PURPOSE
m; no.1 1961–
Bombay

QUEST
Journal of ideas
b; vol.1,no.1–101 1956–76
Bombay. 148 Mahatma Gandhi Road, Bombay 1
ISSN 0018–7437

CA/U–1: no.49–101   CB/U–1: no.56–101 LO/N12: no.49–101   LO/U14: vol.1,no.3– 101

QUILL
m; no.1 1974–
New Delhi. Tulika Prakashan – Quill, 5c–14 New Rohtak Rd.
ed. M. C. Bhandari

ROOPVATI
þ; no.1 1970–
Delhi. Pritam Singh, Pleasure Garden Market, Chadni Chowk, Delhi 6.
ed. Mrs Kailash Puri

SCHOLAR
An illustrated monthly journal devoted to literature, science and art
m; vol.1,no.1 1925–?
Palghat, Kerala
ed. E. H. Parameswaran

LO/N12: vol.1,no.1 – vol.4,no.11

SHAMA'A
A magazine of art, literature and philosophy
q; vol.1,no.1– vol.8,no.4 1920–8
Madras. Mount Rd.
ed. Mrinalini Chattopadhyay

LO/N–1   LO/N12

SHANKAR'S WEEKLY
w; vol.1,no.1–vol.28,no.15 1947–75
New Delhi. Odeon Bldg., Connaught Place, New Delhi, 1
ISSN 0037–3281

SOLILOQUY
Magazine of prose and poetry
q;
New Delhi. R-867 New Rajinder Nagar, New Delhi 110060
ed. Sarabjeet Seth

SRI AUROBINDO MANDIR ANNUAL
q; 1967–
Calcutta

TARAPOREVALA'S INDIAN LITERARY
REVIEW
see INDIAN LITERARY REVIEW

THOUGHT
w; vol.1,no.1— vo.27,no.26 1949—75
Delhi. Siddhartha Publication (Pvt) Ltd., 35
Netaji Subhas Marg. Delhi 6.
ed. S. K. Tripathi
ISSN 0040—6449

CA/U—1   OX/U—1: vol.4,no.12— vol.27,
no.26

TOUCH STONE
m; no.1 1960—
Jullundur, Punjab

TRANSITION
q; vol.1,no.1 1967—
Calcutta. Basanti Library, 22/1 Bidhan Sarani
ed. Arup K. Datta
ISSN 0041—1205

TRIFLER
♭; vol.1,no.1—14 1823—4
Calcutta

LO/N—1   LO/N12

TRIVENI
A journal of Indian renaissance
q; vol.1,no.1 1926—
Machilipatnam. Triveni Press
ed. N. B. Rao
ISSN 0041—3135

DR/U—4: vol.27,no.1   LO/N12: vol.1,no.1—
vol.13,no.1, vol.19,no.1—   LO/U14: vol.25,
no.4, vol.26,no.3—

UNILIT
q; vol.1,no.1 1961—
Secunderabad, A. P. Viswa Sahiti, 208 New
Bhoiguda, Secunderabad 3
ed. Pothukunchi Sambasivarao
ISSN 0041—6762

UNITED ASIA
b; vol.1,no.1 1948—
Bombay. United Asia Publications
eds. G. S. Pohekar and U. R. Rao

LO/N12

VAGARTHA
A critical quarterly of Indian literature
q; no.1 1973—
New Delhi. Joshi Foundation, N—3 Panchsheel

Park, New Delhi 110017
ed. Meenakshi Mukherjee

LD/N—1

VAK
A review of literature and the arts
f; no.1—8 1958—62
New Delhi

DR/U—4   LO/N12

VISHWA BHARATI QUARTERLY
q; 1923—32   new series vol.1,no.1 1935—
Birbhum, West Bengal. P.O. Santiniketan
ed. Ashin das Gupta
ISSN 0042—7195
Also called VISVA-BHARATI QUARTERLY

CA/U—1   DR/U—4: n.s. vol.1,no.1—
vol.33,no.3/4

WASTE PAPER
A hungry generation newsletter
♭
Howrah, West Bengal

WRITERS' WORKSHOP CALCUTTA. LITERARY
READER
a; 1972—
Calcutta. Writers' Workshop, 162/92 Lake
Gardens 45, Calcutta 700045
ed. P. Lal

Academic and Critical

ALLAHABAD UNIVERSITY MAGAZINE
t; 1921—?
Allahabad, U.P. Dept. of English, Allahabad U.
ed. K. K. Mehrota

LO/N12: vol.18,no.1—2   OX/U—1: vol.11—
12,14

ALLAHABAD UNIVERSITY STUDIES
a; vol.1, 1925—
Allahabad, U. P.

LO/N12: (incomplete)   LO/S65: vol.4, 10—1

BULLETIN OF THE DEPARTMENT OF
ENGLISH, UNIVERSITY OF CALCUTTA
♭; vol.1,no.1— vol.6,no.4 1959—64   new series
vol.1,no.1 1965—
Calcutta
eds. S. C. Sen and Amalendu Bose
ISSN 0008—0691

LD/U—1: vol.3,no.1/2, vol.6,no.1—4, new series vol1,no.1—2, vol.6,no.3, vol.7,no.1—2
LO/U—1: vol.4,no.12—

CALCUTTA UNIVERSITY MAGAZINE
m; vol.1,no.1—5 1864
Calcutta

LO/N12

CALCUTTA UNIVERSITY MAGAZINE
A monthly newspaper and review
m; 1898—?
Calcutta. 24—1 Wellesley St.

LO/N12 1898—1901 (incomplete)

COMMONWEALTH NEWSLETTER
þ; c.1976—
Manasagangotri, Mysore. Assn. of Commonwealth Literature and Language Studies (ACLALS), U. Mysore, Manasagangotri 570006

ENDEAVOUR
m; 1967—
Kanpur, U.P. Christ Church College
ed. K. K. Sehgal
ISSN 0013—7170

ENGLISH ASSOCIATION JOURNAL
a; 1965—
Pilani, Rajasthan. Dept. of English, Birla Institute of Technology

GAUHATI UNIVERSITY JOURNAL
þ; vol.1,no.1 1950—
Gauhati, Assam
ed. Maheswar Neog

LO/N12   LO/U14   OX/U—1

HEENAYANA
Literary and cultural quarterly
q; no.1 1974—
Calcutta. 33-D Sreemohan Lane, Calcutta 700026
ed. Subhas Ghosal

INDIAN JOURNAL OF ENGLISH STUDIES
a; vol.1,no.1 1960—
New Delhi. Indian Assn. of English Studies, Orient Longman Ltd., 3/5 Asaf Ali Road, New Delhi, 1
ISSN 0537—1988

LO/N—1   LO/U—1

JADAVPUR JOURNAL OF COMPARATIVE LITERATURE
a; no.1 1961—
Calcutta. Dept. of Comparative Literature,

Jadavpur U., Calcutta 32
ed. Naresh Guha
ISSN 0448—1143

LO/U14: no.3—

JOURNAL OF THE KARNATAK UNIVERSITY: HUMANITIES
a
Dharwar, Mysore. Karnatak U.

JOURNAL OF THE MAHARAJA SAYAJIRAO UNIVERSITY OF BARODA
þ; vol.1,no.1 1952—
Baroda, Gujarat
ed. G. G. Dadlani

CA/U—1: vol.2,no.1—   LD/U—1: vol.9,no.1
LO/N12   LO/S65: vol.2,no.2— vol.13,no.2
LO/U14   OX/U—1

KAKATIYA JOURNAL OF ENGLISH STUDIES
a; vol.1,no.1 1976—
Warangal, A. P.   Kakatiya U., Vidyaranyapuri, Warangal 506 009
ed. Satyanarain Singh

LO/S26: vol.2,no.1—

LITERARY CRITERION
f; vol.1,no.1 1957—
Bombay. Popular Prakashan, 35-C Tardeo Rd., Bombay 400034
ed. C. D. Narasimhaiah
ISSN 0024—452X

CB/U—1: vol.8,no.1—   LD/U—1: vol.6,no.3—
vol.11,no.1   LO/S26: vol.7,no.3, vol.11,no.2—
NR/U—1: vol.7,no.1—

LITERARY HALF-YEARLY
f; vol.1,no.1 1960—
Mysore, A. P. Mysore U. Literary P., Mysore 12
ed. H. H. Anniah Gowda
ISSN 0024—4554

CB/U—1: vol.1,no.1, vol.4,no.1—   DR/U—1
LD/U—1: vol.1,no.2, vol.3,no.2, vol.4,no.1, vol.5,no.1, vol.6,no.1, vol.7—9, vol.11—12, vol.13,no.1, vol.14   LO/N12   LO/S26:
vol.12,no.2—   LO/U14

LITTCRIT
A half-yearly periodical reflecting Indian response to literature
f; vol.1,no.1 1975—
Tiruneveli, Tamil Nadu. Alwarkurichi 627412
ed. P. K. Rajan

LO/S26: vol.2,no.2—

OSMANIA JOURNAL OF ENGLISH STUDIES
a; 1960–
Hyderabad, A.P. Dept. of English, Osmania U.
ed. Vasant A. Shahane

LD/U–1: vol.2,no.1, vol.8,no.2   LO/U–1:
vol.5–

PATNA UNIVERSITY JOURNAL
q; vol.1,no.1 1944–
Patna, Bihar
ed. K. Ahmed

CA/U–1: vol.1,no.2–   LD/U–1: vol.7,
vol.9–11,no.1–2, vol.13,no.1–2, vol.15–16
LO/N–1: vol.1,no.2–   LO/N12: vol.7,no.1–
LO/U14: vol.1,no.2–

RAJASTHAN JOURNAL OF ENGLISH STUDIES
f; vol.1,no.1 1963–
Sikar, Rajasthan. U. Rajasthan

TAGORE STUDIES
a; 1969–
Calcutta. c/o Ms. Pronoti Mukerji, 4 Elgin Rd.,
Calcutta 20
ed. Somendra Nath Bose
ISSN 0082–1454

Drama

ENACT
The theatre magazine
m; vol.1,no.1 1967–
Delhi. Everest P., 4 Chamelian Road
ed. Raginder Paul
LO/S26: vol.32/33–   LO/S65: vol.25–31
LO/U14

IMPACT
ƀ;
New Delhi. National School of Drama and Asian
Theatre Institute

NATYA
Theatre arts journal
q; vol.1,no.1 1958–
New Delhi

THEATRE IMPACT
b; 1951–?
New Delhi. National School of Drama and Asian
Theatre Institute

THEATRE NEWS
m; vol.1,no.1–3 1935
New Delhi. Little Theatre Group

Fiction

LEVANT
An English quarterly of creative writing
ƀ; no.1 1966–
Calcutta. Chintamoni Das Lane, Calcutta 9
ed. S. Datta

RUPAMBARA
Collection of contemporary Indian writing
q; c.1960s
Calcutta. 26 Prataparditya Rd., Calcutta 26
ed. Swadesh Bharati
ISSN 0035–9963

SHORT STORY MAGAZINE OF INDIA
m; 1963
Madras

Poetry

DIALOGUE POETRY MAGAZINE
m; no.1 1968–
Calcutta. 5 Pearl Road, Calcutta 17
ed. Pritish Nandy
Supersedes DIALOGUE CALCUTTA (q.v.)

LO/U–2

EKAK
The premier poetry journal
q
Calcutta

BENGALI INTERNATIONAL
b; no.1 1972–
Calcutta. 170–2 Raja Rammohan Sarani, Calcutta 9
ed. Samir De

DIALOGUE CALCUTTA
b; ?–1968
Calcutta. 5 Pearl Rd.
ed. Pritish Nandy
ISSN 0012–2270
also called DIALOGUE INDIA Superseded by
DIALOGUE POETRY MAGAZINE (q.v.)

LO/N12: no.2–12   LO/U–2: no.13–18

EZRA
A magazine of neo-imagiste poetry
ƀ; no.1–5 1967
Bombay. Ezra/Fakir P.
ed. Arvind Krishna Mehrotra

LD/U–1: no.3,5   LO/U–2: no.1–3

FAKIR
z(1 issue); no.1 1967
Bombay. Ezra/Fakir P.
ed. Arvind Krishna Mehrotra

LO/U—2

GRAY BOOK
f; vol.1,no.1 1972—
Cuttack, Orissa. Gray Book Pubs., P.O. Box 39,
Cuttack 1
ed. Biyot K. Tripathy

LO/U—2

INDIAN VERSE
The voice of the Indian poets
q; vol.1,no.1 1972—
Calcutta. 9—3 Tamer Lane, Calcutta 9
ed. S. Roy

LAVA
An international journal of modern poetry
ɸ
New Delhi. 26/53 W.E.A., New Delhi 110005
ed. G. P. Vimal

MISCELLANY
b; no.28 1968—
Calcutta. Writers' Workshop, 162—92 Lake
Gardens, Calcutta 700045
ed. P. Lal
ISSN 0026—5896
Supersedes WRITERS' WORKSHOP MISCEL-
LANY (q.v.)

CB/U—1: no.28—   LD/U—1; no.18—36,43

OCARINA
A bi-monthly journal of poetry and aesthetics
b; vol.1,no.1 1970—
Madras. Tagore Institute of Creative Writing,
'Diparun', T-29B Seventh Ave., Besant Nagar,
Madras 600090
ed. Amal Ghose

LO/U—2

POET
An international monthly
m; vol.1no.1 1960—
Madras. 20-A Venkatesan St., Madras 17.
ed. Krishna Srinivas
ISSN 0032—194X

LD/U—1: vol.4,no.10— vol.13,no.3
LO/S26: 1968   LO/U—2

POETRY INDIA
q; vol.1,no.1— vol.2,no.2 1966—7

Bombay. Retreat, Bellasis Road, Bombay 8
ed. Nissim Ezekiel
ISSN 0032—2075

LD/U—1   LO/U—2

SKYLARK
q; c.1970s
Aligarh, U.P. Kothi Zamirabad, Raghubirpuri,
Aligarh 202001
ed. B. Mirza

LO/S26: no.27—

SPARK
f; no.1 1975—
Calcutta. 9A Sarat Banerjee Rd., Calcutta 700029
ed. S. K. Adhikari

TORNADO
ɸ; no.1—6 1967—71
Bombay. No Where P., Govind Niwas, Sarojini
Rd., Vile Parle, Bombay 56
ed. Pavankumar Jain
ISSN 0040—9499

LO/U—2

VRISHCHIK
m; vol.1,no.1 1969—
Baroda, Gujarat. 4 Residency Bungalow, University Office Compound
eds. Gulam Sheikh and B. Khakhar

LO/U—2: vol.3,no.10—

WRITERS' WORKSHOP MISCELLANY
b; no.1—27 1961—8
Calcutta. 162—92 Lake Gardens, 700045
ed. P. Lal
Superseded by MISCELLANY (q.v.)

LD/U—1: no.3,7,18—27   LO/U—2

Sri Lanka

(formerly Ceylon)

BUDDHIST ANNUAL OF CEYLON
a; vol.1,no.1— vol.4,no.2 1920—32
Colombo

BH/U—1: vol.1,no.2— vol.4,no.1
CA/U—1: lacks vol.1,no.4, vol.2,no.2
ED/N—1   LO/N—1: vol.1,no.2— vol.4,no.1
LO/S65: vol.1,no.2— vol.4,no.1   LO/U14:

vol.1,no.1,3, vol.2,no.2—4, vol.3,no.1
OX/U—1: vol.2,no.1,3—4— vol.4,no.2

CEYLON JOURNAL OF THE HUMANITIES
f; 1970—
Peradeniya. Dept. of English, U. Sri Lanka
Supersedes UNIVERSITY OF CEYLON
REVIEW (q.v.)

LO/N12   LO/S65   LO/U—1
LO/U14   OX/U—1

CEYLON LITERARY REGISTER
m; vol.1—7 1886—93
Colombo
Superseded by MONTHLY LITERARY
REGISTER (q.v.) Title then reverts to CEYLON
LITERARY REGISTER 1931—6 (q.v.)

LO/N—1: vol.2,no.32,34,36—38, vol.3,no.3—5,
11—12,20—23   OX/U—1: vol.1—2

CEYLON LITERARY REGISTER
vol.1,no.1— vol.4,no.12 1931—6
Colombo
Supersedes MONTHLY LITERARY REGISTER
(q.v.)

CEYLON MAGAZINE
m; vol.1,no.1— vol.2,no.13 1840—2
Colombo. Herald P.

LO/N—1   LO/S65   OX/U—1

CEYLON OBSERVER PICTORIAL
a
Colombo. Associated Newspapers of Ceylon

CEYLON REVIEW
A monthly magazine of literary and general
interest
m; vols.1—3 1893—6;   new series vol.1,no.1—
vol.7,no.20 1897—1902
Colombo. *Ceylon Review* Offices
ed. J. Scott Coates

LO/N—1: vol.1—3,   new series vol.1—3
LO/S65: new series vol.3,no.1— vol.7,no.12,
vol.7,no.15—20

HARVEST
q; vol.1,no.1— vol.2,no.4 1945—7
Colombo

LO/N—1: vol.2,no.1—4

JANA
The news magazine of resurgent Asia and Africa
m; vol.1—3 1954—7

Colombo. Associated Newspapers of Ceylon

LO/N—1   LO/S65   OX/U—1

KOLAYA
ƀ; 1975—
Vidyalankara. U. Sri Lanka

MODERN CEYLON STUDIES
ƀ; vol.1,no.1 1970—
Peradeniya. U. Sri Lanka
Supersedes UNIVERSITY OF CEYLON REVIEW
(q.v.)

MONTHLY LITERARY REGISTER AND NOTES AND QUERIES FOR CEYLON
vol.1—4 1893—6
Colombo
Supersedes CEYLON LITERARY REGISTER
1886—93 (q.v.) Superseded by CEYLON LITER-
ARY REGISTER 1931—6 (q.v.)

OX/U—1

NEW CEYLON WRITING
Creative and critical writing of Sri Lanka
a; 1970—,
North Ryde, N.S.W., Australia. Macquarie U.,
North Ryde, N.S.W. 2113
ed. Yasmine Gooneratne

LD/U—1: 1970—1   LO/S26: 1970—2
LO/S65: 1970—1

NEW LANKA
A quarterly review
q; vol.1 1949—
Colombo

LO/N—1   LO/S65: vol.3,no.1— vol.4,no.3

POETRY PERADENIYA
a; 1957—63
Peradeniya. U. Ceylon

SANKA
ƀ; no.1—2 1958
Colombo

SYMPOSIUM
m; vol.1,no.1— vol.2,no.12 1948—50
Colombo

LO/N—1

TIMES OF CEYLON ANNUAL
a; 1955—
Colombo. *Times of Ceylon*

LO/U14

UNIVERSITY OF CEYLON REVIEW
f; 1942—69
Peradeniya. U. Ceylon
Superseded by CEYLON JOURNAL OF THE
HUMANITIES (q.v.) and MODERN CEYLON
STUDIES (q.v.)

LO/N12: no.1—25

VIDYODAYA
Journal of arts, sciences and letters
f; no.1 1968—
Nugegoda. U. Sri Lanka, Vidyodaya Campus
Library
ISSN 0042—532X

LO/U—1

FORMER COMMONWEALTH COUNTRIES

Pakistan

EDUCATOR
m; 1965—
Lahore. 2 McLeod Road.
ed. G. Rabbani Mirza.
ISSN 0013—2020

ENTERPRISE
m; 1949—
Karachi

IQBAL QUARTERLY
q; vol.1,no.1 1960—
Lahore. Iqbal Academy

DR/U—4   LO/U14: vol.3,no.4—
OX/U—1

ORIENT
A socio-economic cum literary journal
m; no.1 1963—
Karachi. 13/C—C, P.E.C.H.S. Block 2.
ed. Mohammed Umar
ISSN 0048—220X

OUTLOOK
þ; 1973—4
Karachi. Publishers' Combine

PAKISTAN
A literary and cultural review
þ; vol.1,no.1—2 1948
Karachi. Pakistan Publications
Superseded by PAKISTAN QUARTERLY (q.v.)

OX/U—1

PAKISTAN QUARTERLY
q; vol.,1no.1— vol.18,no.2 1949—71
Karachi. Pakistan Publications, P.O. Box 704
Supersedes PAKISTAN (q.v.)

LO/U—1: 1953—   OX/U—1

PAKISTAN REVIEW
Pakistan's national cultural monthly
m; vol.1,no.1 1953—
Lahore. Ferozsons Ltd., 60 Shara-e-Quaid-e-Azam
ISSN 0031—0077

CA/U—1: vol.1,no.5—   LO/N12: vol.1,no.5—
LO/S65: vol.1—10   LO/U14   OX/U—1

PERSPECTIVE
m; vol.1,no.1 1967—
Karachi. Pakistan Pubs., Box 183, Shahrah Iraq,
Karachi 1

ed. M. R. Siddiqui

ED/N—1   LO/S65   LO/U14: vol.3,no.1—
vol.6,no.3

PESHAWAR UNIVERSITY REVIEW
♭; vol.1,no.1 1973—
Peshawar. Peshawar U.P.
ed. Dr. Abdur Rahim

LO/N12   LO/U14

SCINTILLA
q
Karachi. Federation of University Women,
Government College for Women

SIND COLLEGE MAGAZINE
a
Karachi. Sind Muslim College

DR/U—4: 1952—3, 1956—7

TWENTIETH CENTURY
m; vol.1,no.1 1934—?
Allahabad. 8 Nawab Yusuf Rd.

LO/N12: vol.4,no.39— vol.13,no.146 (incomplete)
LO/S65: vol.1,no.1— vol.12,no.12 lacks vol.1,
no.5, vol.7,no.76,79, vol.9,no.101,103,108

UNIVERSITY STUDIES
t; 1964—8
Karachi. U. Karachi

VENTURE
A bi-annual review of English language and
literature
f; vol.1,no.1 1960—
Karachi. Dept. of English, Karachi U.
ed. Syed Ali Ashraf

LD/U—1: vol.1,no.3, vol.2, vol.5,no.1—2, vol.6,
no.1—2   LO/U—2: vol.5,no.2, vol.6,no.1

VISION
m; 1953—?
Karachi. 35—7 Farid Chambers, Victoria Rd.

South Africa

ABYSM
♭; no.1 1974—
Johannesburg. P.O. Box 66226, Broadway

ADAM
A paper for bachelors
m; vol.1,no.1— vol.2,no.13 1920—2
Johannesburg

LO/N—1

AFRICA SOUTH
q; vol.1,no.1— vol.6,no.1 1956—71
Cape Town, African Foundation of South Africa,
Africa South Publications
Superseded by AFRICA SOUTH IN EXILE pub-
lished in London

LD/U—1   LO/S65   LO/U14: vol.2,no.3—
vol.5,no.10   OX/U—9

AFRICAN JOURNAL
A register of facts, fiction, news, literature, commerce and amusement
w; vol.7,no.315— vol.8,no.392 1849—51
Cape Town. Pike
ed. William Layton Sammons
Supersedes SAM SLY'S AFRICAN JOURNAL
(q.v.)

AFRICAN MONTHLY
A magazine devoted to history, exploration,
science, art and poetry
m; vol.1,no.1— vol.7,no.39 1906—10
Grahamstown. African Book Co.
ed. A. Burt

CA/U—1: vol.1—2   LO/N—1   LO/S65
OX/U—1

ALEXANDER ROAD HIGH SCHOOL
MAGAZINE
a; vol.1,no.1 1958—
Port Elizabeth. Alexander Road High School

DE ARTE
q; Pilot Edition 1965   no.1 1967—
Pretoria. Dept. of Fine Arts, U. South Africa
eds. Karin Skawran and Frieda Harmsen

LO/U—2: no.1

BANTU TREASURY
♭; 1957—
Johannesburg. Witwatersrand U.P., Jan Smuts
Ave., Johannesburg 2001
ISSN 0067—4044

BLUESTOCKING
The organ of the South African Association of
University Women
♭; no.1 1930—

Cape Town. South African Assn. of University Women

LO/N—1: no.18—

BOLT
ƀ
Durban. Dept. of English, U. Natal

CAPE OF GOOD HOPE LITERARY GAZETTE
Devoted exclusively to literature, criticism, science and the advancement of useful knowledge
m; vol.1—5 1830—5
Cape Town. W. Bridekirk

LO/S65

CAPE ILLUSTRATED MAGAZINE
m; vol.1,no.1— vol.11,no.8 1890—1900
Cape Town. Dennis Edwards & Co.
Superseded by SOUTH AFRICAN ILLUSTRATED MAGAZINE (q.v.)

LO/N—1   LO/S65: vol.6—8

CAPE MONTHLY MAGAZINE
m; vol.1,no.1— vol.11,no.6 1853—62   New series vol.1,no.1— vol.18,no.110 1870—9   3rd series vol.1,no.1— vol.4,no.6 1879—81
Capetown. Darnell & Murray
Superseded by CAPE QUARTERLY REVIEW (q.v.)

LO/N—1: vol.9, vol.10,no.55,   new series vol.1, no.1— vol.13,no.78   LO/S65: 1857—81
OX/U—1: n.s. vol.1,no.1— vol.18,no.110

CAPE QUARTERLY REVIEW
q; vol.1,no.1— vol.2,no.7 1881—3
Cape Town. J. C. Juta
Supersedes CAPE MONTHLY MAGAZINE (q.v.)

LO/S65   OX/U—1

CAPE TOWN MIRROR
w; vol.1,no.1—43 1848—9
Cape Town. J. H. Collard

LO/S65

CATHOLIC MAGAZINE FOR SOUTH AFRICA
m; vol.11,no.1— vol.35,no.397 1902—24
Cape Town
ed. Revd. F. C. Kolbe
Supersedes SOUTH AFRICAN CATHOLIC MAGAZINE (q.v.)

LO/N—1   LO/S65

CLASSIC
ƀ; vol.1,no.1— vol.3,no.4 1963—71
Johannesburg. Classic Magazine Trust Fund

ed. Barney Simon
ISSN 0009—8302
Superseded by NEW CLASSIC (q.v.)

CB/U—1: vol.3,no.2—4   LO/N19
LO/S65   LO/U14: vol.3,no.2—4
OX/U14: vol.2,no.1— vol.3,no.4

COLONIST
w; no.1—45 1827—9
Cape Town. W. Bridekirk

LO/N—1: lacks no.15,22   OX/U—1: no.1—37

COLONIST
m; 1850—9
Grahamstown

CONTRAST
South African literary journal
t; vol.1,no.1 1960—
Cape Town. 3 Scott Road, Box 3841, Claremont, Cape Town
ed. Jack Cope

LD/U—1   LO/U—1   QL/P—2

CRITIC
A South African quarterly journal
q; vol.1,no.1— vol.5,no.5 1932—9
Rondebosch. Speciality P.

LO/N—1   LO/S65: lacks vol.5,no.2

DARK AREAS
ƀ; no.1 1971—
Glen Osmond

LO/U—2

DIALOGUE
q; vol.1,no.1—2 1968
Cape Town. Students' Representative Council, U. Cape Town
ed. Ben Dekker

LO/U—2: vol.1,no.1   OX/U—1

DIALOGUE
A literary annual for young writers
a; 1971—
Wynberg. P.O. Box 102, Wynberg 7824
ed. Tim Peacock

DRUM
w/m; vol.1,no.1 1951—
Johannesburg. Drum Publications (Pty) Ltd., P.O. Box 3413
Also published monthly in Accra, Nairobi and Lagos, but main literary interest is in early South African issues

Some issues entitled AFRICAN DRUM

LO/N—1   LO/S65: 1951—65 lacks 7 issues
LO/U14   OX/U—9

EASTERN PROVINCE MONTHLY MAGAZINE
m; vol.1,no.1— vol.2,no.24 1856—8
Grahamstown. Godlonton, White & Co.

LO/S65

ENGLISH IN AFRICA
f; vol.1,no.1 1974—
Grahamstown. Institute for the Study of English
in Africa, Rhodes U., Grahamstown 6140
ed. André de Villiers
ISSN 0425—0508

OX/U—1: vol.1,no.1

ENGLISH STUDIES IN AFRICA
A journal of the humanities
f; vol.1,no.1 1958—
Johannesburg. Witwatersrand U.P., Jan Smuts
Ave., Johannesburg 2001
ed. B. D. Cheadle
ISSN 0013—8398

BT/U—1: vol.10—   CA/U—1   DR/U—1:
vol.15—   ED/U—1   LD/U—1: vol.1,no.1,
vol.3,no.1, vol.7—   LO/U—1   LO/U—2
OX/U—1

FOLKLORE JOURNAL
b; vol.1,no.1—, vol.2,no.6 1879—80
Cape Town. South African Folklore Society
ed. Saul Solomon

FORUM
South Africa's independent journal of opinion
w/m; vol.1,no.1— vol.14,no.28 1938—51   New
series vol.1,no.1— vol.10,no.6 1952—64
Johannesburg/Cape Town

LO/U—8: (lacks vol.9,no.44, vol.13,no.1—31;
n.s. vol.2,no.1)

FORUM
f; vol.1,no.1— vol.4,no.1 1967—8
Grahamstown. Students' Representative Council,
Rhodes U.

OX/U—1: vol.4,no.1

GROOTE SCHUUR
b; 1938—63
Cape Town. Students' Union, U. Cape Town
Supersedes UNIVERSITY OF CAPE TOWN
QUARTERLY (q.v.)

LD/U—1: 1957—63   LO/N—1   LO/S65:
1946, 1948   OX/U—1

IZWE
b; vol.1,no.1— vol.3,no.20 1971—4
Johannesburg. P.O. Box 86, Crown Mines

JEWISH AFFAIRS
m; vol.1,no.1 1945—
Johannesburg. South African Jewish Board of
Deputies

LANTERN
w; vol.1,no.1— vol.15,no.634 1877—89
Cape Town
eds. Thomas M'Combie and A. A. Geary

LO/N—1: no.2—235   LO/S65: no.211

LANTERN
Criticism of the contemporary scene
z(1 issue); no.1 1899
Johannesburg

LANTERN
Journal of knowledge and culture
w; vol.1,no.1—2 1949—
Pretoria. Foundation for Education, Science and
Technology

MUSA
z(1 issue); no.1 1949
Cape Town

LO/N—1

NEW AFRICAN
The radical monthly
m; no.1 1962—
After 1965, published in London
Cape Town. Insight Publications
ed. Lewis Nkosi

LO/U—8

NEW CLASSIC
q; no.1 1975—
Johannesburg. Ravan P. P.O. Box 31134, Braam-
fontein, Johannesburg 2001
ed. Barney Simon
Supersedes CLASSIC (q.v.)
ISSN 0009—8302

OX/U—1   OX/U14

NEW COIN POETRY
b; vol.1,no.1 1965—
Grahamstown. Grahamstown Poetry Society
ed. Guy Butler

121

ISSN 0028—4459

LO/S65   LO/U—2   OX/U—1

NEW NATION
m; vol.1,no.1 1967—
Pretoria. New Nation Publications, Box 3039,
Pretoria
ed. Denis Worrall
ISSN 0028—6370

NEWS OF THE CAMP
A journal of fancies, notifications, gossip and
general chit-chat
ƥ; no.1—4 1880—1
Pretoria. Military camp during the Transvaal War
eds. Charles Du-Val and Charles Deecker

LO/N—1   LO/S65

OPHIR
f; no.1—23 1967—76
Johannesburg. Ravan P., P.O. Box 31134, Braam-
fontein, Johannesburg 2001
eds. Walter Saunders and Peter Horn

BT/U—1: no.5,7,   LO/U—2   OX/U—1:
no.5

OPINION
w; vol.1,no.1— vol.59,no.30 1903—61   New
series vol.1,no.1—3 1962
Durban
Sometimes called INDIAN OPINION

OUTSPAN
South Africa's weekly for everybody
w; vol.1—59,no.1—1577 1927—57
Bloemfontein

POETRY SOUTH
f; no.1 1972—
Newlands, Cape. 50 Almond St.
ed. Michael Norris

PURPLE RENOSTER
South African literary quarterly
ƥ; no.1—12 1956—73
Johannesburg
ed. Lionel Abrahams

BT/U—1: no.6—12   LD/U—1: no.1—8
LO/U—2: no.7—12

REALITY
A journal of liberal opinion
b; vol.1,no.1 1969—
Pietermaritzburg. Reality Pubs., Flat 2, Temple
Chambers, Carlyle Arcade

RHODIAN
f; vol.1,no.1 1906—
Grahamstown. Rhodes U. Coll.

LO/S65: vol.6,no.1—4, vol.21,no.1—

SAM SLY'S AFRICAN JOURNAL
w; vol.1,no.1— vol.6,no.314 1843—9
Cape Town. William Leyton Sammons
Superseded by AFRICAN JOURNAL (q.v.)

LO/N—1: vol.2—3

S'KETSH
Journal of Black Theatre
ƥ; vol.1,no.1 1972—
Soweto, Johannesburg. S'Ketch Pubs., P.O. Box 78

SNARL
A critical review of the arts
ƥ; vol.1,no.1 1974—
Johannesburg. Ravan P., P.O. Box 31134, Braam-
fontein, Johannesburg 2001
ed. Joyce Ozynski

SOMEWHERE BEYOND
U.C.T. Poetry Journal
z(1 issue); no.1 1970
Cape Town
ed. Ahmed Essop

OX/U—1

SOUTH AFRICAN BOOKMAN
q; no.1—13 1910—5
Pretoria. South African Home Reading Union

LO/S65: no.5

SOUTH AFRICAN CATHOLIC MAGAZINE
m; vol.1—10 1891—1901
Cape Town
Superseded by CATHOLIC MAGAZINE FOR
SOUTH AFRICA (q.v.)

LO/N—1

SOUTH AFRICAN COLLEGE MAGAZINE
ƥ; vol.1—18 1900—17
Cape Town. Salesian Institute
Superseded by UNIVERSITY OF CAPE TOWN
QUARTERLY (q.v.)

LO/S65: vol.17,no.2—3, vol.18,no.3—4

SOUTH AFRICAN FRIEND
q; vol.1,no.1— vol.4,no.8 1907—14
Johannesburg

Superseded by SOUTH AFRICAN QUARTERLY
(q.v.)

LO/S65: vol.3

SOUTH AFRICAN ILLUSTRATED MAGAZINE
An artistic monthly
m; vol.11,no.9— vol.13,no.3 1900—1
Cape Town. Dennis Edwards & Co.
Supersedes CAPE ILLUSTRATED MAGAZINE
(q.v.)

LO/S65: vol.12,no.11, vol.13,no.3

SOUTH AFRICAN MAGAZINE
A contribution to colonial literature
m; vol.1,no.1— vol.3,no.12 1867—9
Cape Town
eds. J. S. Bond and W. M. Foster

LO/S65: vol.1,no.1—2,4—11, vol.3,no.2—11

SOUTH AFRICAN MAGAZINE
m; vol.1,no.1— vol.2,no.3 1906—7
Cape Town
eds. C. H. Crane and Eric France

LO/N—1: vol.1,no.1— vol.2,no.2   LO/S65

SOUTH AFRICAN P.E.N. YEAR BOOK
♭; 1954—60
Cape Town. International P.E.N. (South African
Centre)

HL/U—1: 1954   LO/N—1

SOUTH AFRICAN QUARTERLY
q; vol.1,no.1— vol.7,no.4 1914—26
Johannesburg
ed. J. D. Rheinaut Jones
Supersedes SOUTH AFRICAN FRIEND (q.v.)

CA/U—1: vol.2,no.1— vol.7,no.4   LO/N—1:
vol.2,no.1— vol.7,no.4   LO/S65

SOUTH AFRICAN QUARTERLY JOURNAL
q; 1st series vol.1—5 1829—31   2nd series vol.
1—4 1833—5   3rd series vol.1 1836
Cape Town. South African Literary and Scientific
Institution

LO/N—1

STANDPUNTE
b; no.1 1945—
Cape Town. Tafelberg Publishers, Box 879
ed. P. G. du Plessis
ISSN 0038—9730

CA/U—1: no.9—   LO/N—1

THEORIA
A journal of studies in the arts, humanities and
social sciences
f; no.1 1947—
Pietermaritzburg. U. Natal

BH/U—1: no.1—2   CA/U—1: no.1—2
CB/U—1   DR/U—1: no.3—   LO/S65:
no.1—17   NW/U—1   SH/U—1: no.29—

THESAURUS
a; vol.1—5 1965—70
Cape Town. Student Writers' Society, U. Cape
Town

TREK
m; vol.4,no.5— vol.16,no.8 1939—52
Johannesburg
Supersedes SOUTH AFRICAN WOOL AND
PRODUCE REVIEW

LO/N—1: vol.36,no.44—   LO/U—2: vol.14,
no.10—2, vol.15,no.2,no.5

UNIVERSITY OF CAPE TOWN QUARTERLY
f; vol.1,no.1— vol.20,no.4 1918—37
Cape Town. Students' Council
Supersedes SOUTH AFRICAN COLLEGE
MAGAZINE (q.v.) Superseded by GROOTE
SCHUUR (q.v.)

LO/N—1: 1932—6   LO/S65: vol.2,no.4—
vol.9,no.4

UNISA
a; 1946—
Pretoria. U. South Africa

UNISA ENGLISH STUDIES
t; vol.1,no.1 1962—
Pretoria. U. South Africa

VOORSLAG
m; vol.1,no.1—11 1926—7
Pretoria

LO/N—1: vol.1,no.2—9   LO/S65: vol.1,
no.1—9

WASTE PAPER BASKET OF THE OWL CLUB
♭; 1921—34
Cape Town

WURM
♭; vol.1,no.1—12 1966—70
Pretoria

LO/U—2: vol.1,no.4—11

Sudan

ADAB
Journal of the Faculty of Arts, University of
Khartoum
q; vol.1,no.1 1972–
Khartoum, Sudan. Khartoum U.P.

LO/U14

Title Index

Index

Index